Driving to Stony Lonesome

Publication is made possible in part with the generous support of Susan Houseworth Herrel and Ann Houseworth Massing in honor of the lifelong friendship of their mother, Barbara Rogers Houseworth, with the authors.

JACK WELPOTT'S
INDIANA PHOTOGRAPHS,
1936–1959

Driving to Stony Lonesome

Jack Welpott

FOREWORD BY JO ANN B. FINEMAN

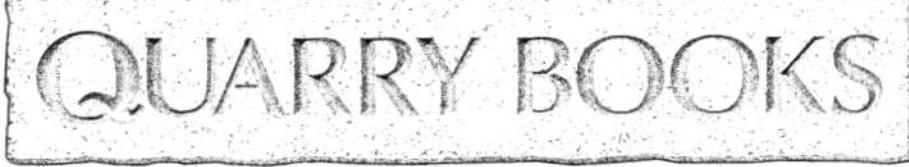

AN IMPRINT OF
INDIANA UNIVERSITY PRESS
BLOOMINGTON AND INDIANAPOLIS

This book is a publication of

Quarry Books

an imprint of
Indiana University Press
601 North Morton Street
Bloomington, IN 47404-3797 USA

http://iupress.indiana.edu

Telephone orders	800-842-6796
Fax orders	812-855-7931
Orders by e-mail	iuporder@indiana.edu

The paper used in this publication meets the minimum requirements of American National Standard for Information Sciences—Permanence of Paper for Printed Library Materials, ANSI Z39.48-1984.

Printed in China

Library of Congress Cataloging-in-Publication Data

Welpott, Jack, date
Driving to Stony Lonesome : Jack Welpott's Indiana photographs, 1936–1959 / Jack Welpott ; foreword by Jo Ann B. Fineman.
p. cm.
ISBN-13: 978-0-253-21866-7 (pbk.)
ISBN-10: 0-253-21866-7 (pbk.)
1. Welpott, Jack, 1923– . 2. Photographers—Indiana—Biography. 3. Photography—Indiana—History—20th century. I. Title.
TR140.W427A3 2006
770.92—dc22
[B] 2006009679

1 2 3 4 5 11 10 09 08 07 06

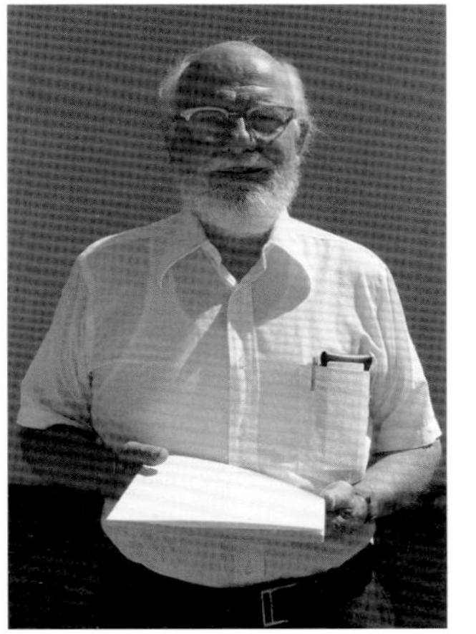

Henry Holmes Smith came to teach at Indiana University in 1947. He had been an associate of Moholy Nagy at the New Bauhaus in Chicago and was, for a time, an editor of the magazine Mini Cam. Henry was an early innovator in color photography, having perfected a method that he called Tricolor Collage. He was also a published cartoonist and writer. He influenced a whole generation of young photographers, many of whom went on to establish reputations in the field. Henry Holmes Smith played a pivotal role in the evolution of photography as a fine art in the mid twentieth century.

My dear Dad was a ubiquitous cameraman of the snapshot variety.

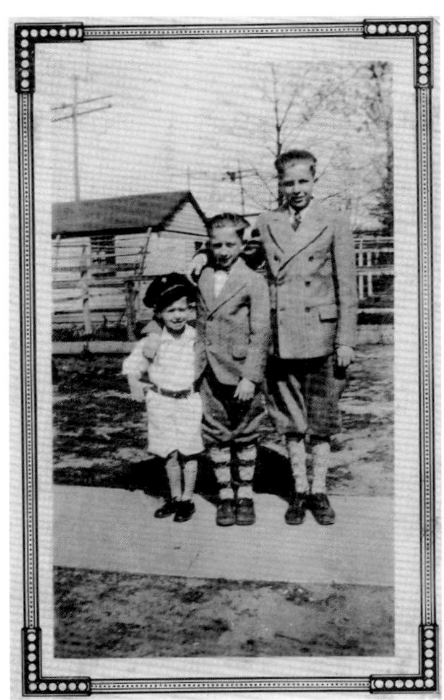

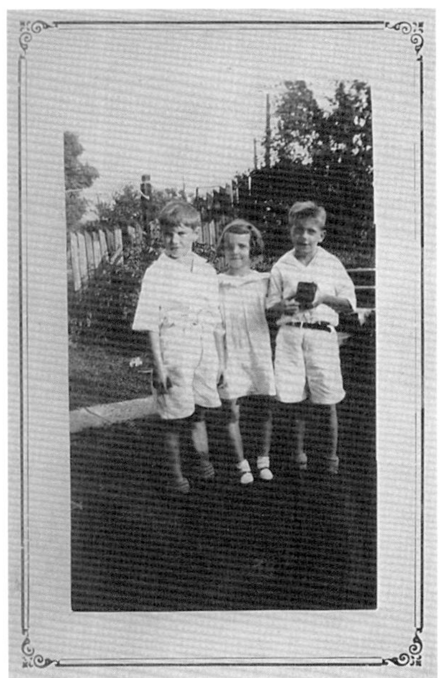

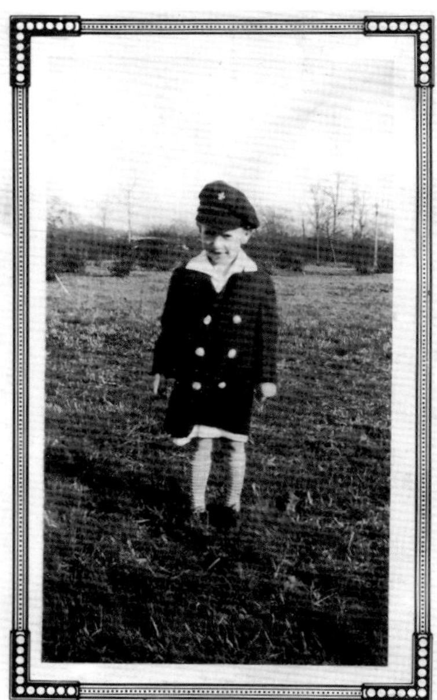

PHOTOGRAPHY IS MY PASSION.
THE SEARCH FOR TRUTH MY OBSESSION.

ALFRED STIEGLITZ

Contents

Foreword

There is a real place called "Stony Lonesome," a place of reality and, as these images attest, a place of fantasy and of the unique artistic merging of the real world and the inner eye of the artist-photographer. It may be that all artistic photography is a paradox—it is at the same time a record of an absolute reality and an exposition of the inner experience of the artist, and in most cases, that of the human subject. It is a momentary realized experience of the artist-as-photographer, as the photographer merges his largely unconscious, internal, affective, and intrapsychic view of the outer reality before his lens with the indelible stamp of his subjective eye.

This, for me, means that the artist-as-photographer—more than any other—is able to combine the literal, concrete world with an inner perception and create a new and unique image which can never be replicated. No matter how many posed images the photographer makes, each one will be distinct and quite literally will never exist again. The photographer's inner eye forms an unconscious image upon outer reality, thereby creating an image that is neither real nor unreal, but one that is not only a record of what IS, but a revelation of the photographer's inner eye in that instant of recognition. The artist-photographer captures an illusion and makes it visible to the viewer.

There are those, and I include myself, who attempt to study and understand the creative process, despite Freud's warning that the psychoanalyst should not, and could not, truly fathom the mystery of artistic creativity. There is much with which to agree in that admonition, so it is with a certain amount of humility on my part that I undertake to make these remarks and offer words of deep appreciation for the art of Jack Welpott, from the view of a fond friend of many years, and incidentally, a psychoanalyst.

As I have viewed and pondered these images, absorbed them both visually and in my own inner memories with a recognition of the world of my childhood and adolescence, I not only become aware of a sense of nostalgia and desire for that earlier time, but am repeatedly struck by Jack's ability to find and record that instant when the human beings in these photographs open themselves to reveal their hidden selves beneath the exterior. It is as though a curtain were flung aside that allows us to see something that can never be exactly the same ever again. Jack's genius—and I use the word in its true meaning—is to seize and know that moment. Such a blending of the conscious mind and unconscious perception cannot be taught or learned—it is simply the quality of the mind and the eye *knowing;* we, the viewers of these images, cannot have any idea of how that internal event takes place, and really, should not know. We are given a glimpse of a human being we have never, and probably will never, actually encounter in real life. But we have that internal vision of someone which bursts upon us and engraves itself onto our own inner eye and memories, so that in reverie we are able to recall that person—whether the sometimes somber Indiana children, the stern-faced men, the quiet elderly twins facing the world with their old black dog, the grinning boy in his porch swing, or any of the others. Even the weathered barn walls and the textured brick have that quality of evanescence—they will never quite reflect the same light again.

The personal identities have shown themselves, and Jack has known exactly when to record those selves, not judgmentally but with the solemn patience of the seer who knows when the truth appears. Remarkably, there is nothing invasive or controlling about these photographs; the active-passive waiting and watching without intrusion is one of the many qualities that can create such art, and I believe as I see these photographs that the children and grownups in them were aware of that quality in Jack. He was utterly and deeply respectful of their humanity and also utterly non-judgmental; neither was he imposing any reality of his own upon the people he viewed.

Again, those of us who lamely attempt to shed some light on the creative art and on the artist have formed some theoretical propositions—articulated in several different versions—that the artist has the innate capacity to, as one analyst has put it, "regress in the service of the ego." That sounds fine as far as it goes, but I would also add that it is far more complex and must include the capacity to suspend the barrier between the conscious self and the unconscious levels of the mind, without becoming fixed in either. Many, if not most, human beings are unable to move between conscious and cognitive, and unconscious and affective perception, without a sense of dissonance, anxiety, and a strong need to cling to one or the other realm. In night dreams, unless they become too undisguised and reveal dangerous truths about ourselves, we have a glimpse of that internal dichotomy, which is the daily life of the artist, and especially of the artist-photographer. To risk a leap—which I perhaps have no right to do—all those weekends with the family and Dad with his box camera formed one core of Jack's identity—and family may be a key concept. They were together, probably no more nor less conflicted about their relationships than most families, but as Jack says, Dad's camera *held* them together—with much laughter and happiness, whatever other relational conflicts there may have been. It was only when Jack, as he "imitated Dad" in "snapping, snapping, snapping," supposedly inadvertently snapped before the posed photograph could be taken by his father, that he truly realized his ability to see something most of the world could not see, and to have the sudden knowledge of what he saw. The ladies, thinking that Dad had clicked his shutter, began laughing, breaking out of their posed rigidity, and walking toward Dad and Jack as Dad's shutter finally clicked. This allowed Jack to "see and know" an image uniquely original.

I use the word "know" not as a felt cognitive experience, but as that unconscious sense of the moment, which has never left Jack. And there is Uncle Cal as well—he of the fast cars and show girls, a radio performer and photographer. How on earth, in southern Indiana in the late forties, did Uncle Cal appear? We only knew of such romantic strangers in the movies we saw on Saturdays at the downtown Indiana and Princess theaters. However, Uncle Cal was a formative personality for Jack. When Jack was nine—only NINE—Uncle Cal showed him the magic transformation of a blank piece of paper into a photograph. That early sense of magic has never left Jack, as each image he makes becomes an evocation of magic—alone in the darkroom, revealing his "evidence of being there."

Jack mentions his darkroom door sign: "I've gone to find myself. If I get back before I return, keep me here." He has always kept himself there, in the magical darkroom where he knows exactly who he is and exactly what he does. Not many of us can truly say and feel that about ourselves.

Jo Ann B. Fineman
Santa Fe, New Mexico

Preface: Driving to Stony Lonesome

Stony Lonesome is a bend in the road, with nothing much to set it apart from other bends in the road. Like so many places in southern Indiana at mid twentieth century it was surely stony, placed as it is in limestone country. It is fair to say it was also lonely with a lot of trees and some limestone outcroppings, and very quiet, an eternal quiet. It was the name that got me. It has been said that Edgar Allan Poe, when asked his favorite words in the English language, replied, "Cellar door." Nice, but I will take Stony Lonesome—sheer poetry. It seems a metaphor for life. A life contains some stony outcroppings and each of us gets our share of loneliness. There are many poetic places on Indiana back roads: Stone Head, Gnaw Bone, Greasy Creek, Hindustan, Needmore, Bean Blossom, all attesting to the poetic nature of country folk.

I doubt I would have paid much attention to Stony Lonesome without the motivation provided by photography. It sets one off on an odyssey not unlike that traveled by primal humans. One goes from point to point in a linear manner, not looking for that bison or deer on which to gorge, but rather in search of that artifact called a photograph. It is the pleasure of the hunt. One hopes to bring back evidence of being there. My greatest joy was to spend hours driving rural Indiana roads. Often times I didn't know just where I was. I sometimes got good and lost. I quickly learned that when one is lost it is best to just change your destination. If I plunged ahead I would always find a main road that would take me home. That is if I made the right decision to turn left or right. Whatever happened I always managed to find home turf eventually. Getting there was an adventure not unlike Homer's *Ulysses*. Why did it take him ten years to find his way home? Any fool could tell him that all he had to do was sail east and he would get there. A psychiatrist friend has suggested he was really trying to avoid his wife, Penelope.

On Getting There

My dear dad was a ubiquitous cameraman of the snapshot variety. He delighted in planting my mother, my aunts and uncles, my brothers, my grandmother, and all members of the German-Irish family in neat rows, usually twos or threes. He would demand utmost attention and then snap the picture. He had total command of technique. The tip sheet said, "Sun over your left shoulder and don't shake." His instrument was a black contraption otherwise known as a box camera. The film roll went off immediately to the nearest drugstore and within a week he would pick up the deckle-edged masterworks. At the next family gathering, which seemed to always happen Sundays at Granny's house, the prints came out and there was much hilarity over the results. Keep in mind that this was the 1920s. There was no television, no picture magazines except for an occasional silent movie, and photos were mostly seen in the family album or with the aid of a stereopticon, with its many views of the Taj Mahal and scenes from the Wild West.

When I was six or seven, dear Dad came across a small version of his box camera that he gave to me. I was not entitled to any film, just the camera. Even so, I gloried in playing cameraman and went around snapping, snapping, snapping, snapping. I did have a moment of glory that really started out as a disaster. One sunny Sunday, Dad planted Aunt Jane, Mother, and Grandmother in a neat row in the back of Granny's house in St. Louis. As was the custom, they stood stock still awaiting the click of the shutter. I placed myself next to my father with empty box camera in hand, and a fraction of a second before he clicked his shutter I clicked mine. Upon hearing my shutter, the ladies cracked up and started walking toward the camera. My father was annoyed that I had ruined his photo. I was redeemed the following Sunday when this photo came into view. One and all were delighted at this image of laughing ladies walking toward the camera. I do believe that it was my first photograph, made with the assistance of my dear old dad.

The real photographer in the family was my uncle Cal. He was a role model for a kid. He drove fast cars, sang in a band, had his own radio show, dated showgirls, and made photographs. I wanted so much to be like him but I was just a kid. I couldn't do any of those things except make photographs. When I was nine, he took me into his darkroom in Granny's basement and let me watch. He took a blank piece of paper and put it into a tray of liquid and WOW! up came a photograph. I thought I was in the presence of Merlin the Magician. How was it possible that a blank piece of paper could be made into a photograph?

Somehow I managed to scrounge a plastic camera. I think it was called a Bull's Eye. Even though we were in the depths of the Depression, I sometimes bought film. My folks were struggling to keep it together. My father worked for a small loan company and my mother opened a rooming house for Indiana University students. Our house was always a little mad, what with containing my older brothers, my father, my mother, ten students, and me. My father, who had a penchant for practical jokes, compounded the madness. The place was like a circus. We ate a lot of gravy bread, which was like a meat substitute. I didn't mind because I liked gravy bread.

Whenever I could raise a few nickels, I would get some film and click away. Off to the drugstore the roll would go. Waiting for the deckle-edged photos to come back was a source of great excitement. Along the way I obtained a little developing kit for doing film and making contact prints. The directions said, "do it in the dark," so I went into the bathroom and pulled down the shade. That was the first of a thousand mistakes as I tried to learn the craft from tip sheets. As George Bernard Shaw observed, "The photographer is like the cod, he must lay a million eggs in order to bring one to fruition." Photography, like baseball, is about failure. If you think about it, a guy can come to bat ten times, strike out seven times, get a hit three times, and he is a superstar. I struck out a lot and at a tender young age. One has to tolerate a lot of failure to be a photographer or baseball player.

When I was thirteen, an IU student loaned me a miniature Rollie. I can't imagine why he did that. The Rollie was a very high-end camera. Not something that one would loan to a kid. I began photographing life in junior high school. I entered one of my photographs in a competition and to my surprise it won. If that wasn't enough to seal my fate, the first year of *Life* magazine came into our lives. It is hard to imagine today the impact that magazine had. Keep in mind that there were few image stimulations to be had in 1936. Suddenly the whole world was open for view. Only after Dad devoured that magazine could I get my hands on it. I studied with envy the small photos of *Life* photographers in the front of the magazine. There would be Eisenstadt or Stackpole with a Leica or Contax camera around his neck. How I wanted one of those cameras! Then I would study the photographs and marvel that anyone could do that. *Life* transported us from an insular life in a small midwestern town to places all over the world.

One Christmas when I was fourteen, I got Uncle Cal's camera. I think he had abandoned photography in favor of showgirls. The camera was a Recomar—a small-view camera and a real professional instrument. I was ecstatic. I quickly began photographing my friends, but mainly the girls of whom I was becoming increasingly aware. My father fashioned a simple darkroom in our basement and got a plumber friend to make me an enlarger out of sheet metal and a pipe stand. He equipped it in such a way that I could slide my camera onto it to provide a lens for enlarging. I had three small trays, a safe light, and a graduate and I was off and running. Aside from swimming in the quarries during summer and hanging out at Potter's Pool Room during the winters, my leisure time was spent making photographs. I loved it so.

A Day That Will Live in Infamy

My youthful reverie came to a screeching halt on December 7, 1941. Along with a million other guys, I was swept up and sent to war. I ended up being trained to monitor Japanese radio transmissions and landed in the South Pacific attached to the 13th Air Force. When the war ended I was dumped back into my mother's kitchen, where she tried to make up for all the "C" rations I had consumed overseas. Like so many veterans, I hadn't a clue what I was supposed to do as a civilian. When all else failed I would drink with my buddies and celebrate our survival.

Before leaving for service I had put my camera on a closet shelf and did not think to get it down until one night during our frequent celebrations of survival. I attended a drinking party at a fellow vet's house. He got out a camera and a couple of lights and began taking "cheesecake" photographs of the girls. I asked if I could shoot a roll and then promptly forgot the session in favor of drinking more and dancing. About a week later my friend came to me with a proof sheet of what I had done. He thought my efforts remarkable. So did I. I promptly got down my old camera and began making photographs again.

From Lush to Learner

After a time of celebrating my survival, reality began to take hold. Drinking and partying can only take you so far before you turn into the town lush. For want of something better to do I decided to enter Indiana University on the GI Bill. There were so many returning veterans that the school was overwhelmed. In a year the enrollment jumped from a couple thousand to more than twelve thousand. The resources of the school were stretched so thin that one couldn't talk to a faculty advisor. I had to settle for a graduate student. The fellow asked me what I wanted to do with my life. I said, "I dunno, how about music?" "Oh, man, you don't want to major in music. You will just end up being a tuba teacher in some high school." Well, I surely didn't want to end up a high-school tuba teacher, so after a moment's reflection, I opted for the business school, which was what my two older brothers had done. I asked my learned advisor what his major was. He said, "Music!"

Corporation finance, money and banking, marketing, economics—these subjects did not exactly thrill me. I struggled on, doing my best, which was only average. In my spare time I took photographs.

GI Joe

I had a buddy, a fellow amateur photographer named Joe. Joe was a survivor of the Battle of the Bulge and had been seriously wounded. Joe was a poster boy for the rough, tough vet. He was big, and had acquired a certain "don't tread on me" attitude gained in the foxholes in Europe. He told me about a guy who was teaching photography in the art department named Henry Holmes Smith. Joe suggested we sign up for an elective. I packed up some of my prints and went to see Smith. He perused my work and informed me that I could enroll in beginning photography. WHAT! Beginning photography?! I was insulted. Why, I had been making photographs since I was twelve. Some of my prints had blue ribbons on the back. Blue ribbons won at the Ellettsville Fall Festival, mind you. I enrolled anyway, and thus began a ten-year relationship that set me on my path.

Taking a class from Henry was shock city. Henry Holmes Smith had been an associate of László Moholy-Nagy at the New Bauhaus in Chicago. His assignments included photographic investigations into such arcane subjects as reflection, refraction, translucence, opacity, transparency, and modulation of light. We experimented with prisms, mirrors, and all manner of ways light could be modulated. He would take us for walks on campus, find a blank wall with a pipe coming out, and ask the question, "What does that imply?" Joe and I spent many a night trying to hash out just what Henry was getting at. Was he genius or madman?

On the last day of class I chanced by Henry's office. Joe was standing at the door screaming at Henry with all the profanity learned on the battlefield. Henry was matching him in volume if not in blue language. Joe spun around, face livid, and brushed by me exclaiming, "I'll never take another class from that son of a bitch."

When the new semester began I enrolled once again, not sure why. The first semester had left me confused and uncertain. As I awaited the beginning of class, a furtive figure slipped into the chair next to me. It was Joe. He hung his head and said rather sheepishly, "I don't know what there is about this guy. I think he is onto something, and I intend to find out what it is."

This episode points up something about Henry's classes. They were volatile and intense, and at times a little maddening. Henry was forever challenging your value systems. Intense discussion was the norm. One day Henry walked into the classroom with a *Life* magazine under his arm. He threw it down in front of a particularly dense young jock, handed him a marker and told him to go through the magazine and mark everything he wished he had. When the lad was done, Henry sat beside him and questioned each choice until the poor guy was frothing at the mouth. It was a typical Smith performance.

Henry's Myth: A Search for Self

It has been said that Henry was a man with an infinite capacity for righteous indignation. This comment is a comic twist to an otherwise deep journey into self. Really there was nothing righteous about Henry's indignation. It was the fruit of a mythic trip in search of the real H. H. Smith. So as to succeed in this adventure, Henry had honed his senses to such a razor's edge that it must have seemed as if all the madness around him was trying to blunt his instrument. He could certainly rage against the indignities and injustices he saw in the world—and there were many. He suffered for being so finely tuned. Most of us shield ourselves with a thick veneer of indifference. That was not Henry's way. As time passed, Henry's rage turned to ironic wit. He became a wryly funny man—fun to be around. He had sailed into calm waters where he had a clear view of the world, no less indignant but tempered with an amalgam of wisdom. He shared all of this with his students and set many of them on a similar journey. It ran deeper than just learning how to make a photograph; it was a prescription for life.

Increasingly he produced icons of his journey in the form of photographs. These photographs were mythic in character and little understood. His method and soaring intelligence sailed over the heads of contemporary critics. Such a journey cannot be ignored for long. It offers too much of substance for us all.

Dropping Out: Breaking Ties

Meanwhile, back at the IU business school, my grade point average slid down, down, down. I took a class each semester with Henry. I did manage to graduate. In the last semester, the proper protocol was to put on your suit and tie and go to the business school and sign up for interviews with the corporate headhunters that descended on the school. I spent two days peeking into the interviews. Two questions kept coming to mind: "Do I want to talk with that guy?" and "Why would I want to talk with that guy?" My schoolmates were coming out of those interviews excited. They were going to work for General Electric, Standard Oil, NBC, and any number of corporations, with good salaries. I didn't sign up for a single interview. After two days of this, I left the school, walked across the street, and hired on as an IU photographer at a fraction of what I would have made if I had stayed the course. And so began ten years of working for Indiana University and hanging out with Henry Smith. During those years I managed to earn an M.S. degree in visual communication and a Master of Fine Arts degree. I rejoice at the day I stumbled into Henry's class. What luck!

On Doing It

Today, on my darkroom door, there is a sign that says, "I've gone to find myself. If I get back before I return, keep me here." I found that sign in the high country of Arizona, and when I laid eyes on it I thought it the true expression of my life in photography. It has always been a personal quest. A quest with an unknown destination. Photography fleshes out my life and gives it meaning and coherence. For that I am deeply grateful.

I like the process. The way in which it holds together opposites: light and dark, beautiful and ugly, sublime and banal. To make a photograph as honestly as one can generates an artifact that bears witness to one's personal truth. It locks you into the moment, the eternal present. Sometimes there is the physical sensation of light. The world becomes luminous. You get a chance to unite with multiple realities. I have come to realize that it is more than an act of monitoring the world. Sometimes I feel like I am penetrating a void to a parallel universe. Pretty mystical, I suppose. Minor White offered the only advice I can give on photography: "Look at it not for what it is, but for what else it is."

Acknowledgments

What manner of loving souls are these people who have so aided in the making of this book? It could not have happened without the willing assistance of so many. The first and foremost is Carol Isaacs, my niece, who pushed me into going by Indiana University Press on a visit to Bloomington, Indiana, to find out if a book might be possible. She also helped along the way in doing research on these photographs made so many years ago. At Indiana University Press I met Linda Oblack, my sponsoring editor, who suggested that I cover the early years of my photographic odyssey. A book about my Indiana years. Linda exhibited infinite patience as I struggled to rediscover work that had been lost in the files for almost half a century. Bradley Cook of Indiana University Archives also helped in finding old images which are in the IU Archives.

And then there is Ben Nixon, my assistant, who proved a master at finding ancient negatives, and who served as an ongoing helper in every aspect of doing this work. Ben is a fine photographer, a very proactive guy. I doubt if I could have done this without his assistance and counsel.

For over thirty years I taught art at various institutions. In the process I garnered a number of loyal former graduate students who have arrived at mid career. It was my pleasure to teach these folks photography as I knew it, namely silver-based work done in what we now refer to as the "wet" darkroom. They have moved on to digital photography and willingly helped this old dog learn new tricks on the computer. I doubt I could have done this book without digital photography. My dream team consisted of Michael Creedon, John Spence Weir, Bill Kane, Rod Laursen, and John Toupin. I also received help from photographers Richard Blair, Alexis Gerard, and Ira Nowinski. There are also the countless folks who, in a chance conversation, dropped a gem about digital photography which I quickly absorbed. I have been constantly tuned to learn this complex technique. It has enriched my dotage beyond measure.

ONE | Beginnings

My photographic odyssey began when I was thirteen years old. I made this photograph in 1936 and entered it in a contest. It won. No doubt my fate was sealed. The photograph was taken at a Bloomington High School football game.

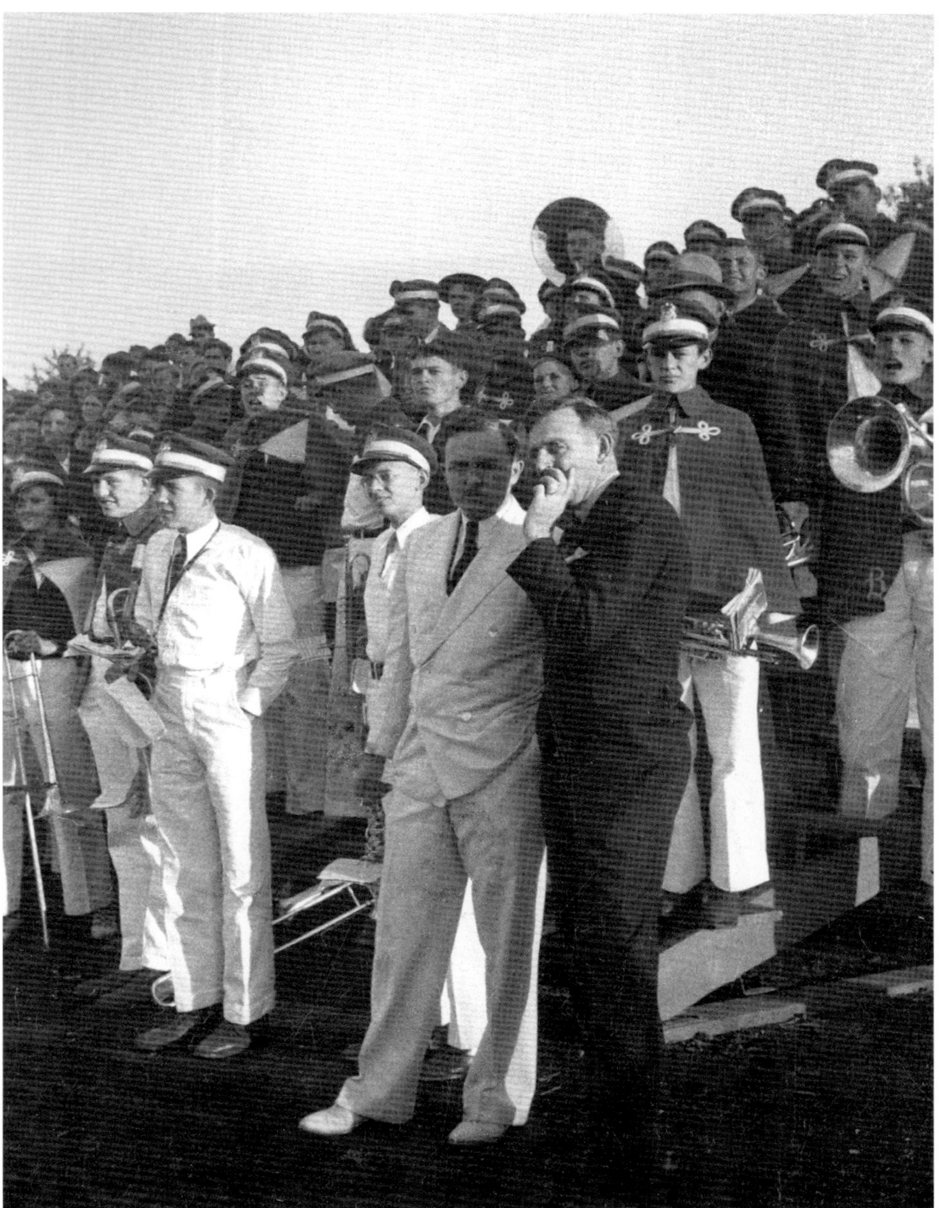

BLOOMINGTON HIGH SCHOOL FOOTBALL GAME, 1936

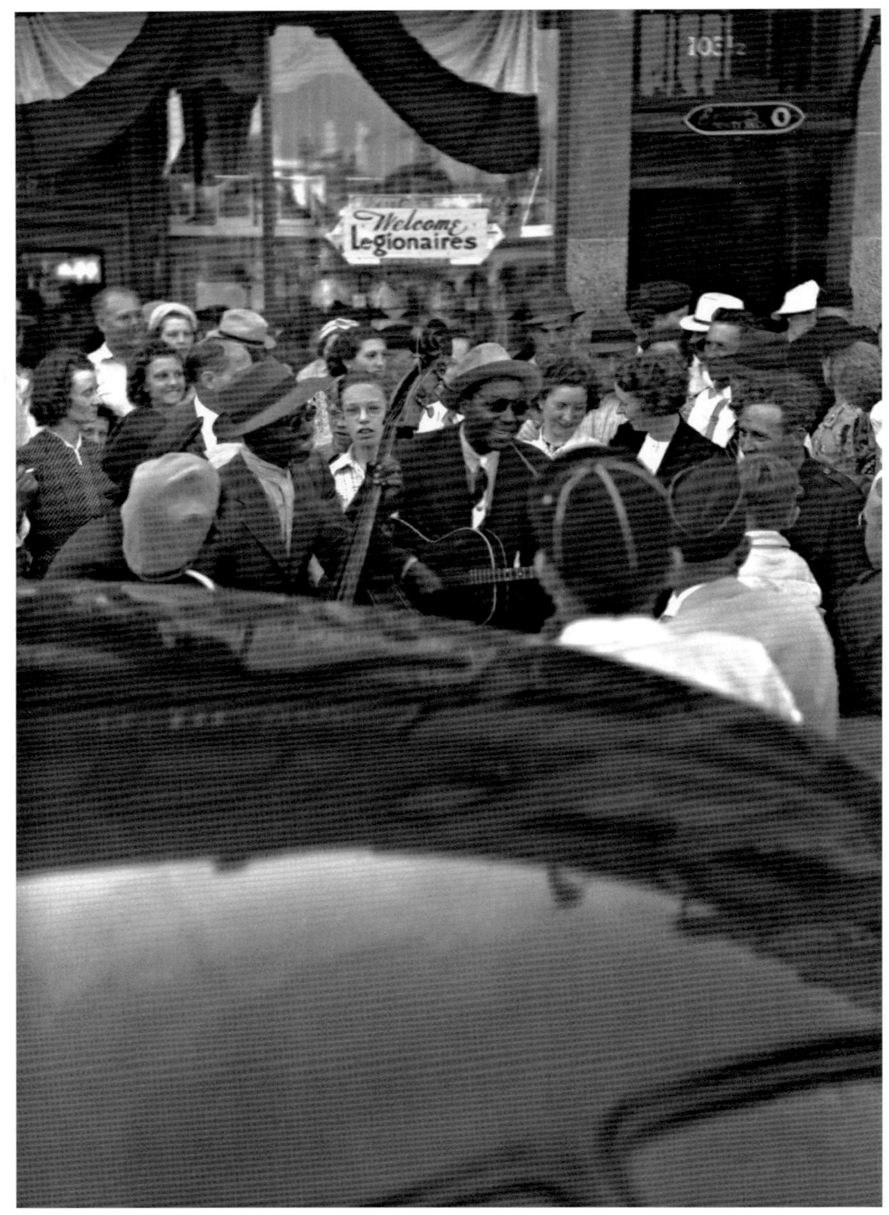

This image was made in 1938 during an American Legion convention held in Bloomington, Indiana.

On November 26, 1936, Life *magazine entered our home. I had to wait until my dad was done with it, after which I devoured it. It made a big impression and influenced my photography.*

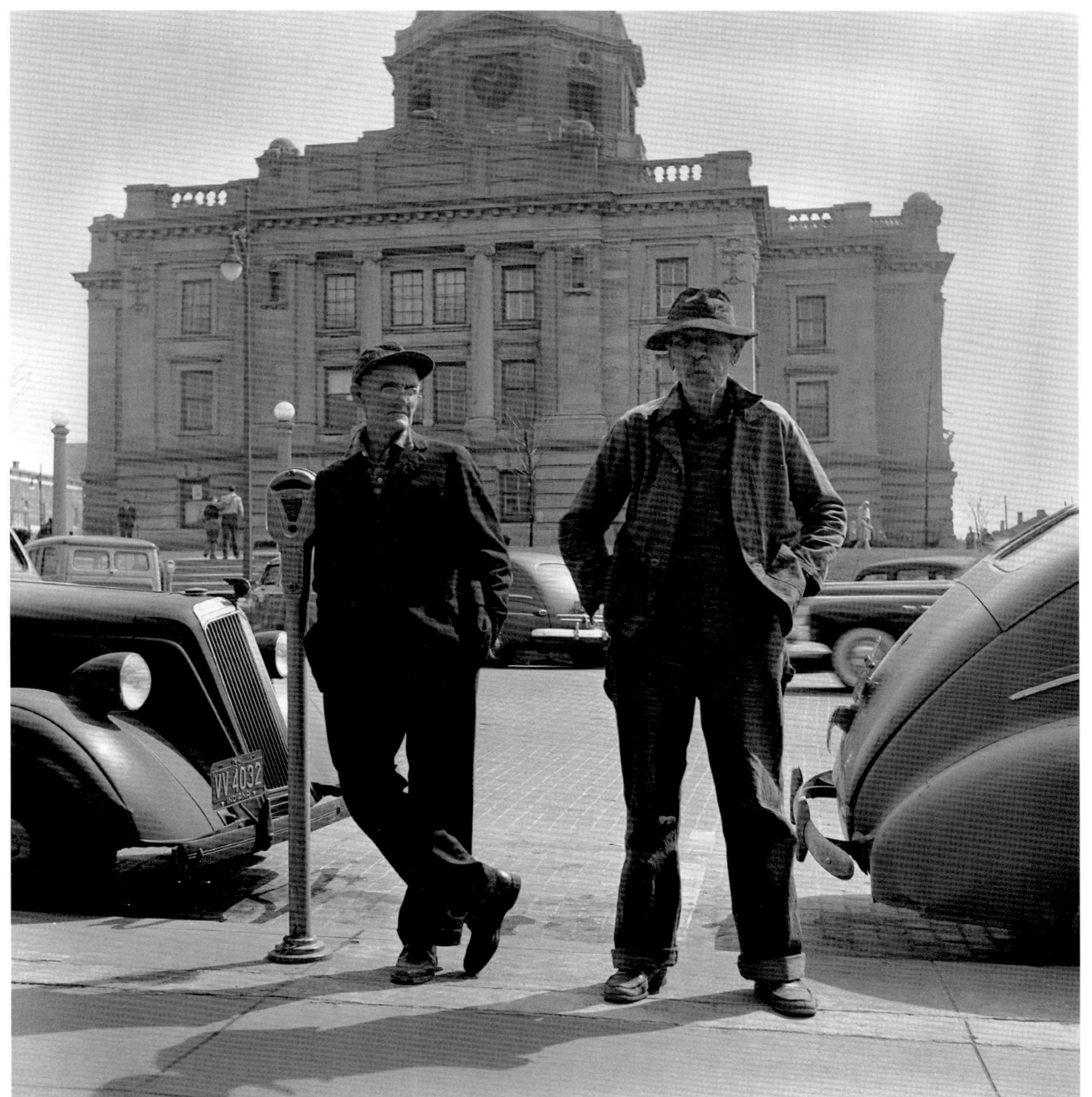

FARMERS ON THE SQUARE, BLOOMINGTON, INDIANA, c. 1950

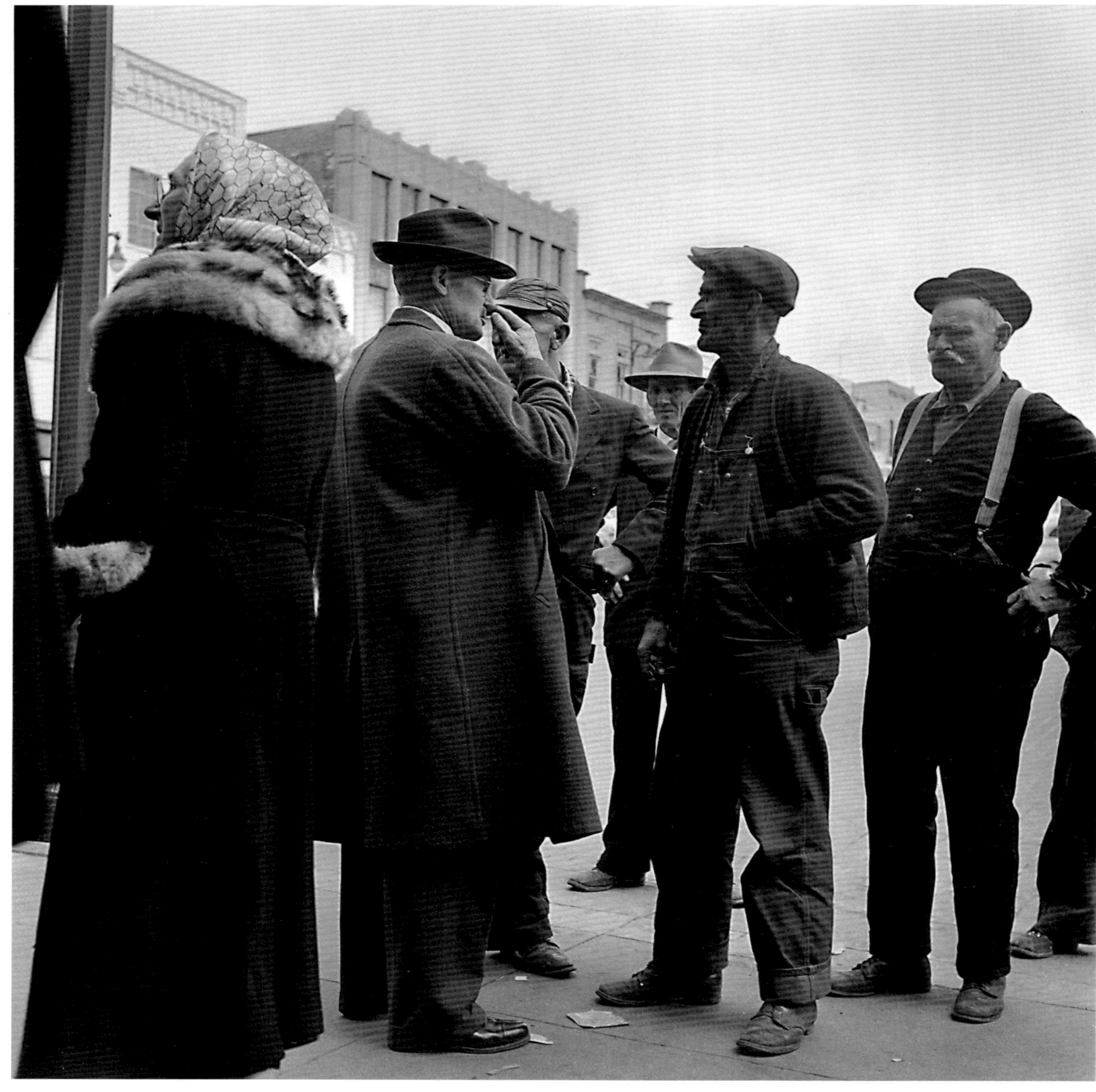

These gentlemen are talking to "the man." He is probably a local banker or the county agent, both of whom had a heavy influence on their lives. The county agent helped them in their farming and the bankers tided them over in bad years. During the Great Depression years it was tough going trying to keep the bankers from foreclosing on their farms. It was a love-hate relationship.

 | TALKING TO "THE MAN," BLOOMINGTON, INDIANA, c. 1950

In 1948 I took my first class with Henry Holmes Smith. That class set me off exploring my hometown in ways I had never done before. I haunted the streets and alleys of Bloomington in search of photographs. Bloomington was the county seat and farmers would flood the downtown square on Saturdays. They would do business and talk with their peers while their wives shopped the square. It was a fascinating way to spend Saturdays.

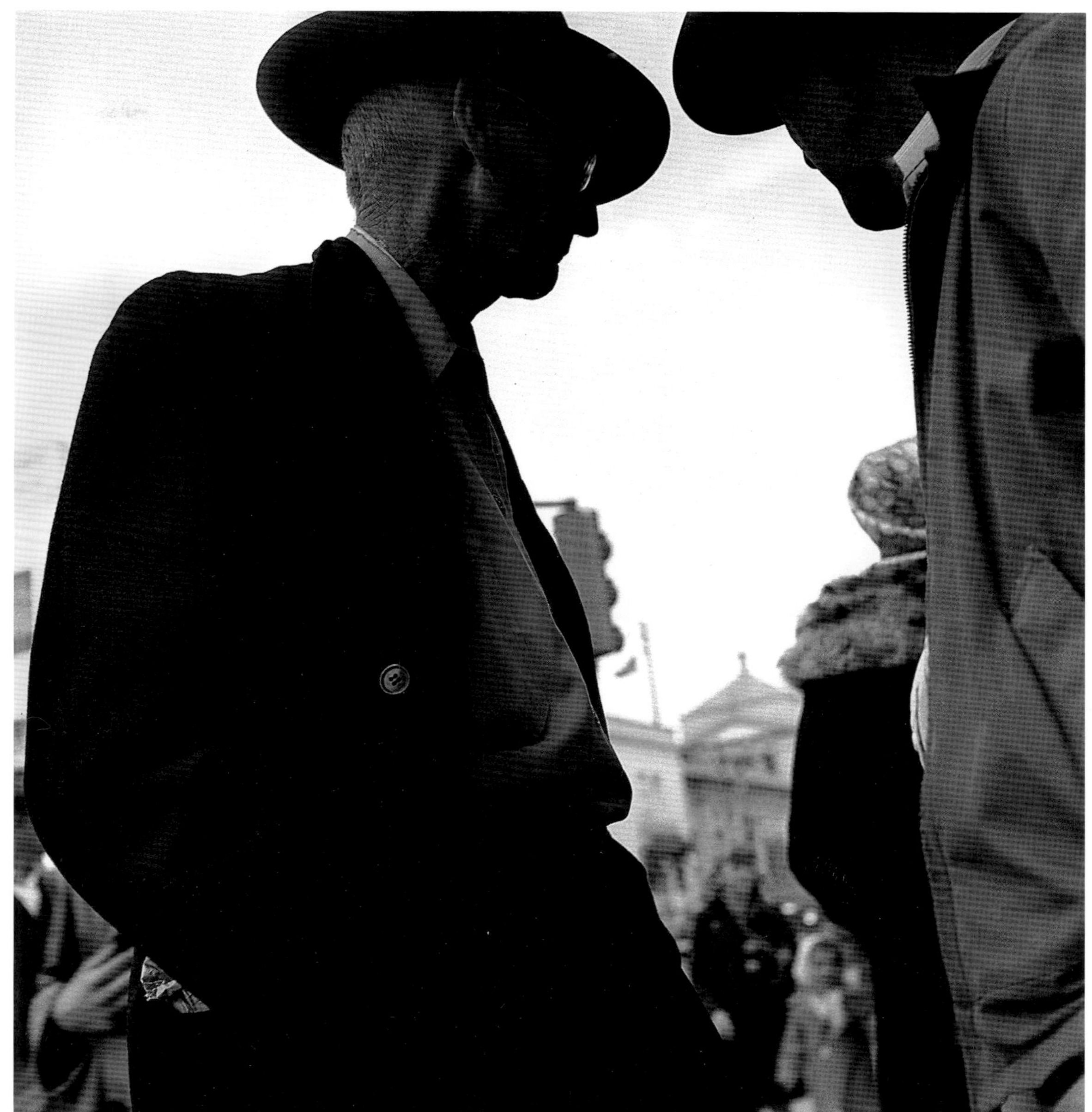

ON THE SQUARE, c. 1948

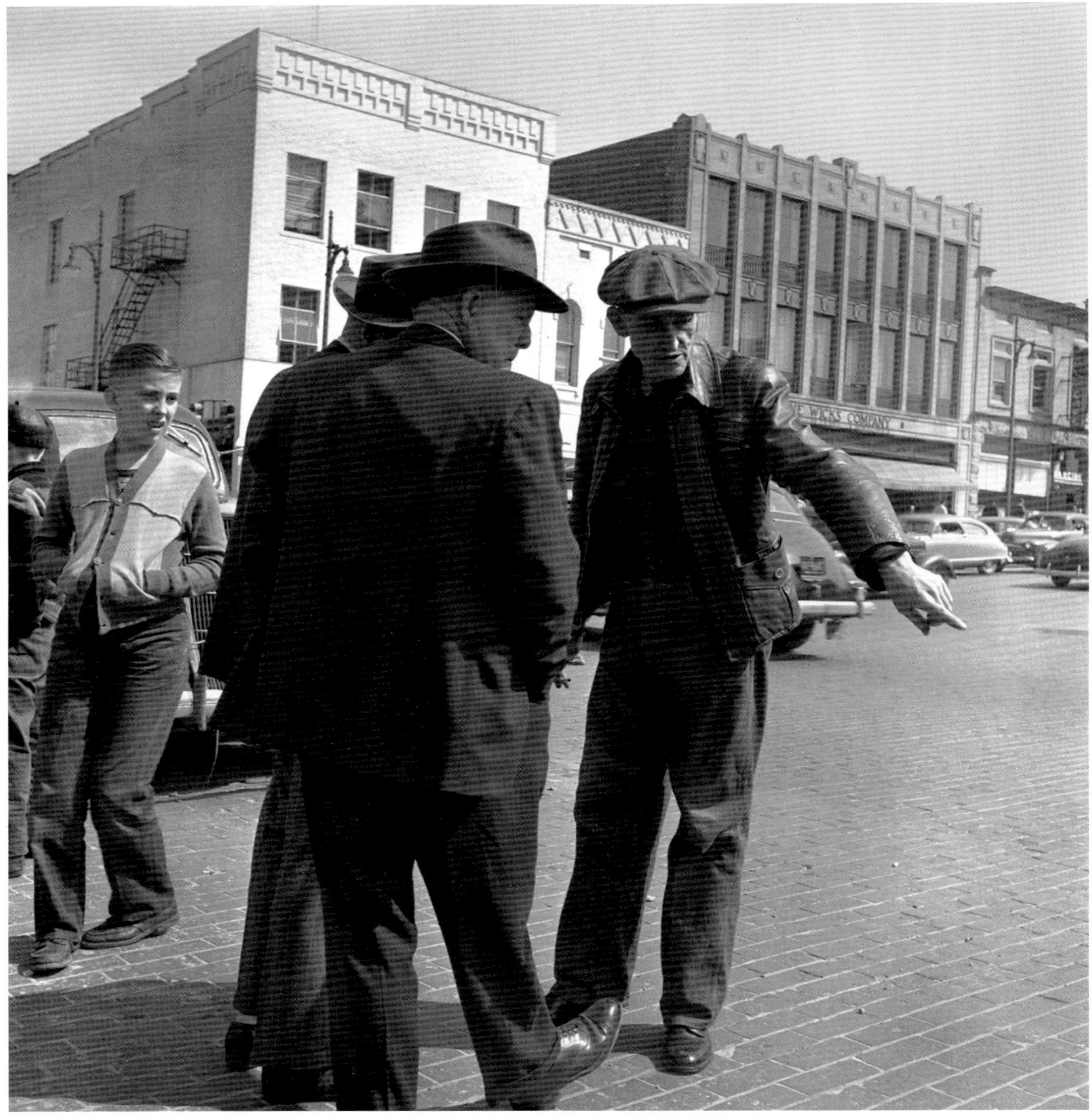

I arrived on the scene after an accident on the square. The gentleman on the right points out to a friend just where things happened, while, in the next photo, the officer does his duty as skeptical citizens look on.

 | IT HAPPENED HERE, ACCIDENT SCENE ON THE SQUARE, BLOOMINGTON, INDIANA, c. 1949

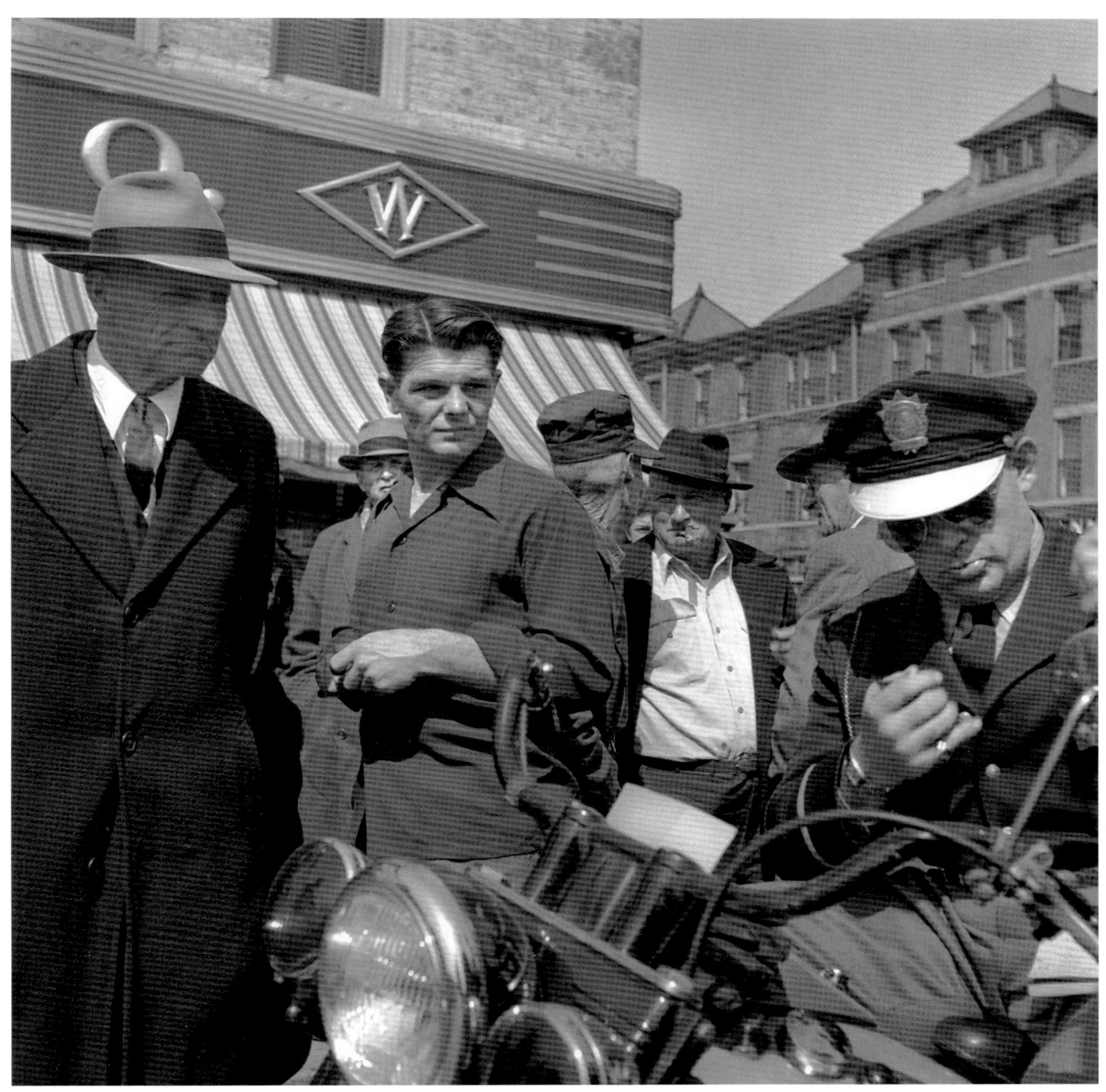

THE BUST, BLOOMINGTON, INDIANA, c. 1949

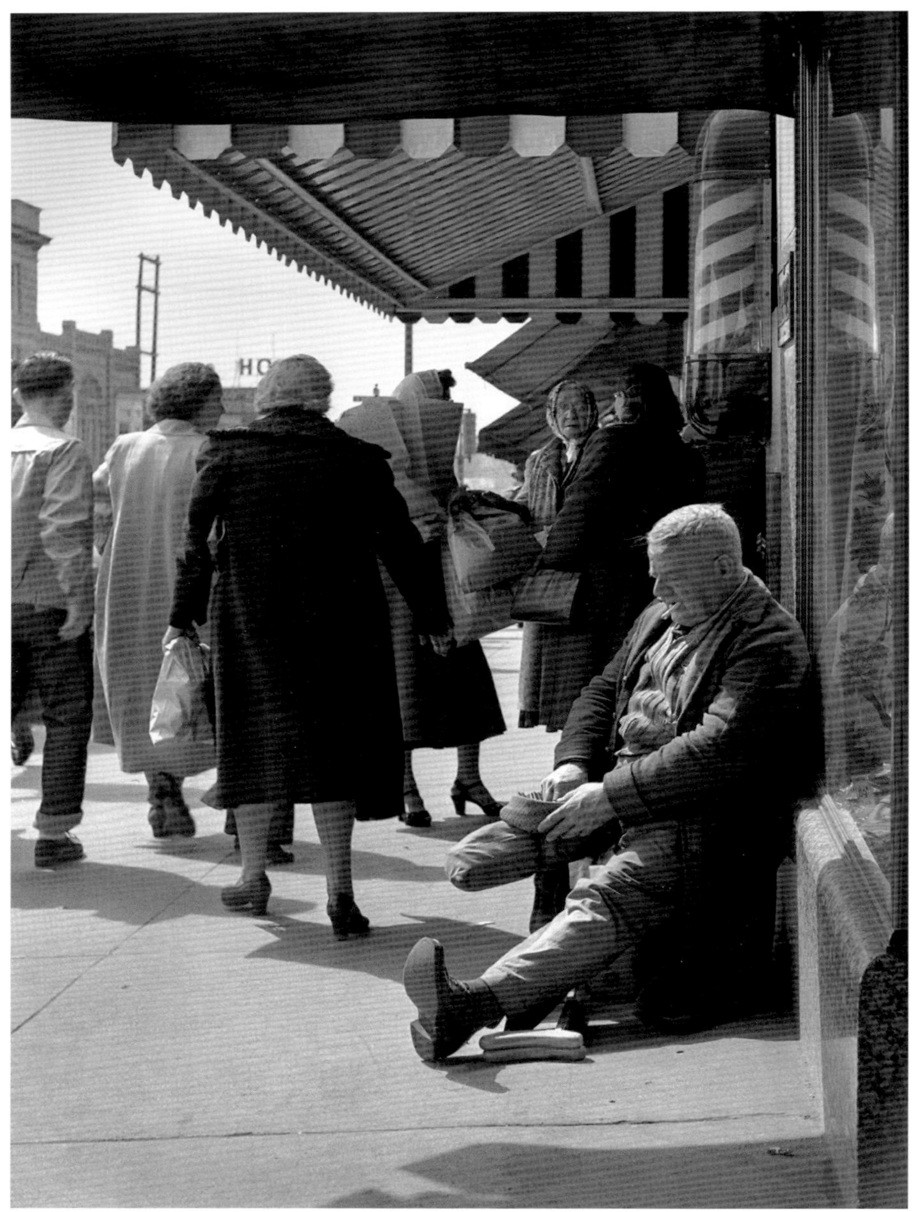

 | SATURDAY ON THE SQUARE, BLOOMINGTON, INDIANA, c. 1949

TWO | Kids

Kids love alleys. While roaming Bloomington's alleys I discovered it was a favorite place to be. In these alleys they could create a private world away from the prying eyes of adults. It was their best sanctuary. Here they were relatively free until such time as they were summoned home. I made a lot of young friends searching the alleys. If you want to see a town as it was a hundred years before, go to the alleys. While people update their storefronts and houses, they often leave the backside as it was many years before.

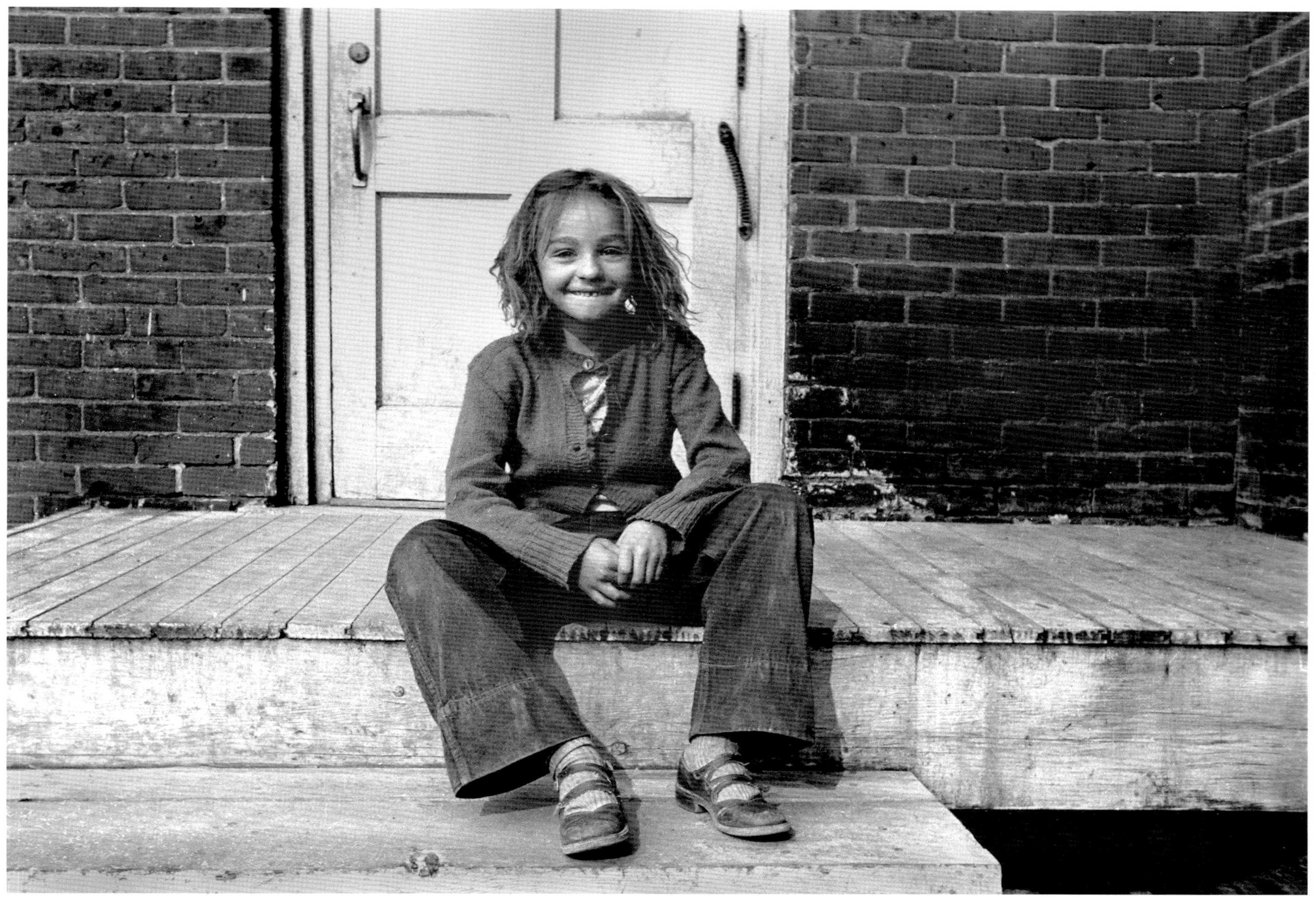

ALLEY GIRL, BLOOMINGTON, INDIANA, 1950

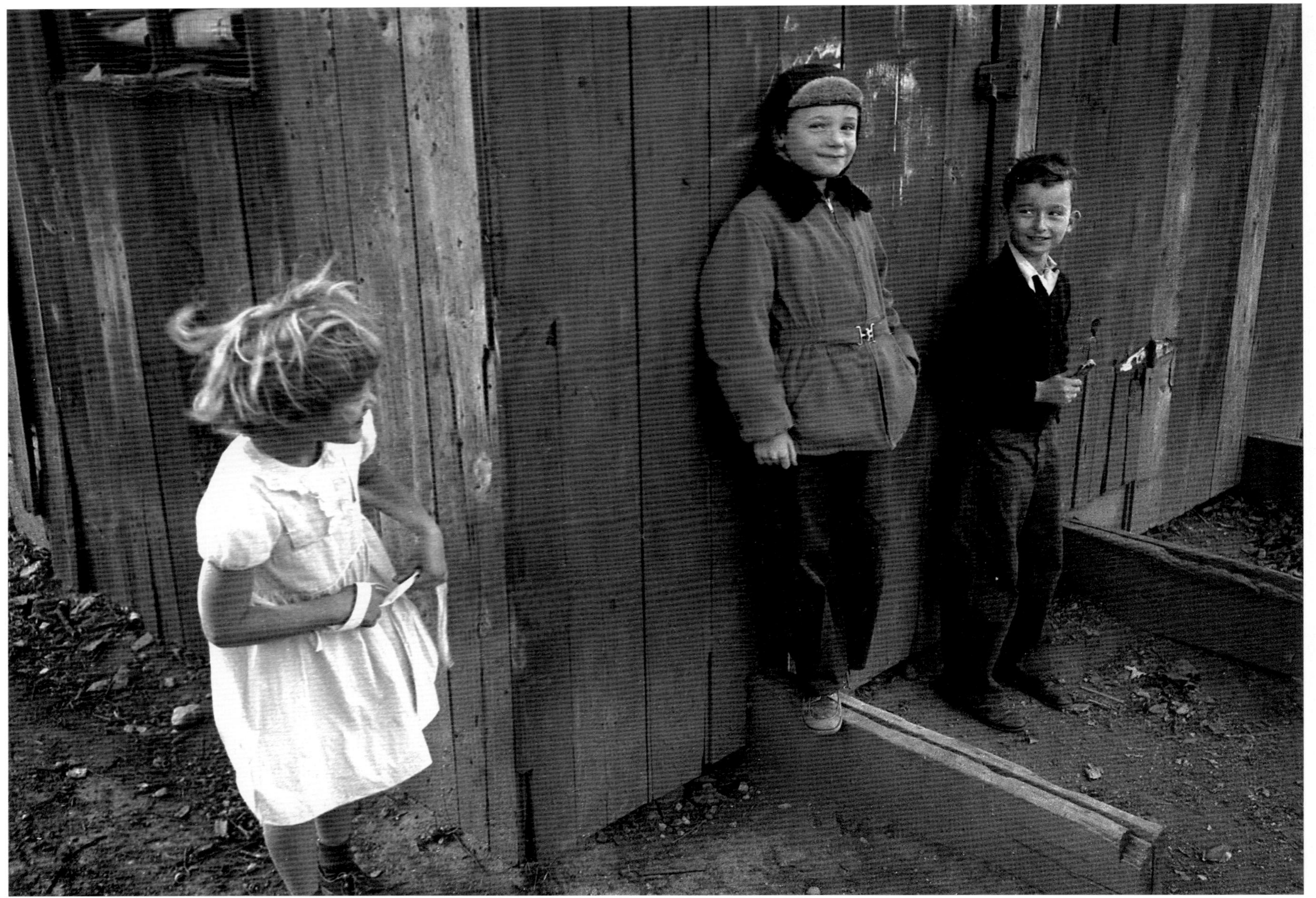

 | THE ENCOUNTER, BLOOMINGTON, INDIANA, c. 1950

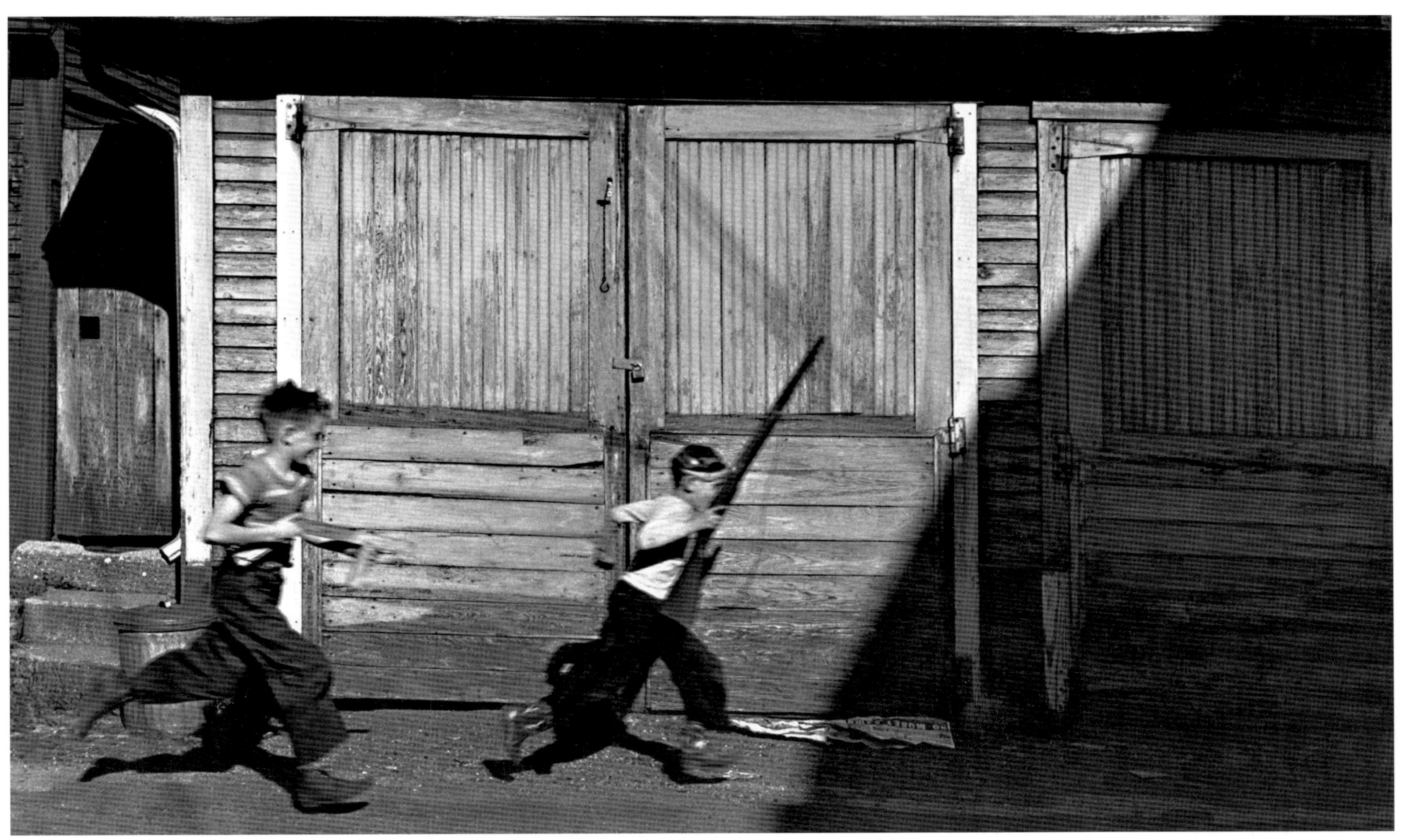

WAR GAMES, INDIANAPOLIS, c. 1952

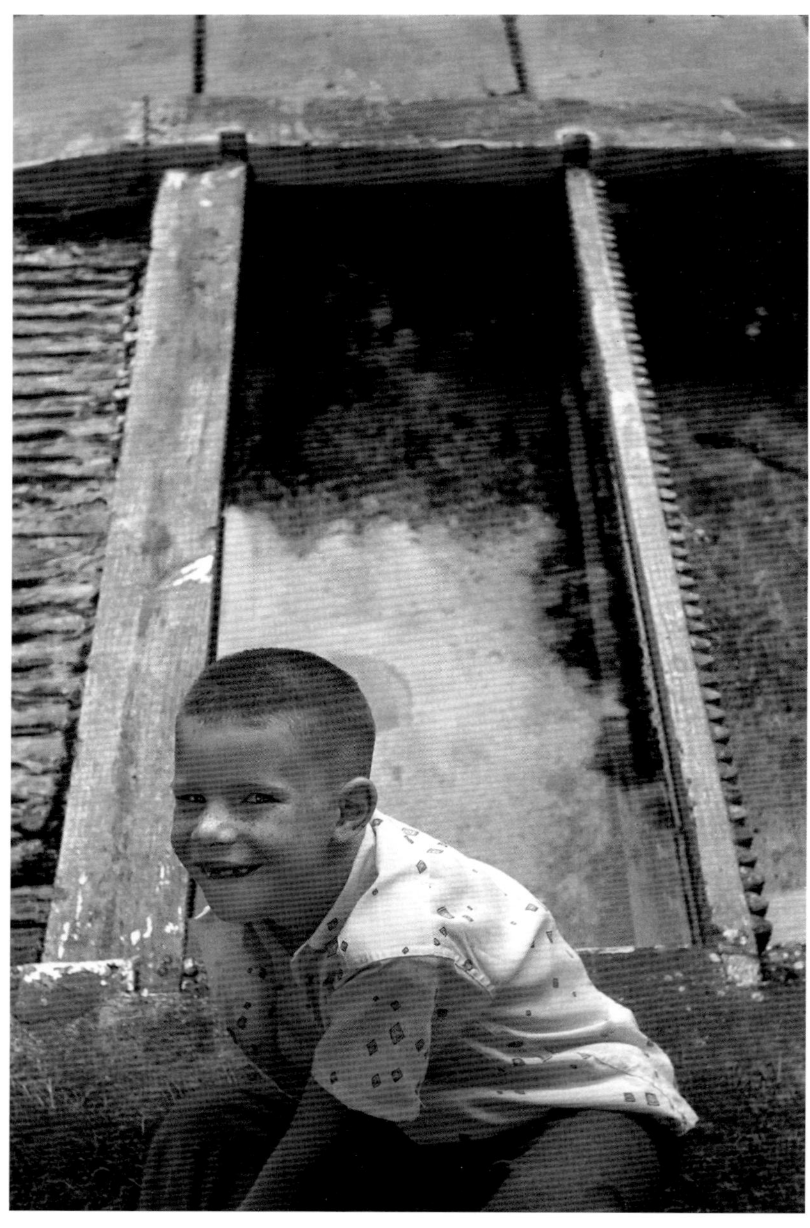

 | QUIZZICAL KID, FOND DU LAC, WISCONSIN, c. 1950

(opposite) The little girl in the cardigan is my daughter, Jan Marie. Here she reacts to her playmates in a most mysterious way. What does it all mean?

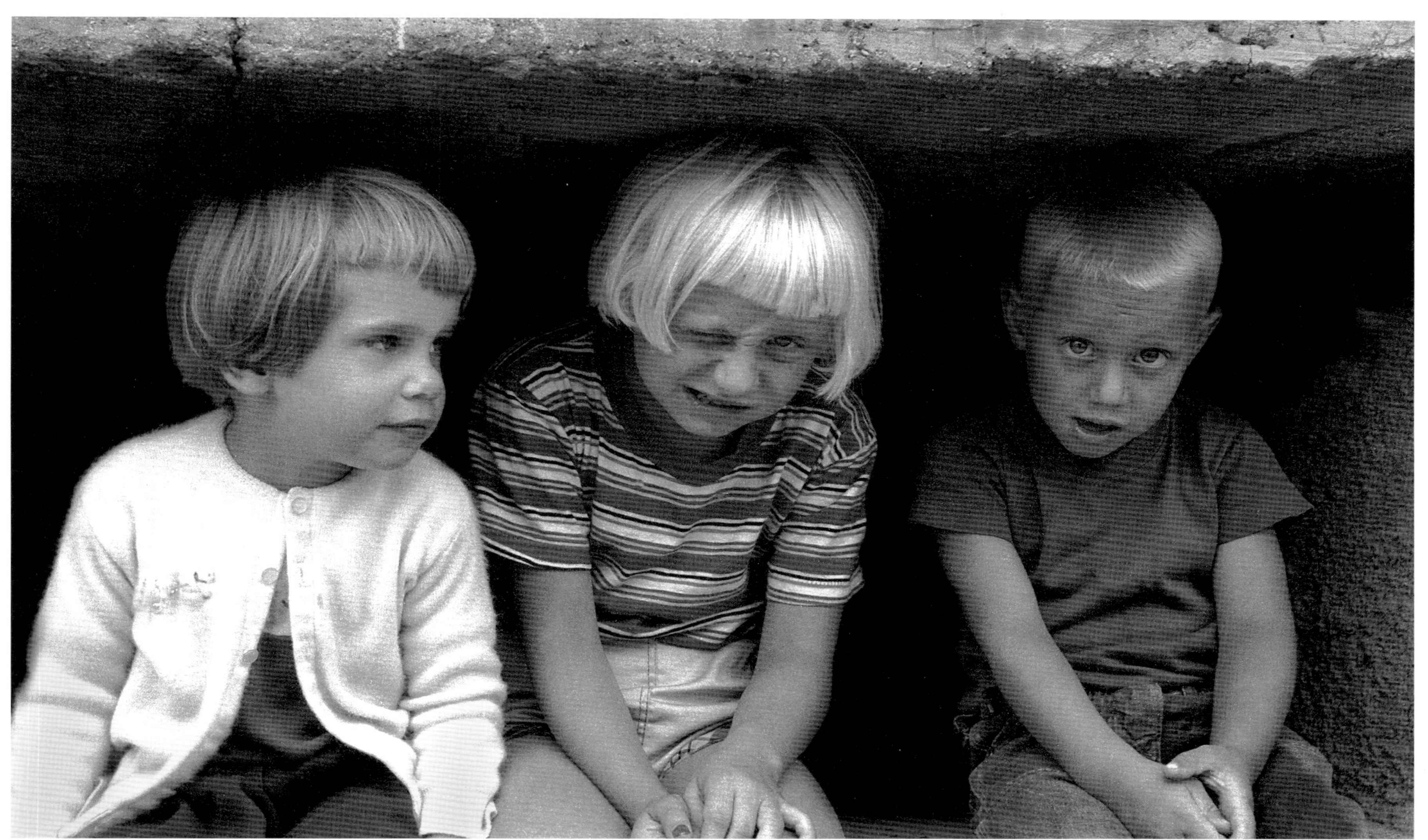

KIDS UNDER PORCH, FOND DU LAC, WISCONSIN, c. 1955

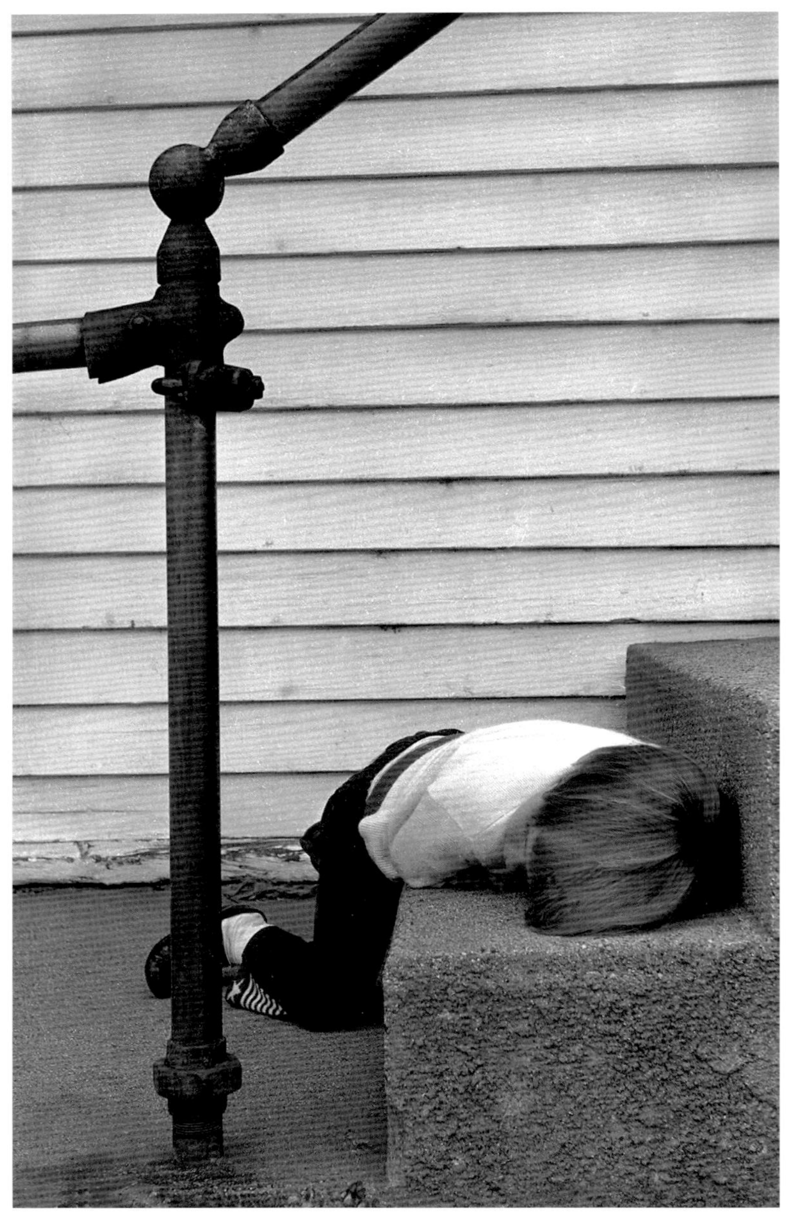

 | JAN MARIE WELPOTT, FOND DU LAC, WISCONSIN, c. 1955

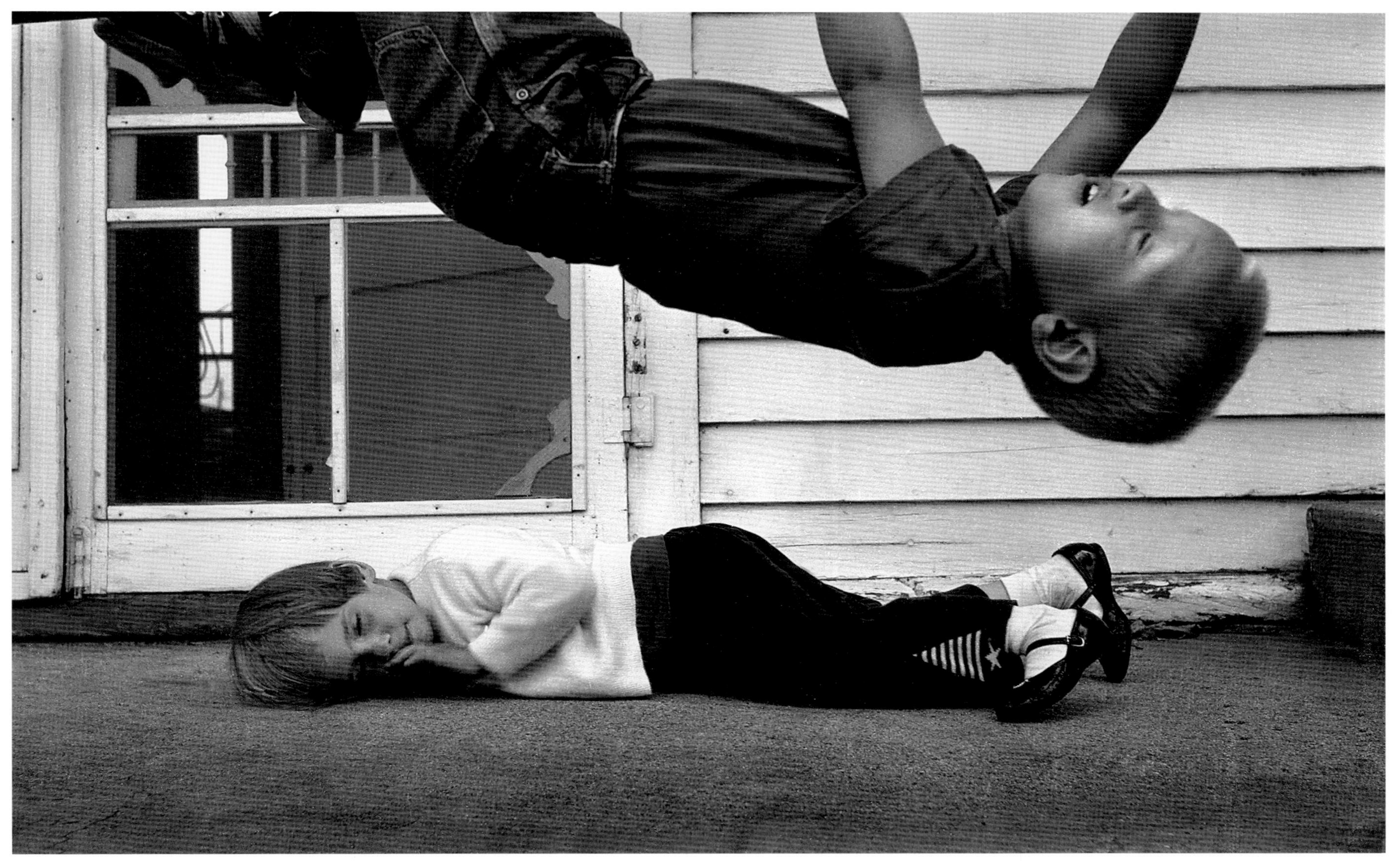

JAN MARIE WITH BOY, FOND DU LAC, WISCONSIN, c. 1955

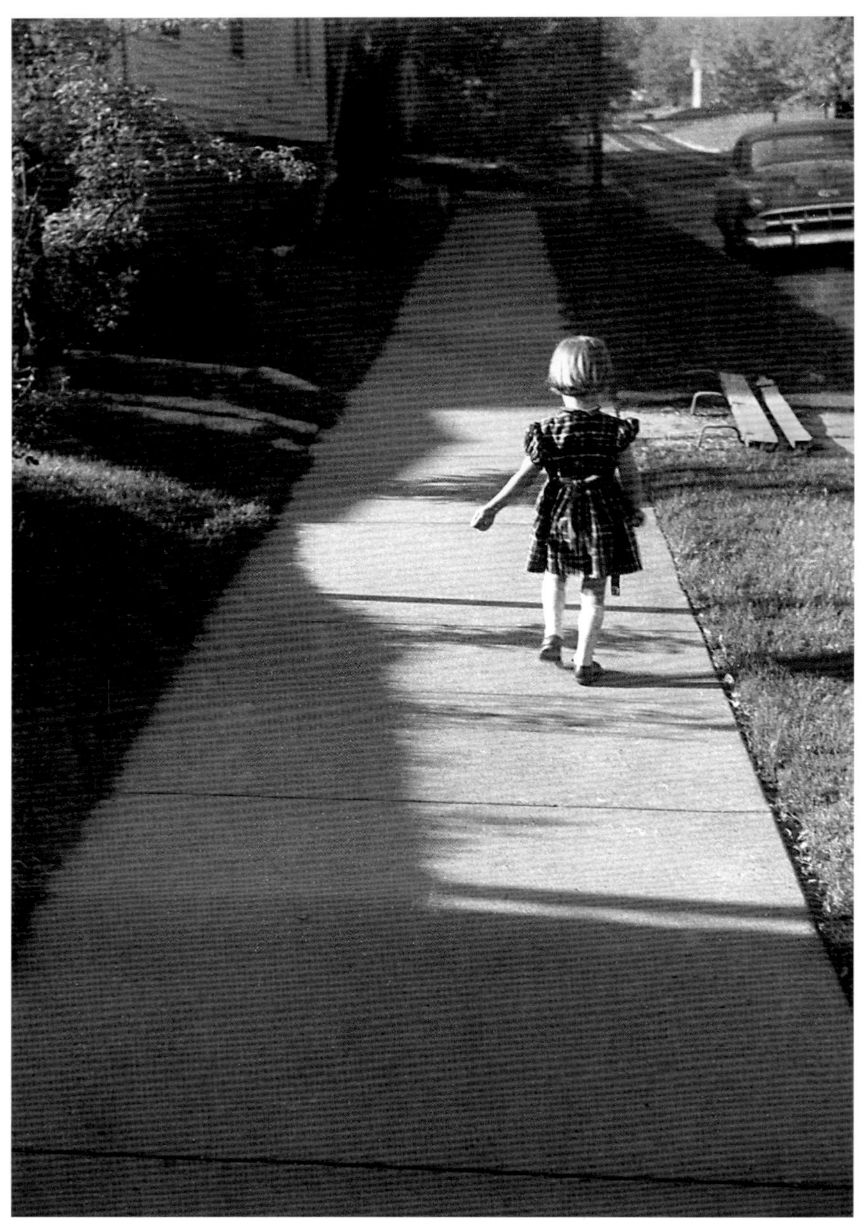

My daughter, Jan Marie, was born a twin. Her twin brother, Jay, died in infancy. It was one of the most difficult times in my life. Jay had a congenital heart defect that today would have been corrected in the womb even before birth. In those days such surgery was unknown.

My late wife, Jean, was a medical doctor. She had to stand by helpless as Jay's life slipped away. It was a most traumatic time.

In this photograph of Jan walking down the street, I have always felt that she is holding hands with her brother. I can't look at it without a flood of emotion.

 | DREAM WALKING, JAN MARIE WELPOTT, BLOOMINGTON, INDIANA, c. 1956

THREE | Indiana University

In 1949 I took a job with Indiana University as a photographer. I worked in that capacity for ten years. Among the many assignments I undertook, some of the most interesting took me into the science labs.

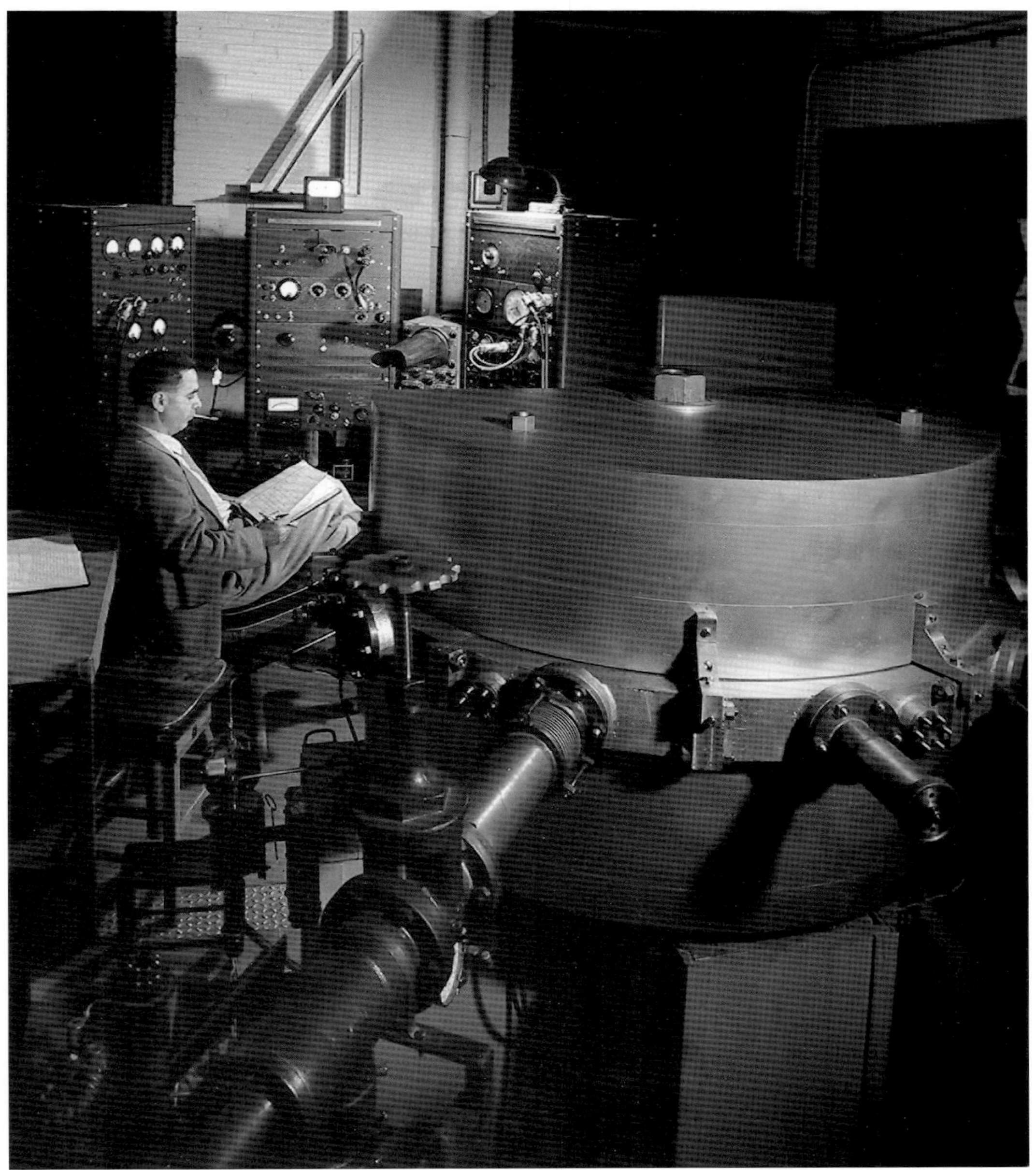

IN THE SCIENCE LAB, INDIANA UNIVERSITY, c. 1955

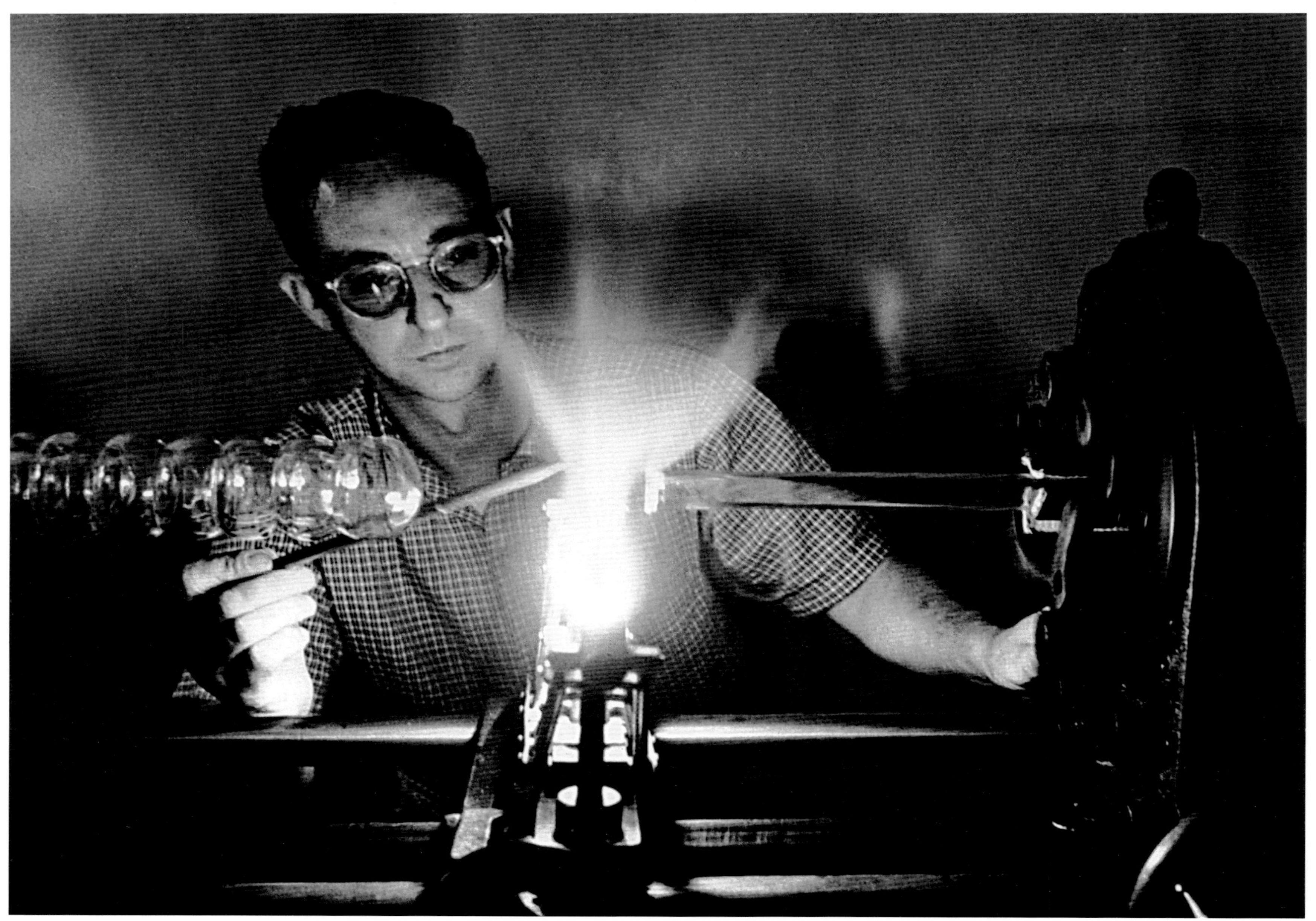

 | GLASS FUSION, INDIANA UNIVERSITY, c. 1955

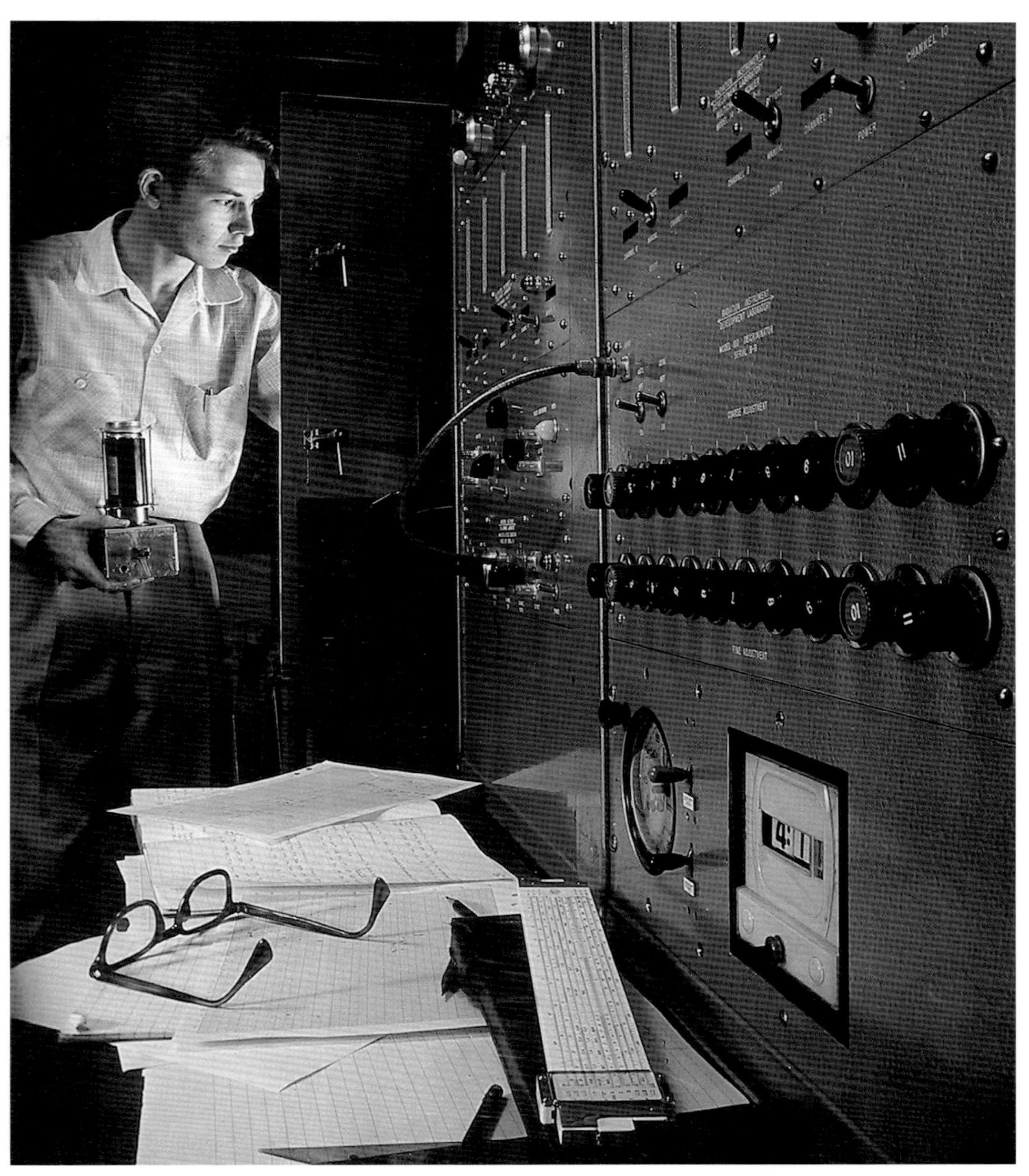

IN THE SCIENCE LAB, INDIANA UNIVERSITY, c. 1955

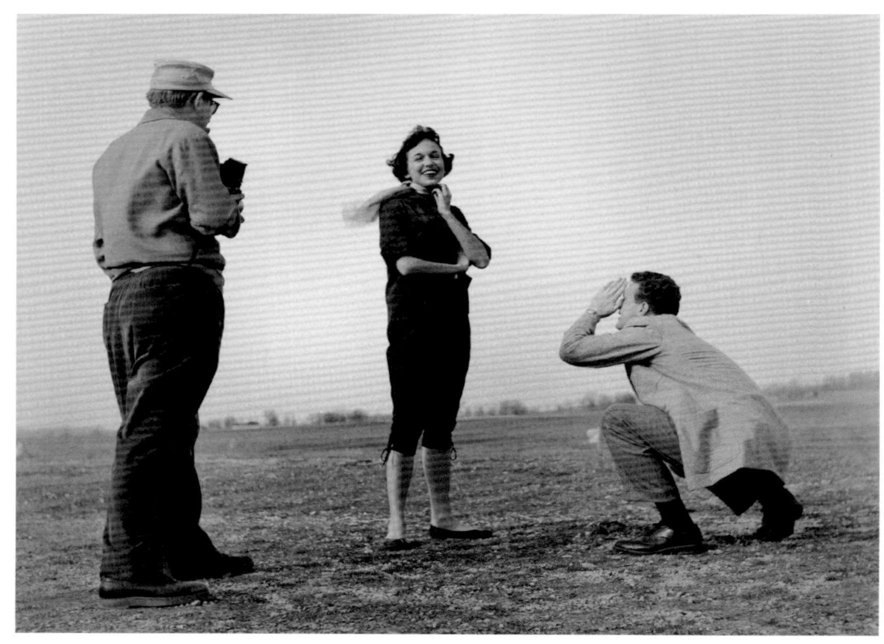

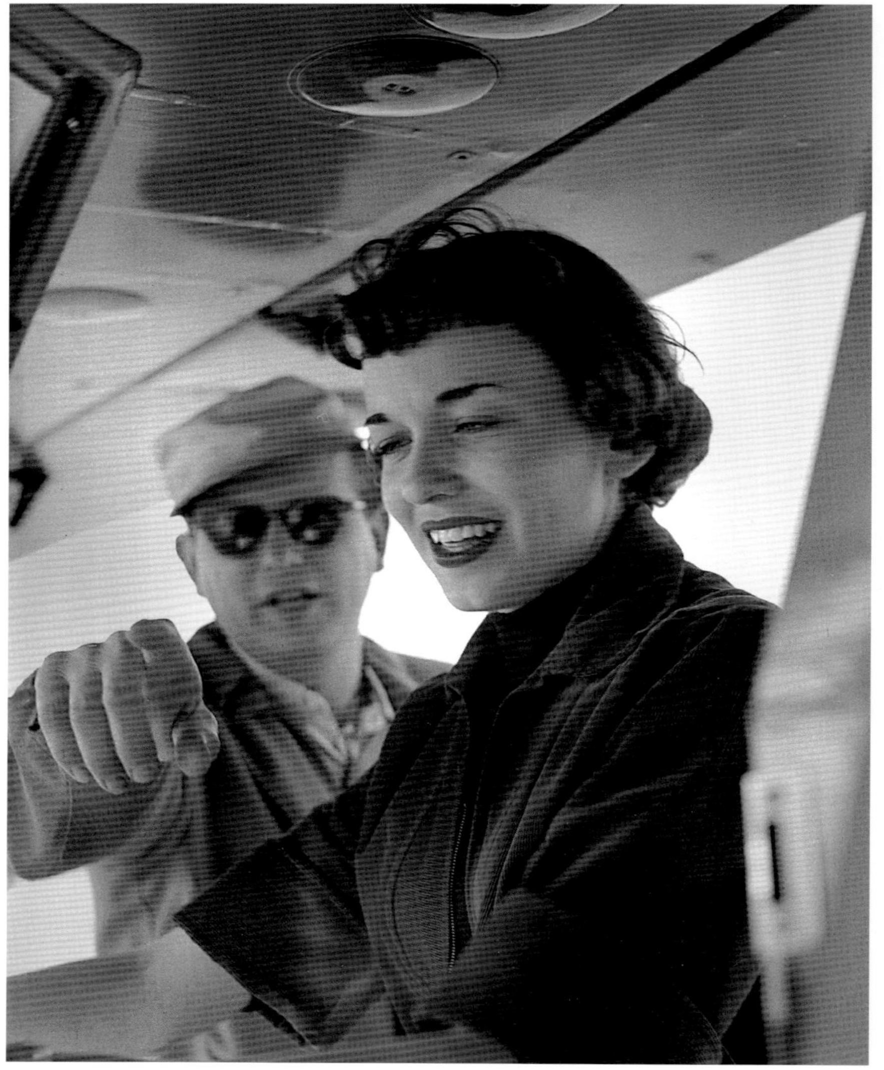

(above) Photographing an Arbutus Beauty. The guy on the right is George Disborough, doing what art directors do. (at right) Jack directs, c. 1955.

PHOTOS BY ROBERT SHAFFER

Working for Indiana University provided the most complete experience for applied photography that a photographer could hope for. Over the years, I did such a variety of work that it boggles my mind, including theater, dance, opera, news bureau, publicity, football, basketball, landscape, architecture, book illustration, documentation of university life, receptions, commencements, faculty portraits, science, celebrities, medical and dental documentation, fashion, and more. It was a remarkable training ground that served me well when I began teaching. Name any specialty and I had been there and done that. The assignments I loved the most were those involving the campus beauties. It is hardly work gallivanting around with attractive young ladies. I suppose it was my favorite duty, if you can call it a "duty."

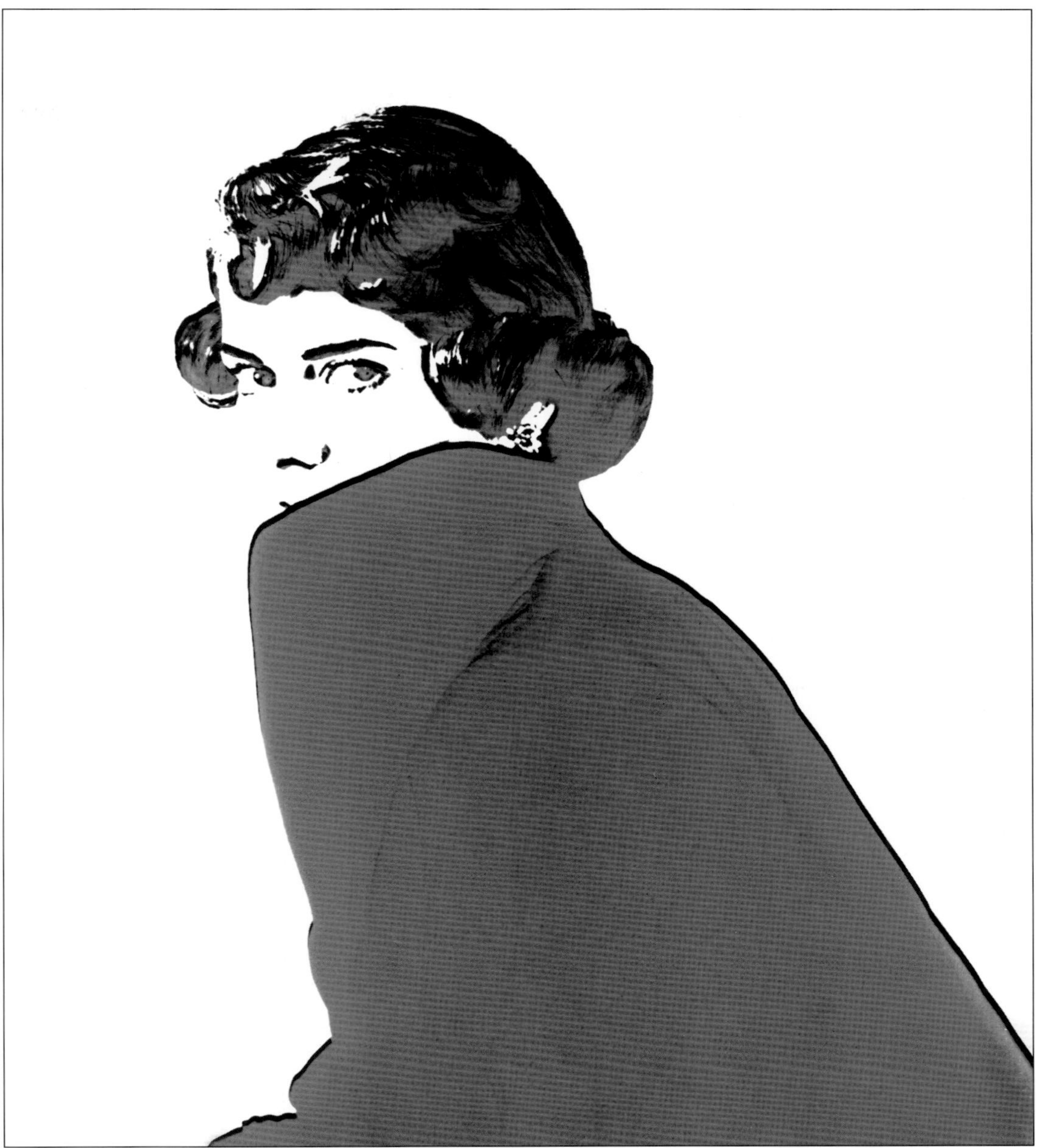

PHOTO DRAWING, c. 1953

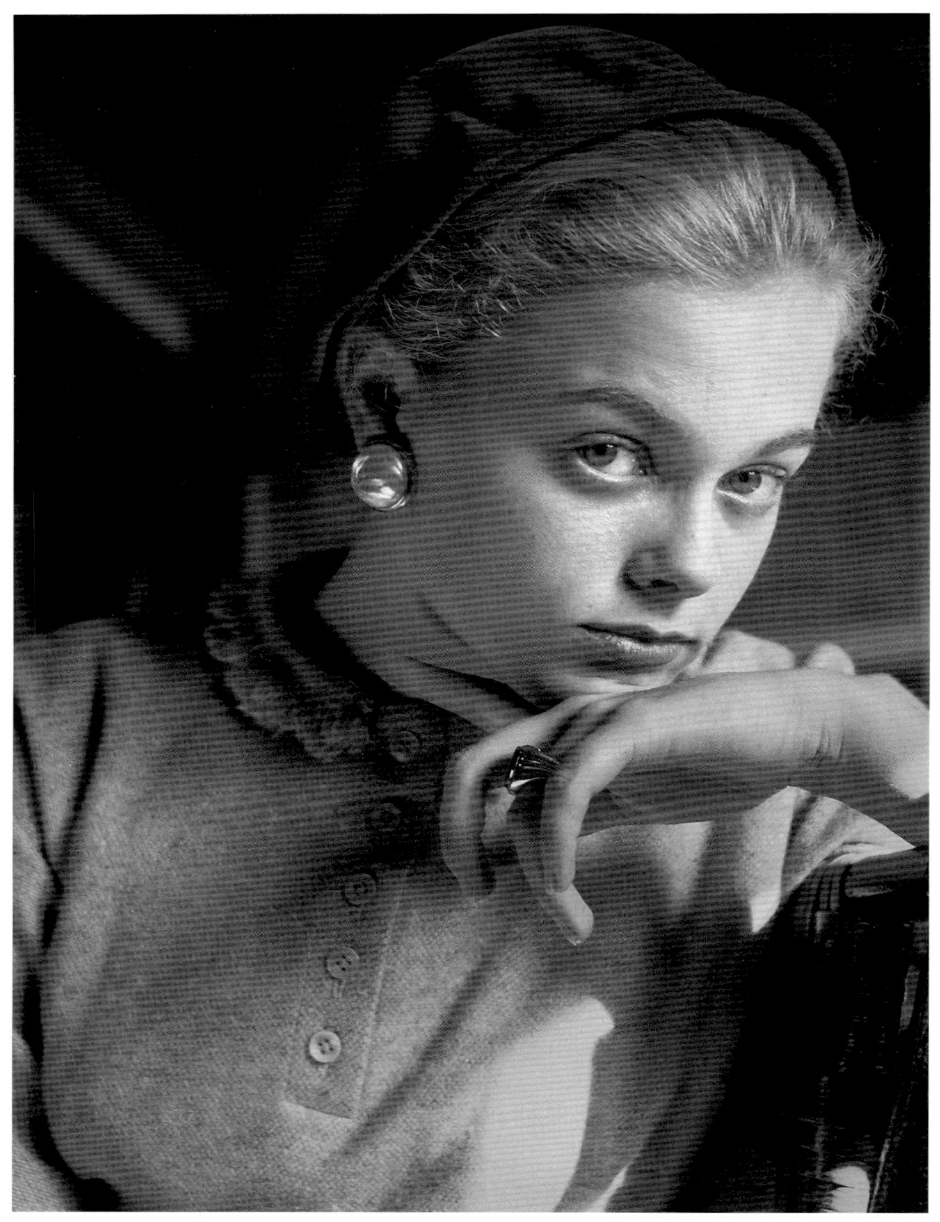

 | PAT WISE, ARBUTUS BEAUTY, c. 1955

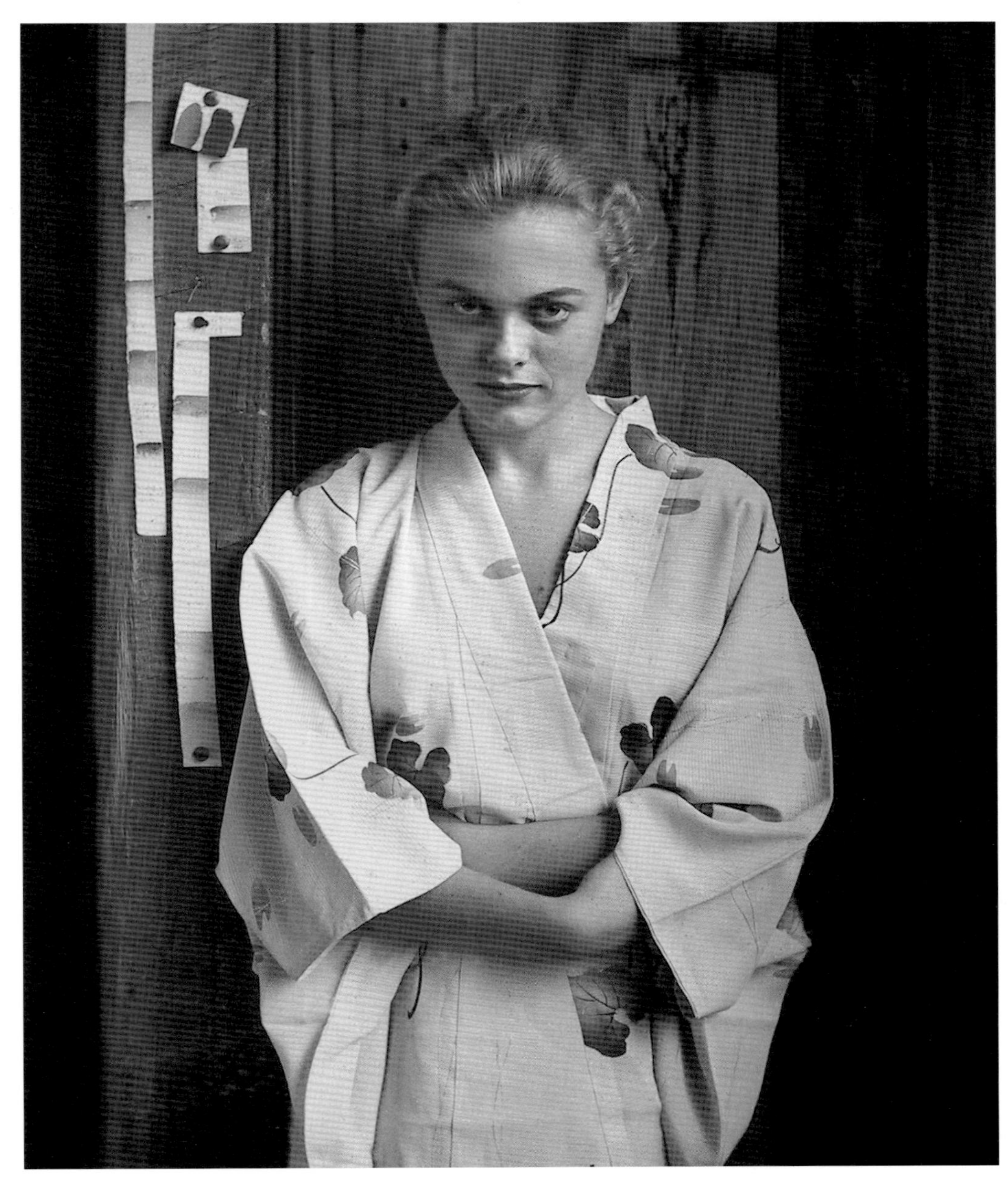

PAT WISE, ARBUTUS BEAUTY, c. 1955

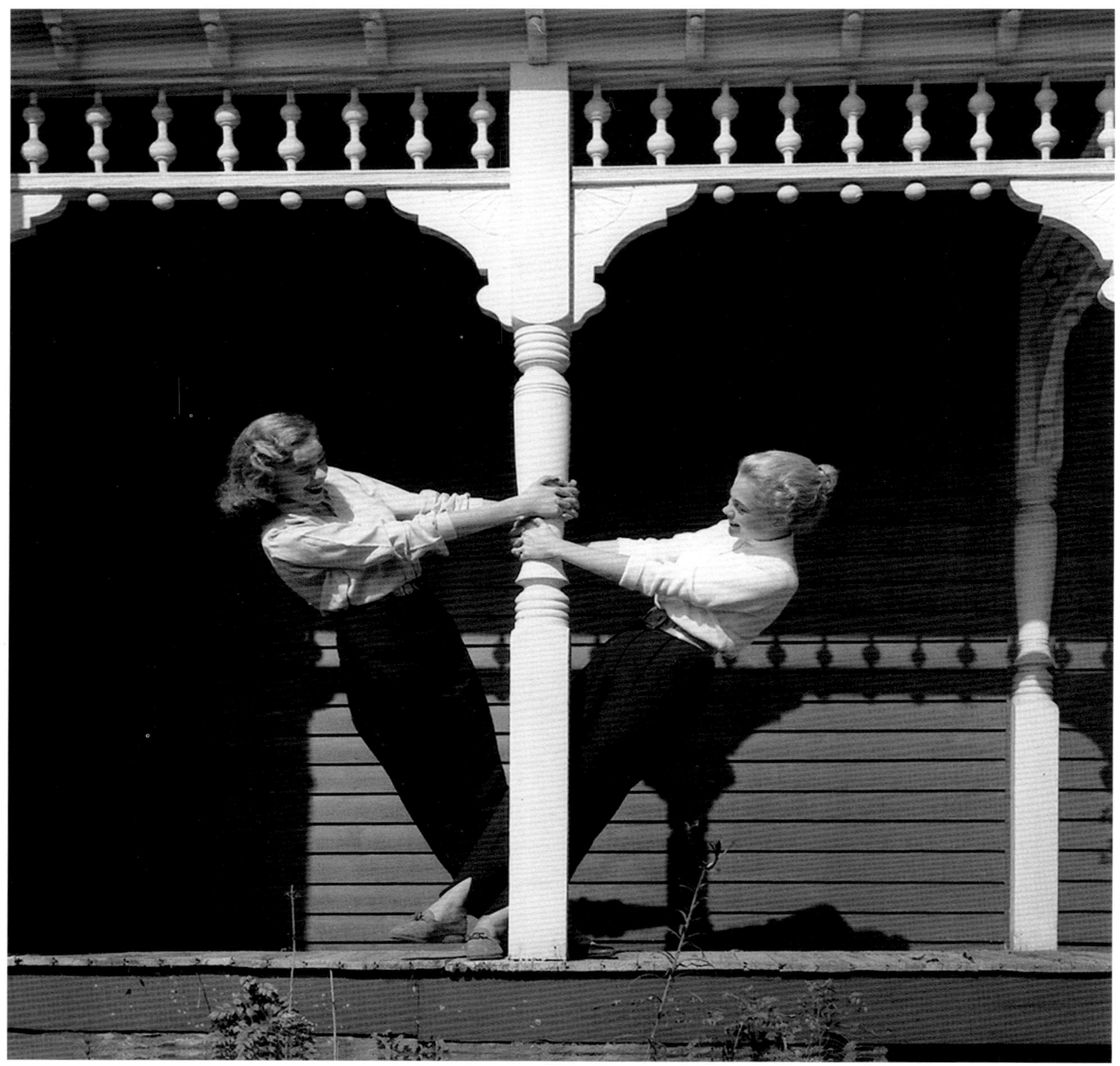

 | DAGNIA BLONIKALNS AND PAT WISE, ARBUTUS BEAUTIES, c. 1955

Carol Mitchell was first runner-up in the Miss America contest as well as Miss Indiana. I was privileged to spend time with Carol photographing her for the Miss America pageant in 1956.

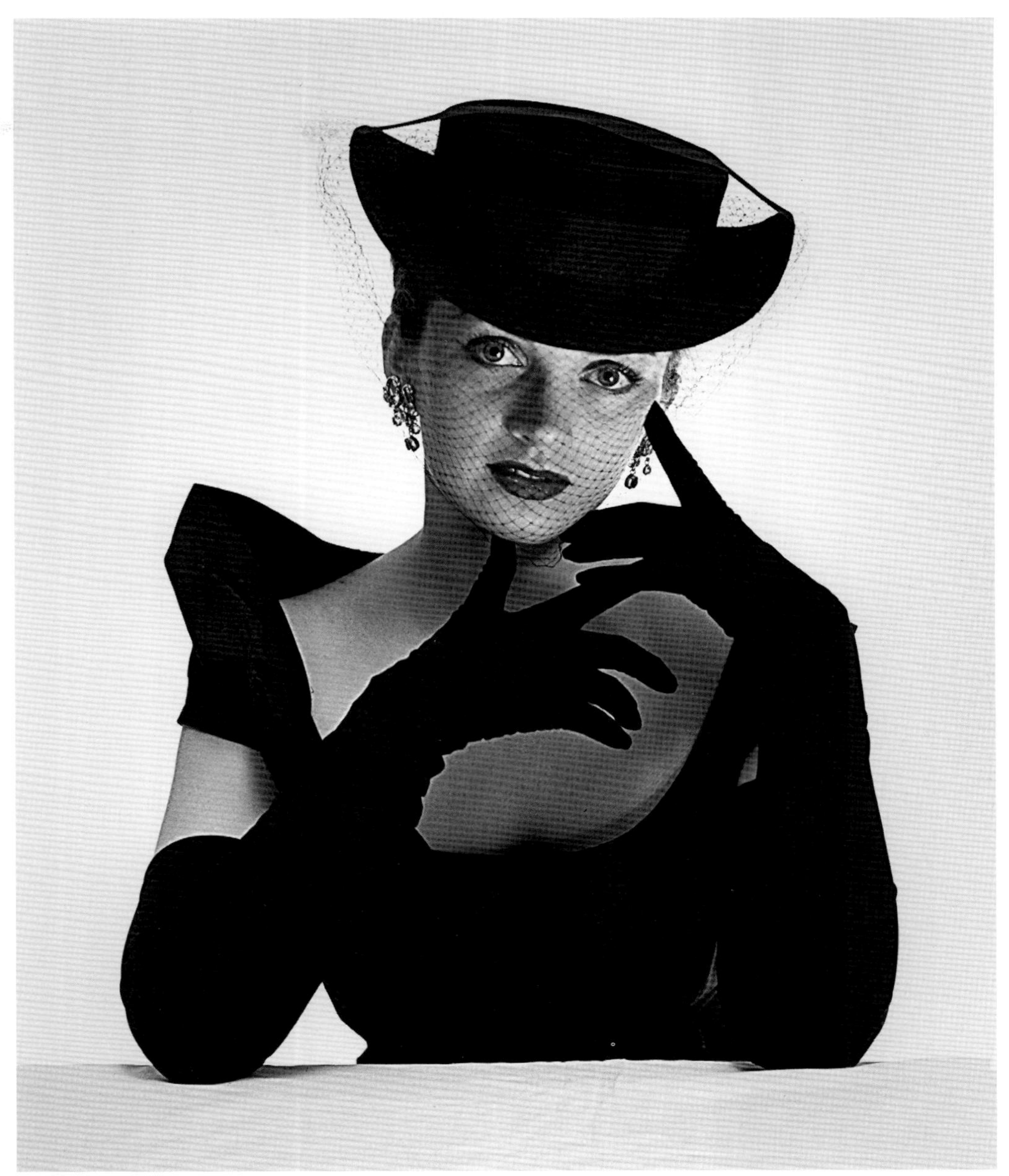

CAROL MITCHELL, MISS INDIANA AND FIRST RUNNER-UP, MISS AMERICA, 1956

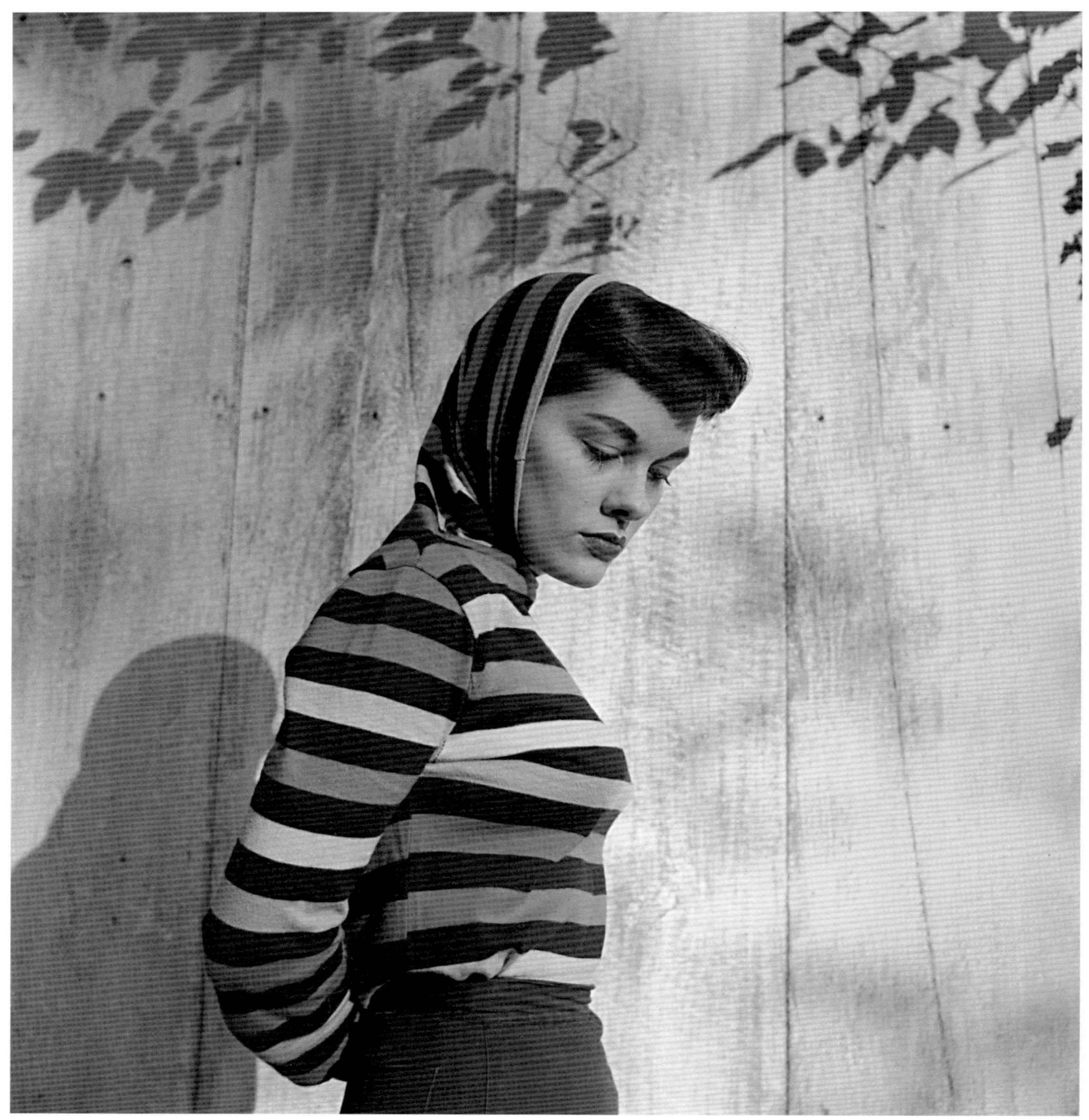

 | CAROL MOELLER, ARBUTUS BEAUTY, c. 1955

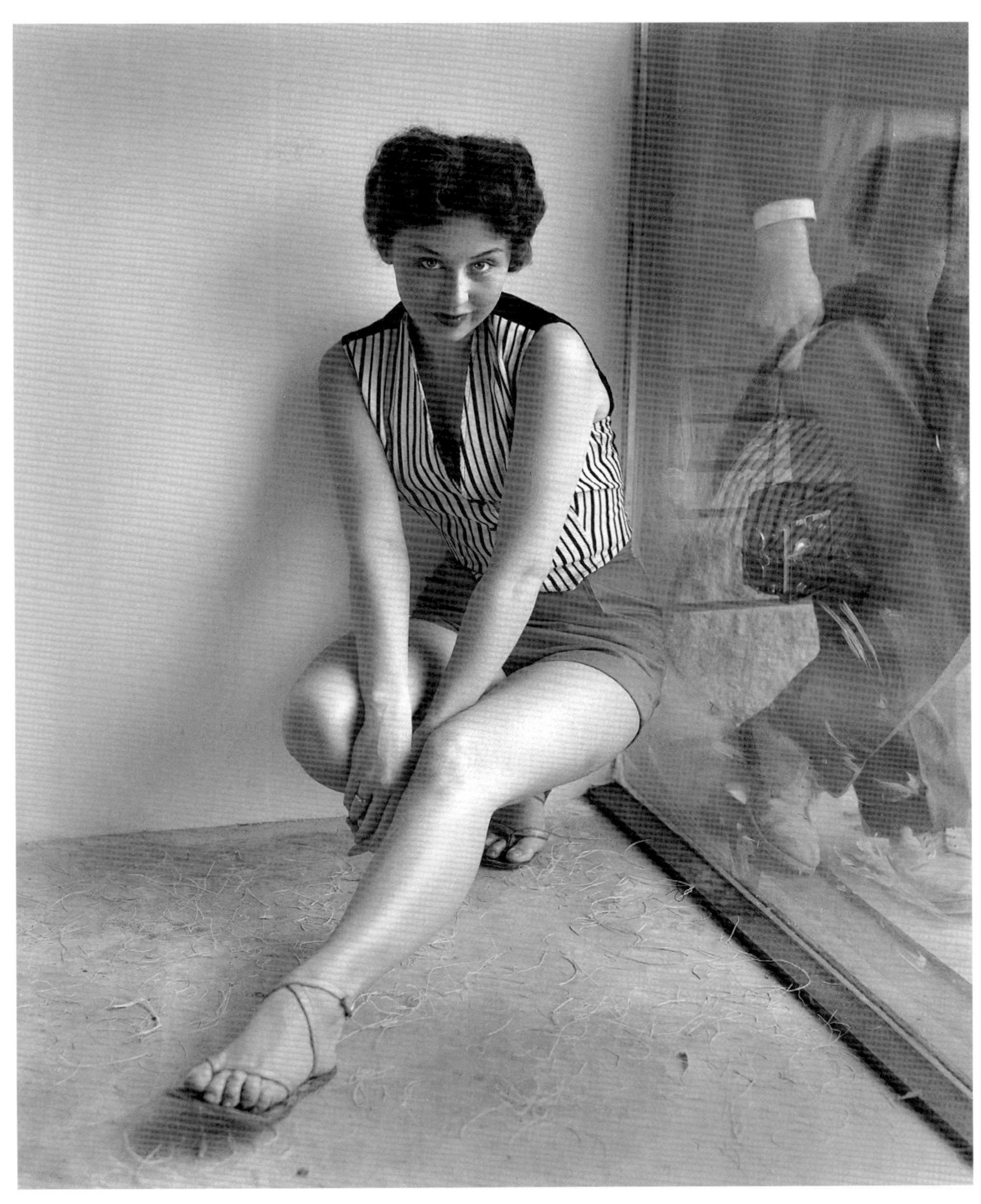

CAROLINE HILL, ARBUTUS BEAUTY, 1954

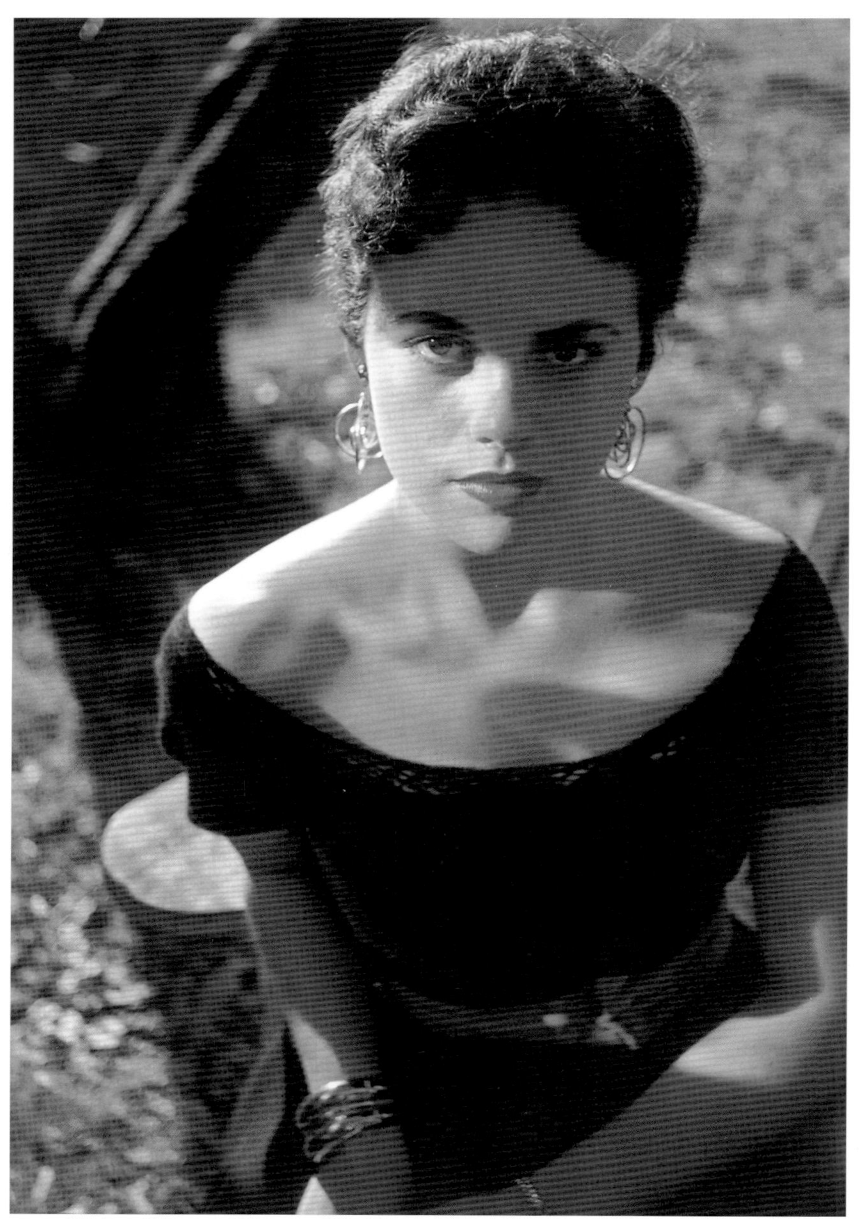

 | CAROLYN JUNE BONNER, ARBUTUS BEAUTY, c. 1955

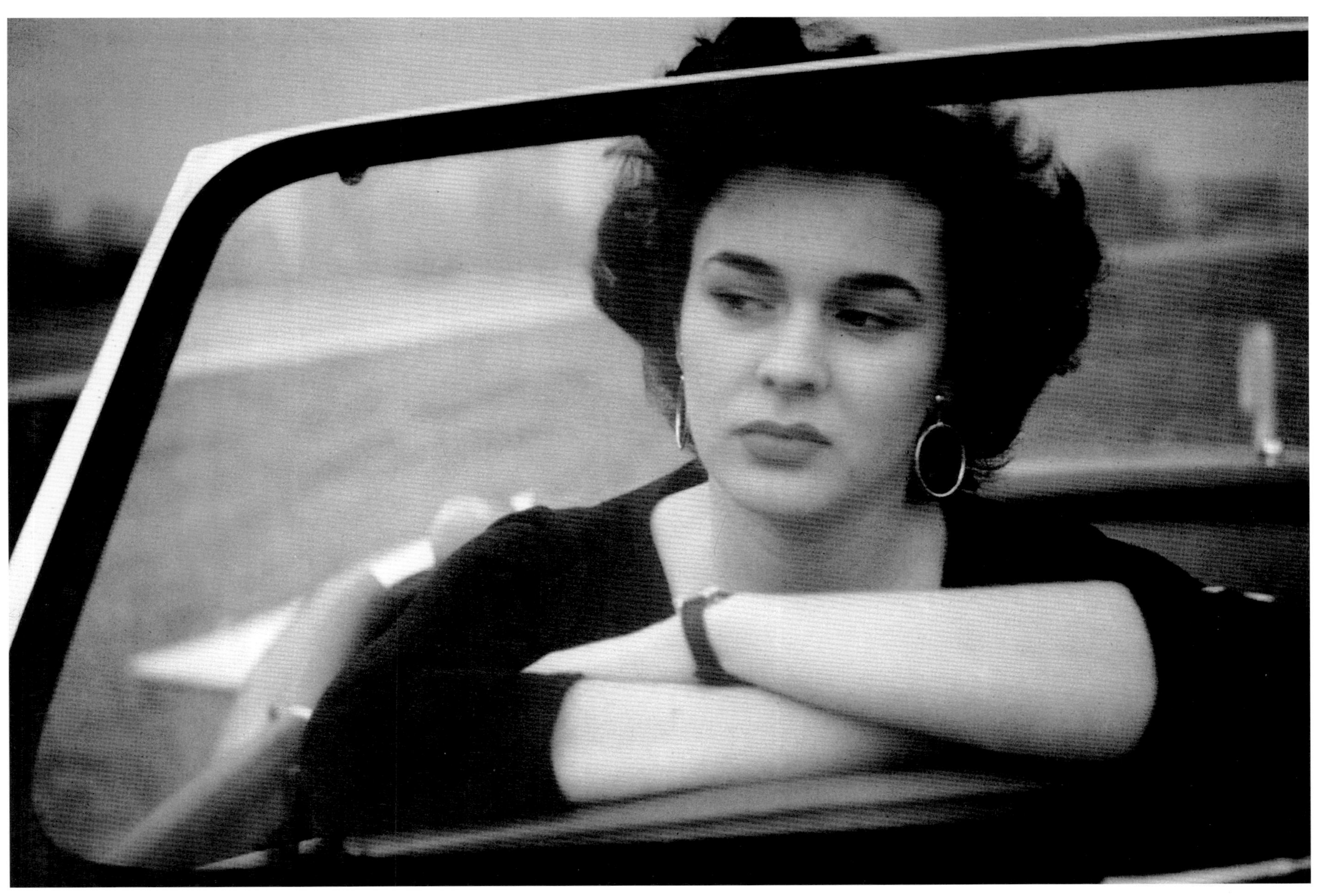

JUDY HAMPTON, ARBUTUS BEAUTY, c. 1955

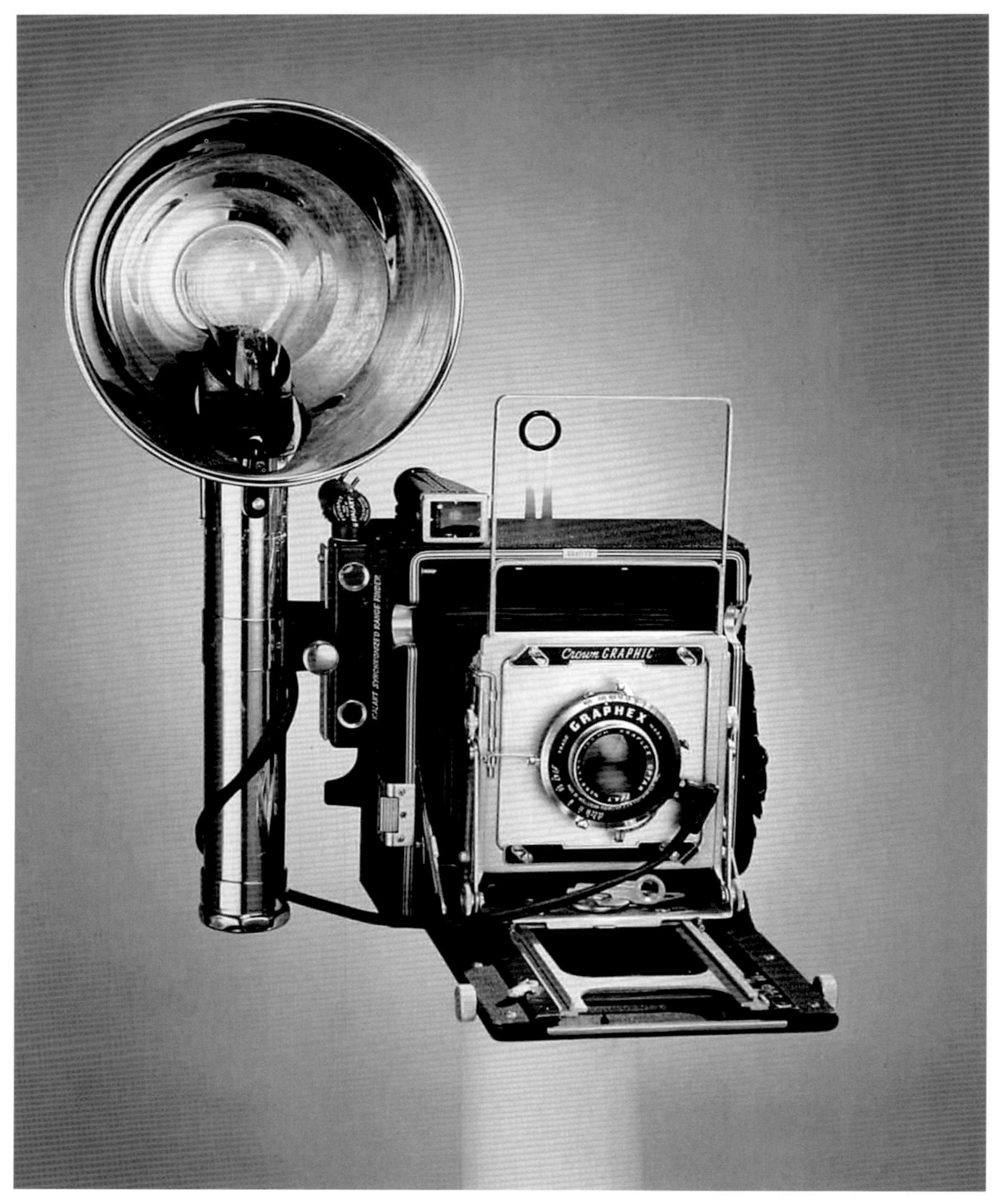

For ten years, this was my weapon of choice while working at the Indiana University Photo Lab.

FOUR | Jefferson City, Missouri, Workshop

In 1951, Henry Holmes Smith urged me to attend a workshop conducted by the University of Missouri School of Journalism. Henry was invited as a member of the staff. Each year the university undertook the documentation of a different town in Missouri. For this workshop, the town was Jefferson City. My primary assignment was to document a bus driver.

The staff, besides Henry, included Russell Lee of Farm Security Administration fame and Arthur Siegel, a renowned Chicago photographer. No one got much sleep that week. We worked all day and discussed the results at night. I became especially interested in the antics of Arthur Siegel and did a documentation of the workshop in process. Some seventeen of my photographs were collected for the Missouri State Archives.

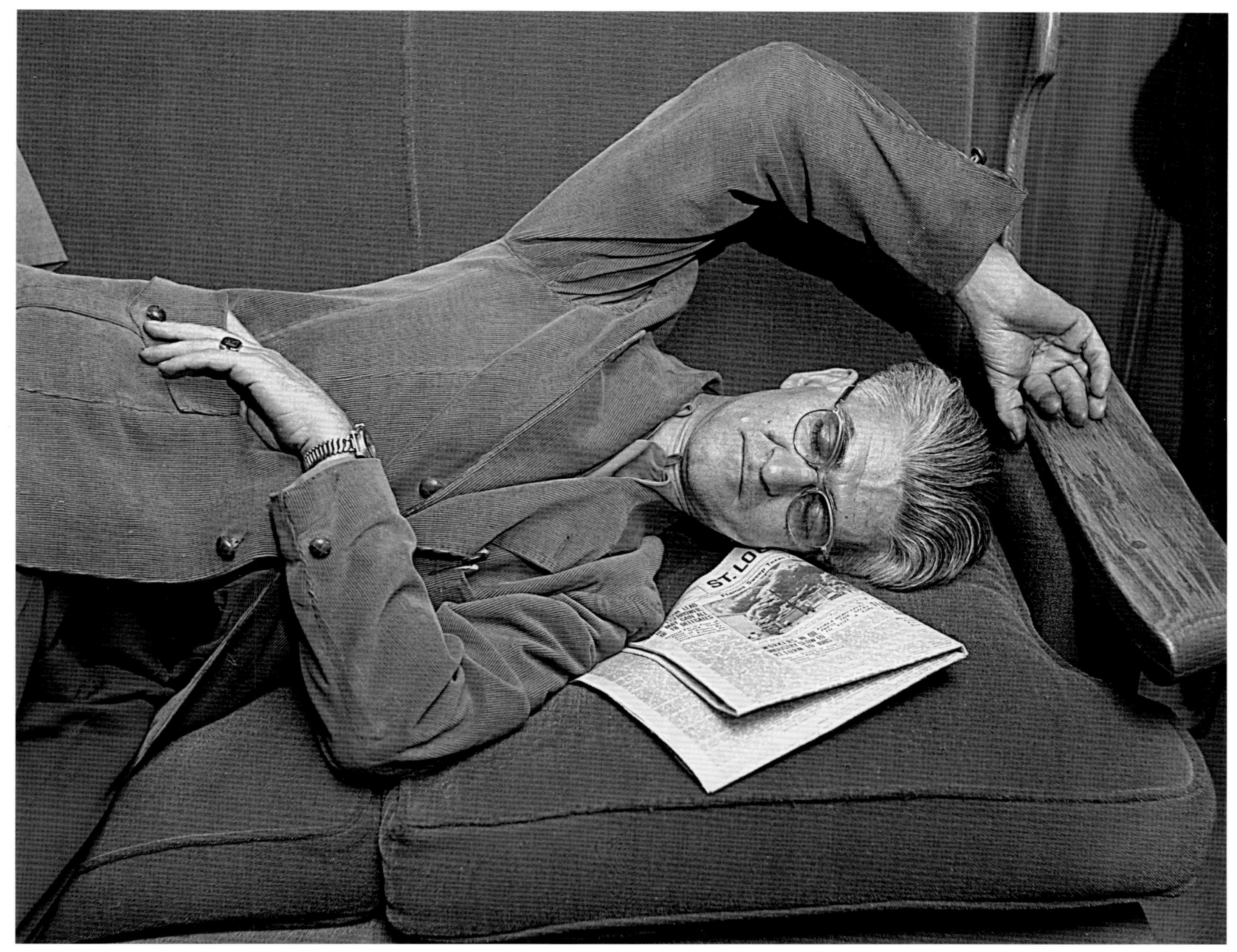

CLIF EDOM, WORKSHOP DIRECTOR, 1952

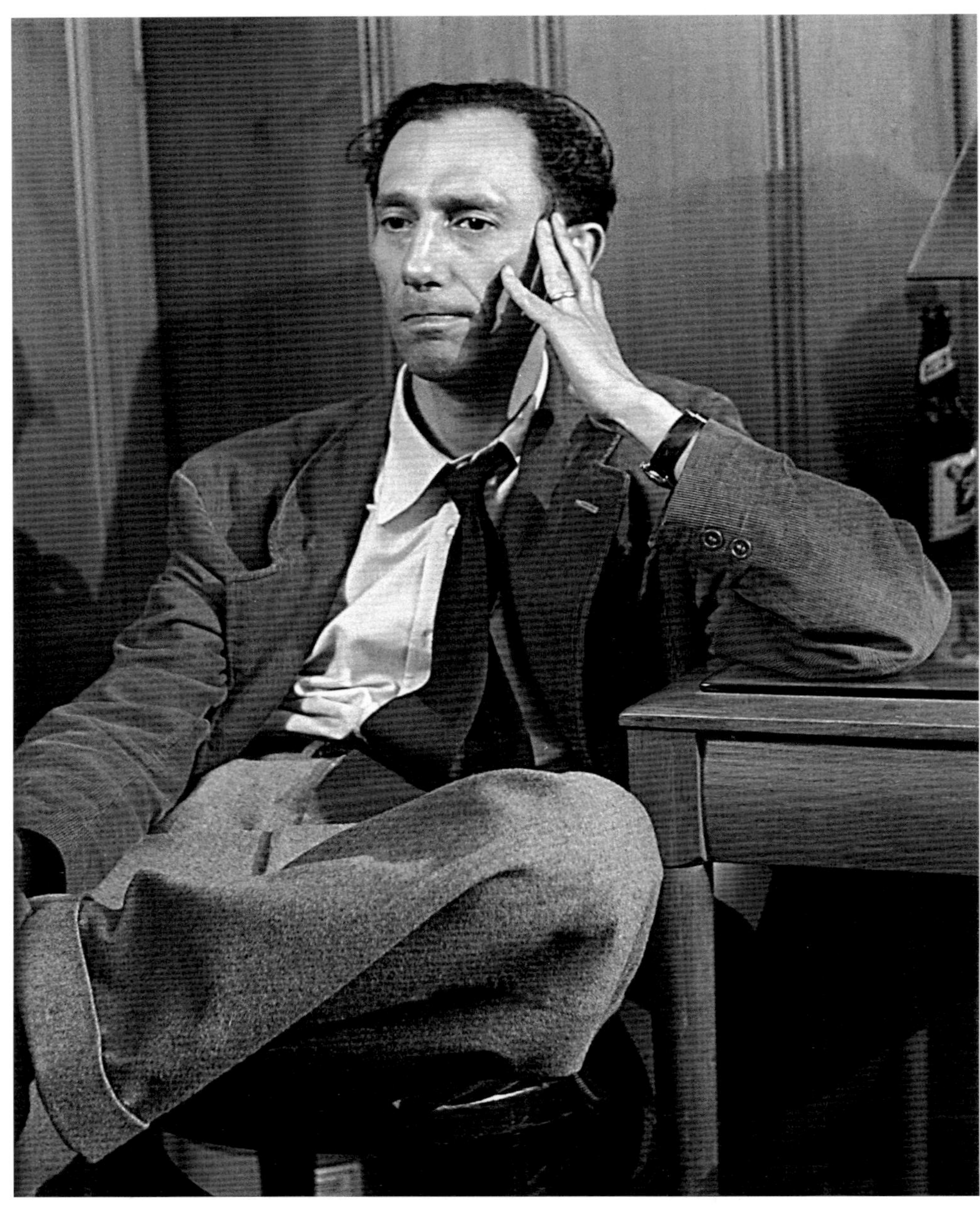

 | ARTHUR SIEGEL, PHOTOGRAPHER, MISSOURI WORKSHOP, 1952

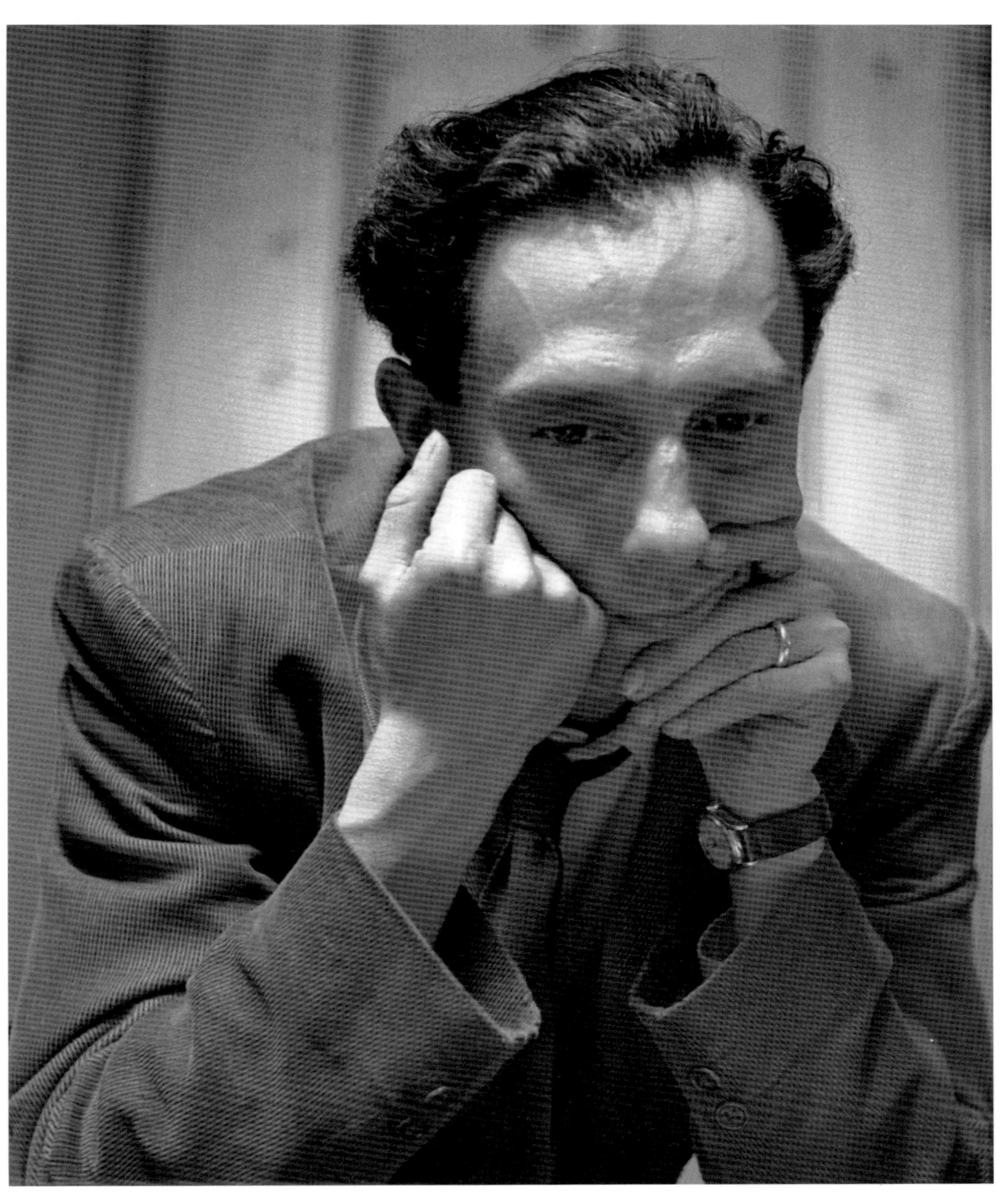

ARTHUR SIEGEL, PHOTOGRAPHER, MISSOURI WORKSHOP, 1952

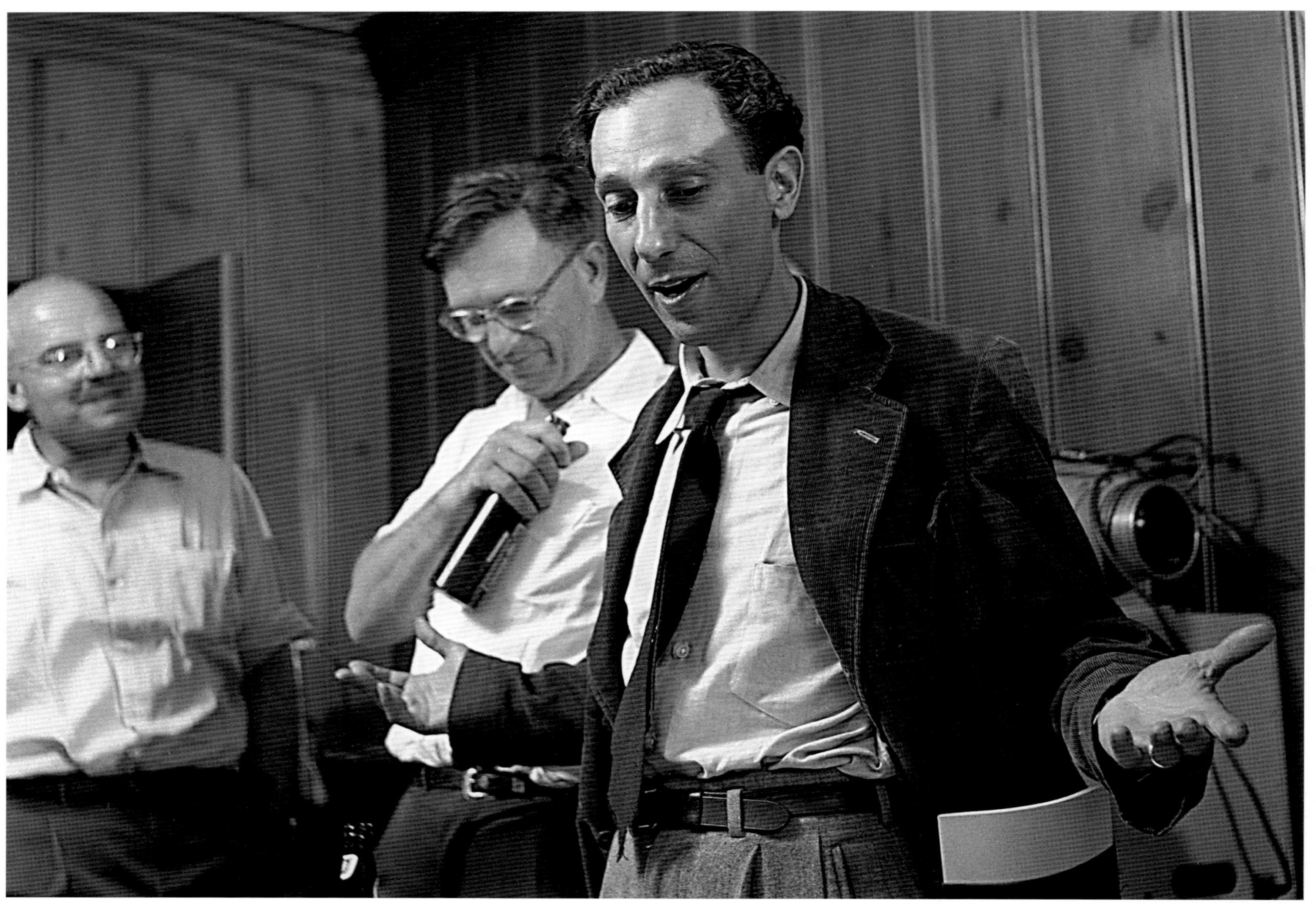

 | LEFT TO RIGHT: HENRY HOLMES SMITH, RUSSELL LEE, ARTHUR SIEGEL AT MISSOURI WORKSHOP, 1952

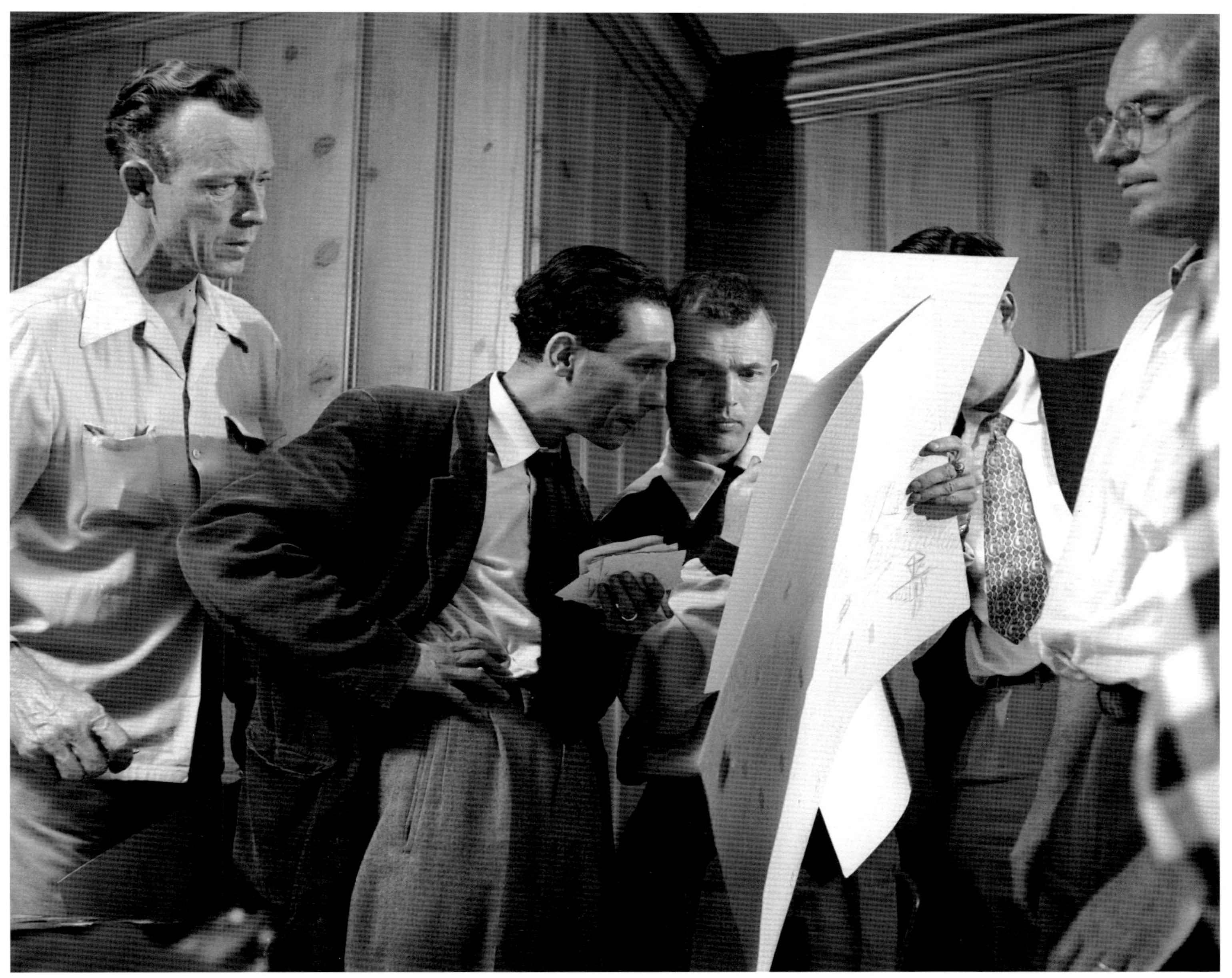

LEFT TO RIGHT: UNIDENTIFIED, ARTHUR SIEGEL, BILL TENNEL, HENRY SMITH AT MISSOURI WORKSHOP, 1952

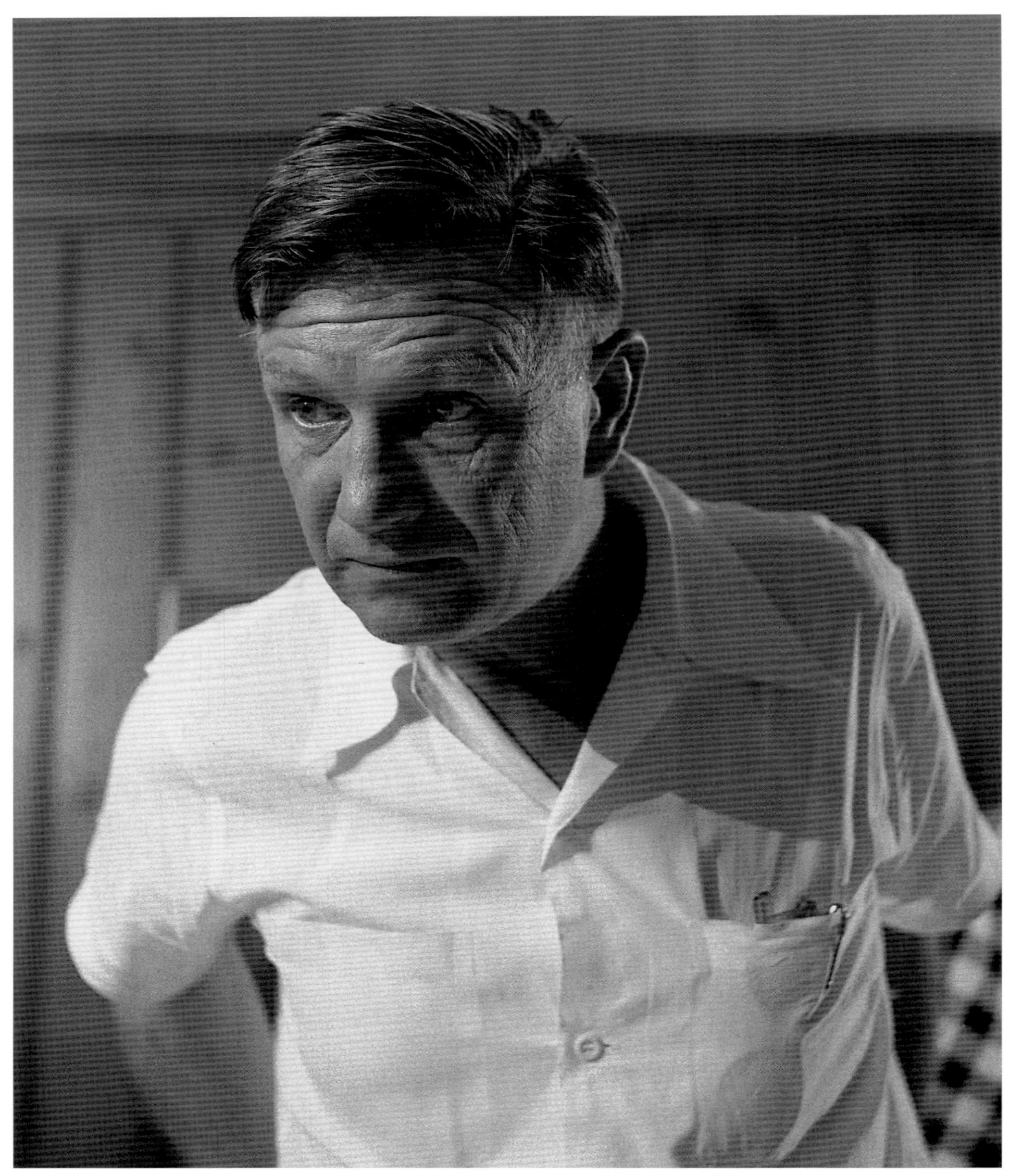

 | RUSSELL LEE, FSA PHOTOGRAPHER, MISSOURI WORKSHOP, 1952

The clock on the wall says quarter to three. That's AM, not PM. We spent our days photographing and our nights discussing proofs. The talks were intense. One moment you were on a high because staff praised you, and the next moment you crashed as they trashed your efforts. There were a lot of bruised egos. The suffering retreated into a bottle of beer.

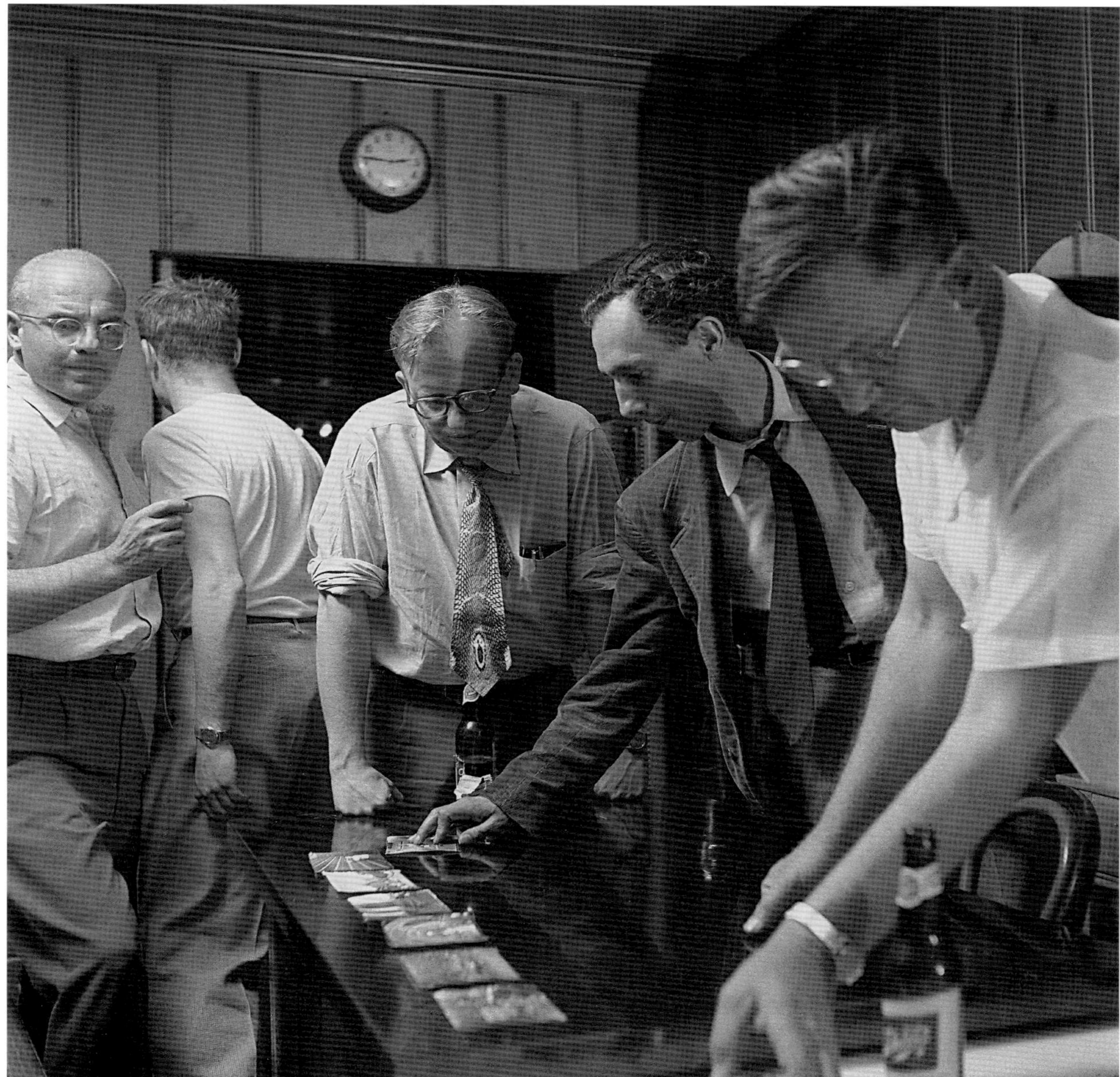

LEFT TO RIGHT: HENRY SMITH, UNKNOWN, JACK WELPOTT, ARTHUR SIEGEL, RUSSELL LEE AT MISSOURI WORKSHOP, 1952

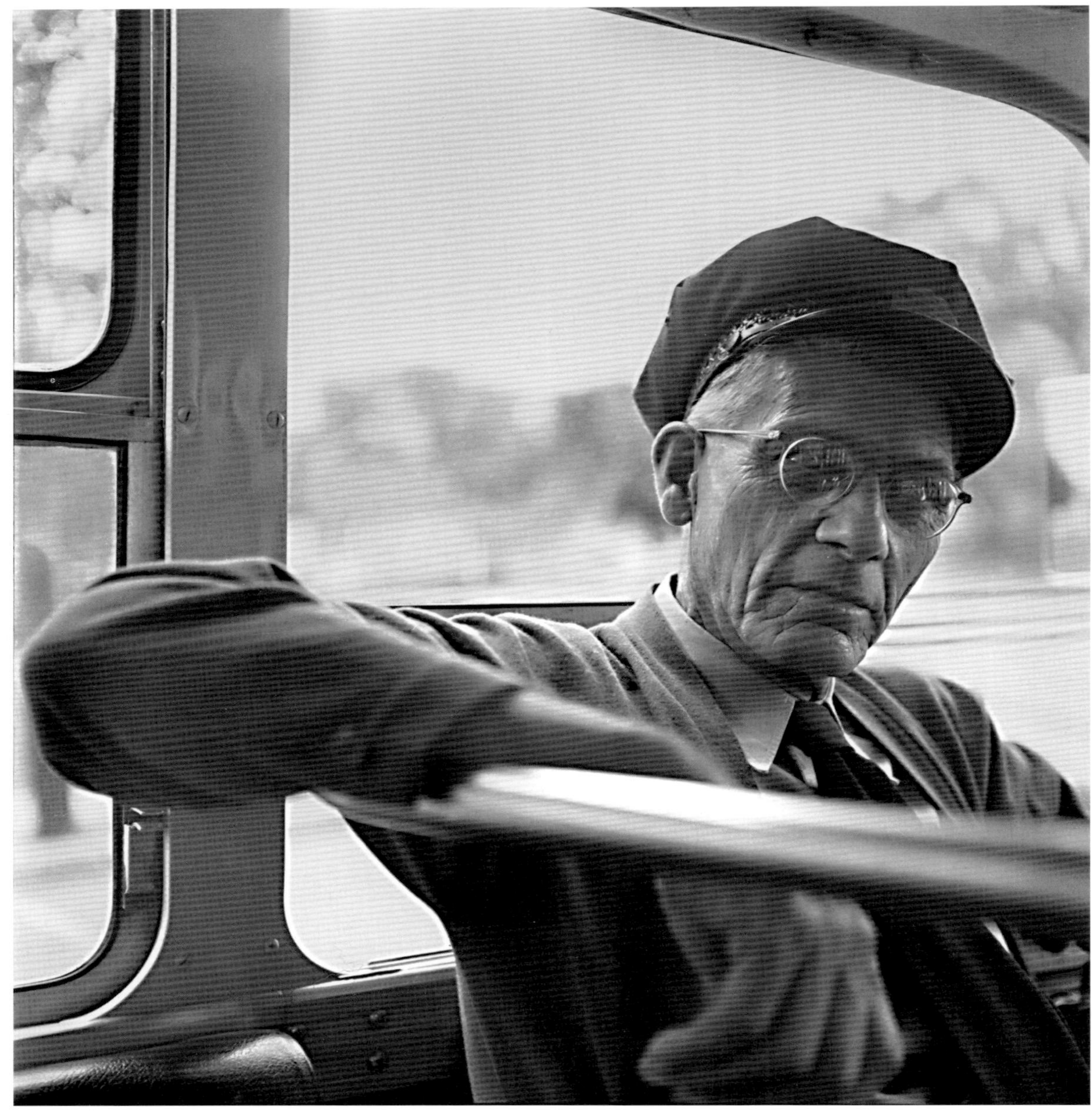

 | MY BUS DRIVER, JEFFERSON CITY, MISSOURI, MISSOURI WORKSHOP, 1952

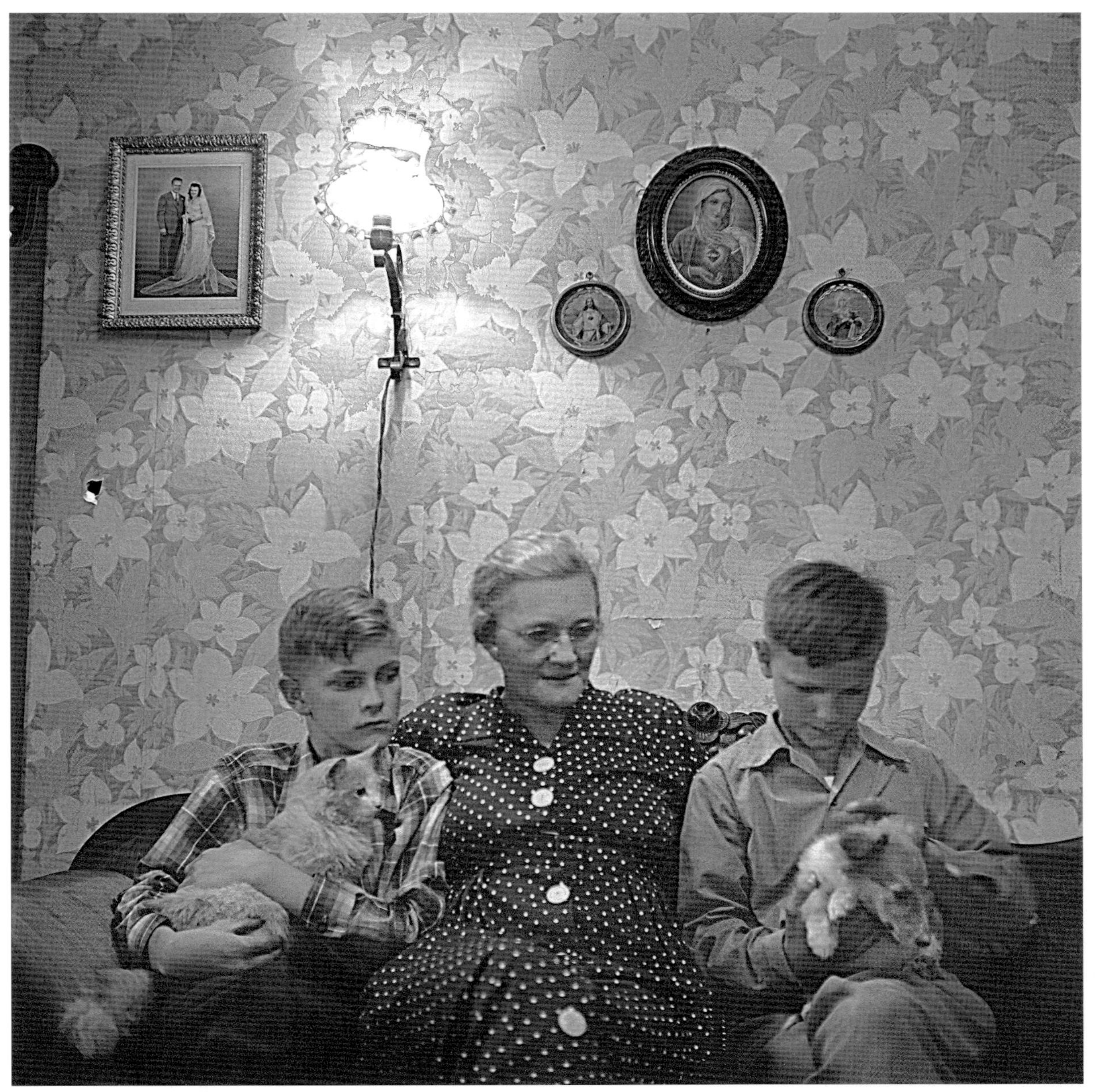

MY BUS DRIVER'S FAMILY, JEFFERSON CITY, MISSOURI, MISSOURI WORKSHOP, 1952

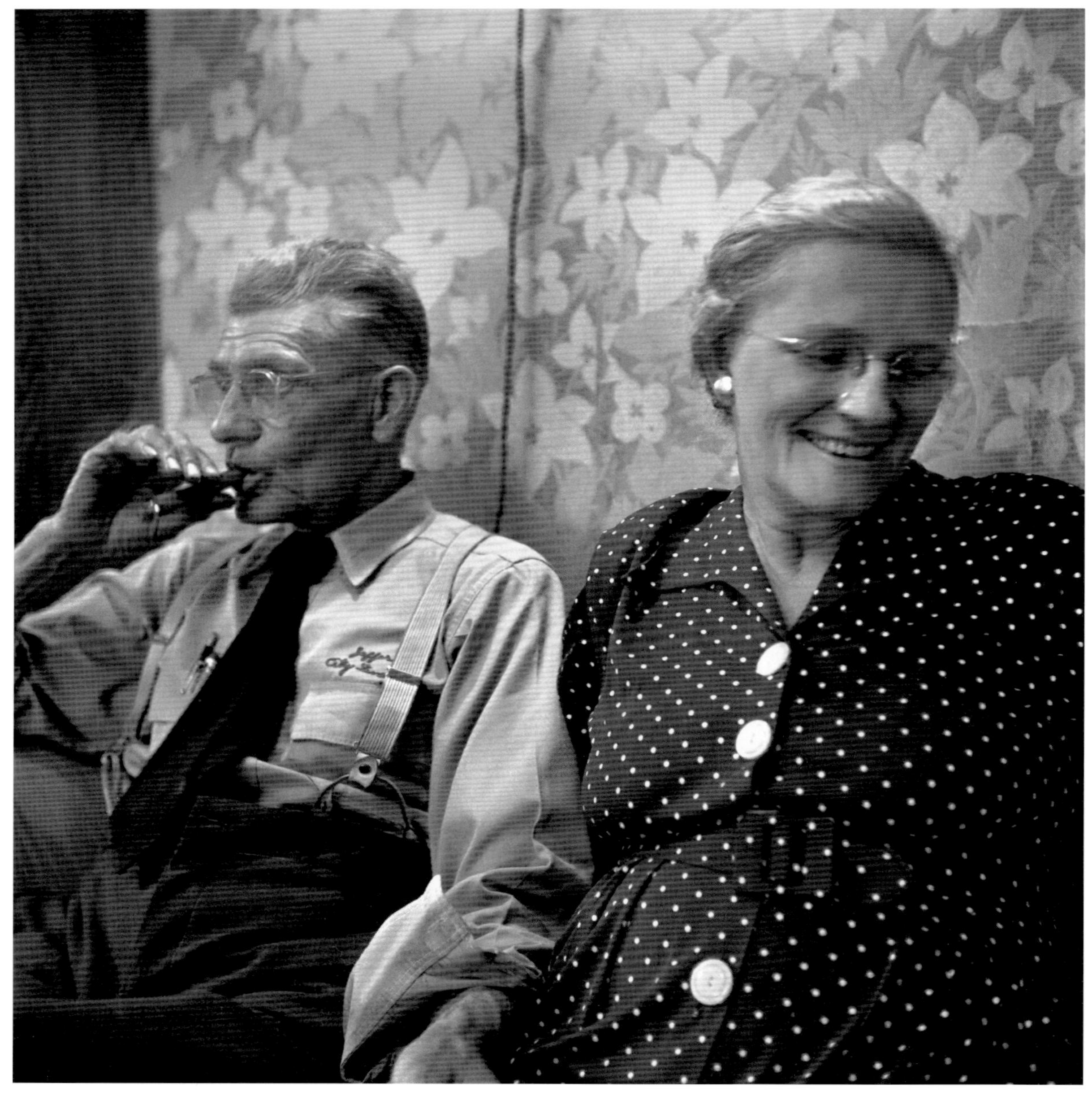

 | MY BUS DRIVER AND HIS WIFE, JEFFERSON CITY, MISSOURI, MISSOURI WORKSHOP, 1952

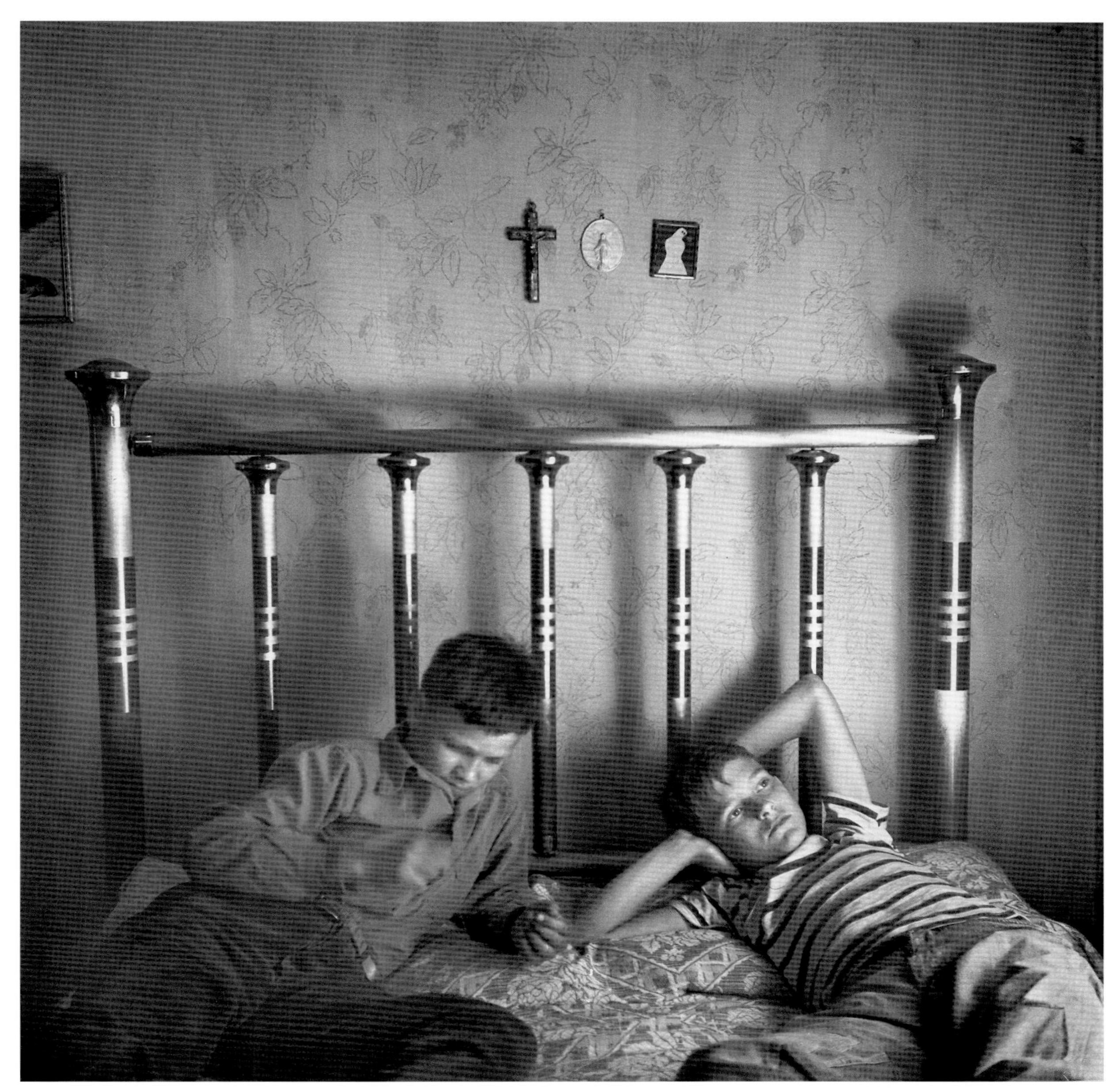

THE BUS DRIVER'S SONS, JEFFERSON CITY, MISSOURI, MISSOURI WORKSHOP, 1952

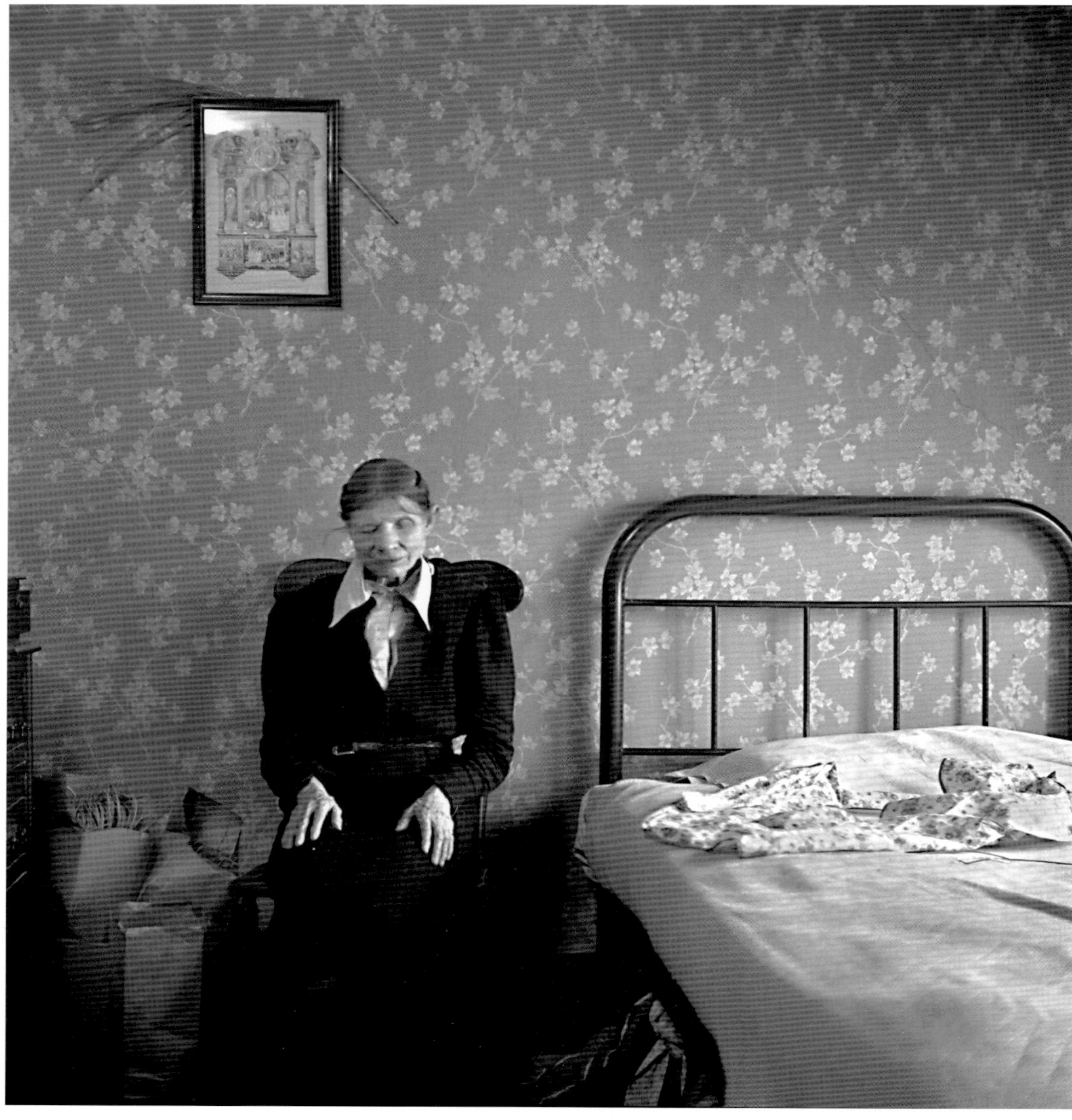

This lady was the aunt who lived in an upstairs room. She was blind and spent her days weaving cane bottoms for chairs.

 BLIND AUNT, JEFFERSON CITY, MISSOURI, MISSOURI WORKSHOP, 1952

There is no artifact so loaded with personal meaning than the bed. Most of us are born in one. We spend one third of our lives sleeping in one. We make love in one. We are sick in one and we die in one. Over the years I have photographed a lot of beds. They are always emotionally charged with the history of events that have taken place therein. This is the bus driver's bed. I find it amazing in its gothic elegance. If it could talk, what poignant tales it could tell.

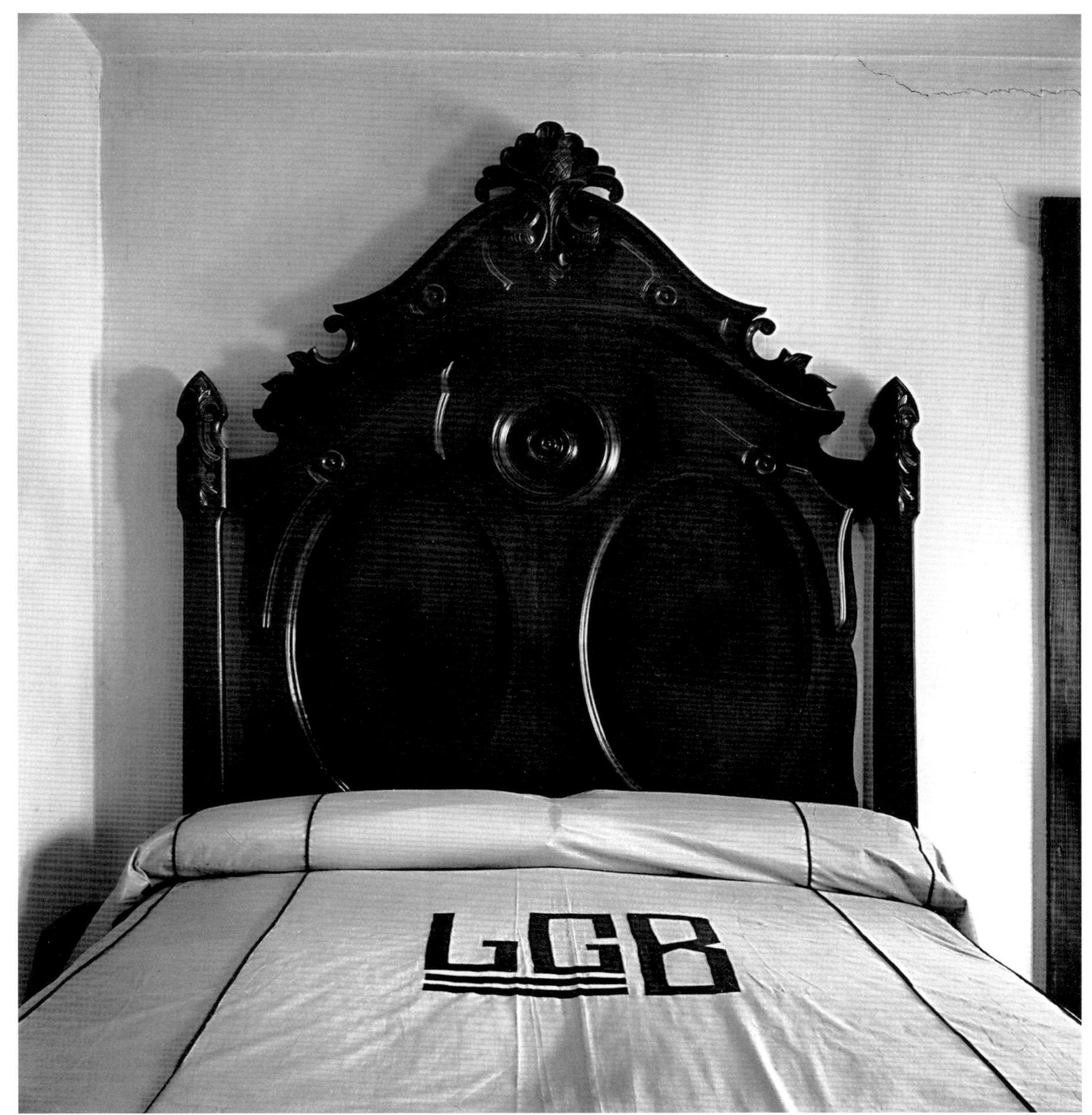

THE BUS DRIVER'S BED, JEFFERSON CITY, MISSOURI, MISSOURI WORKSHOP, 1952

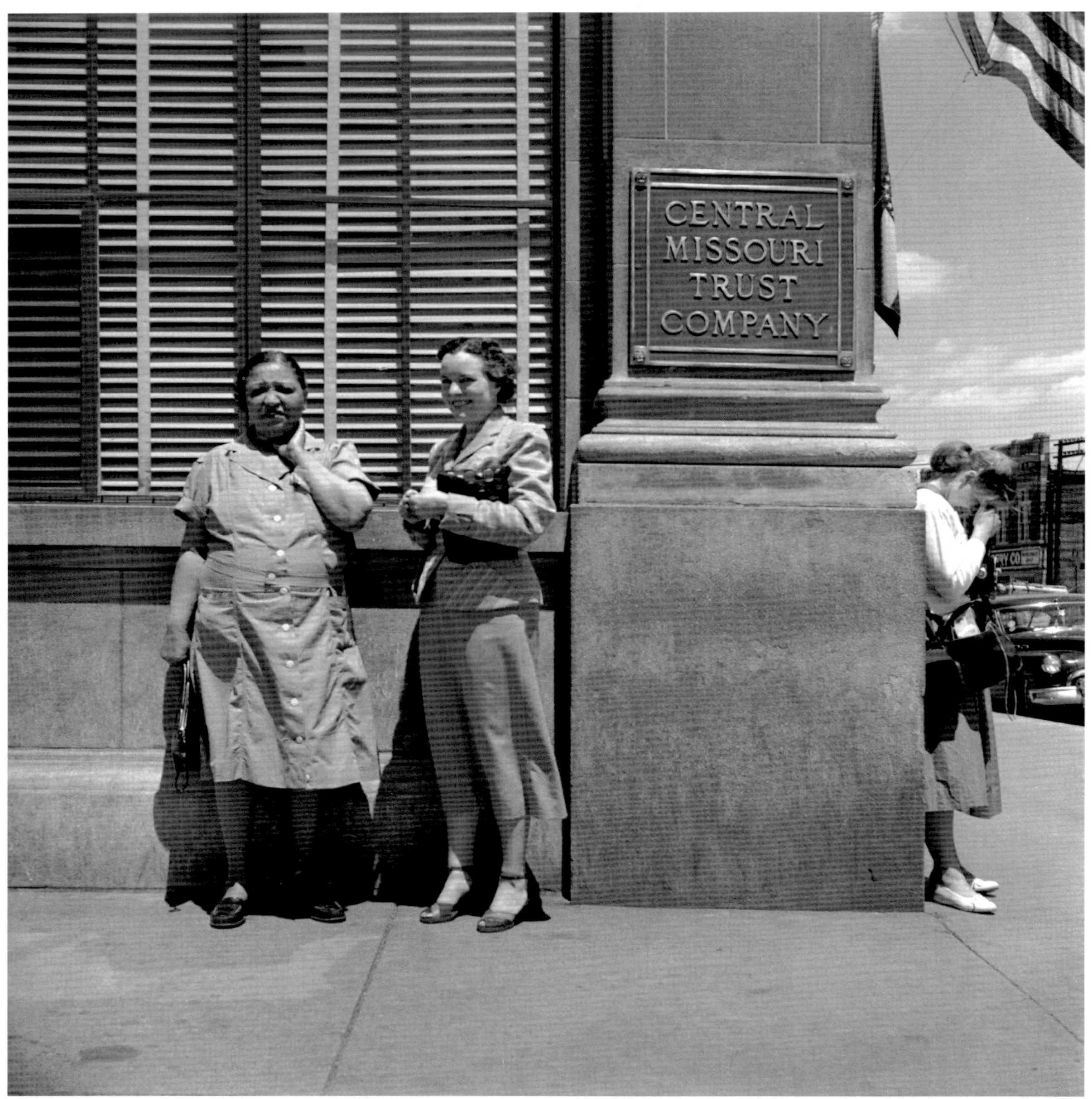

 | WAITING FOR THE BUS, MISSOURI WORKSHOP, 1952

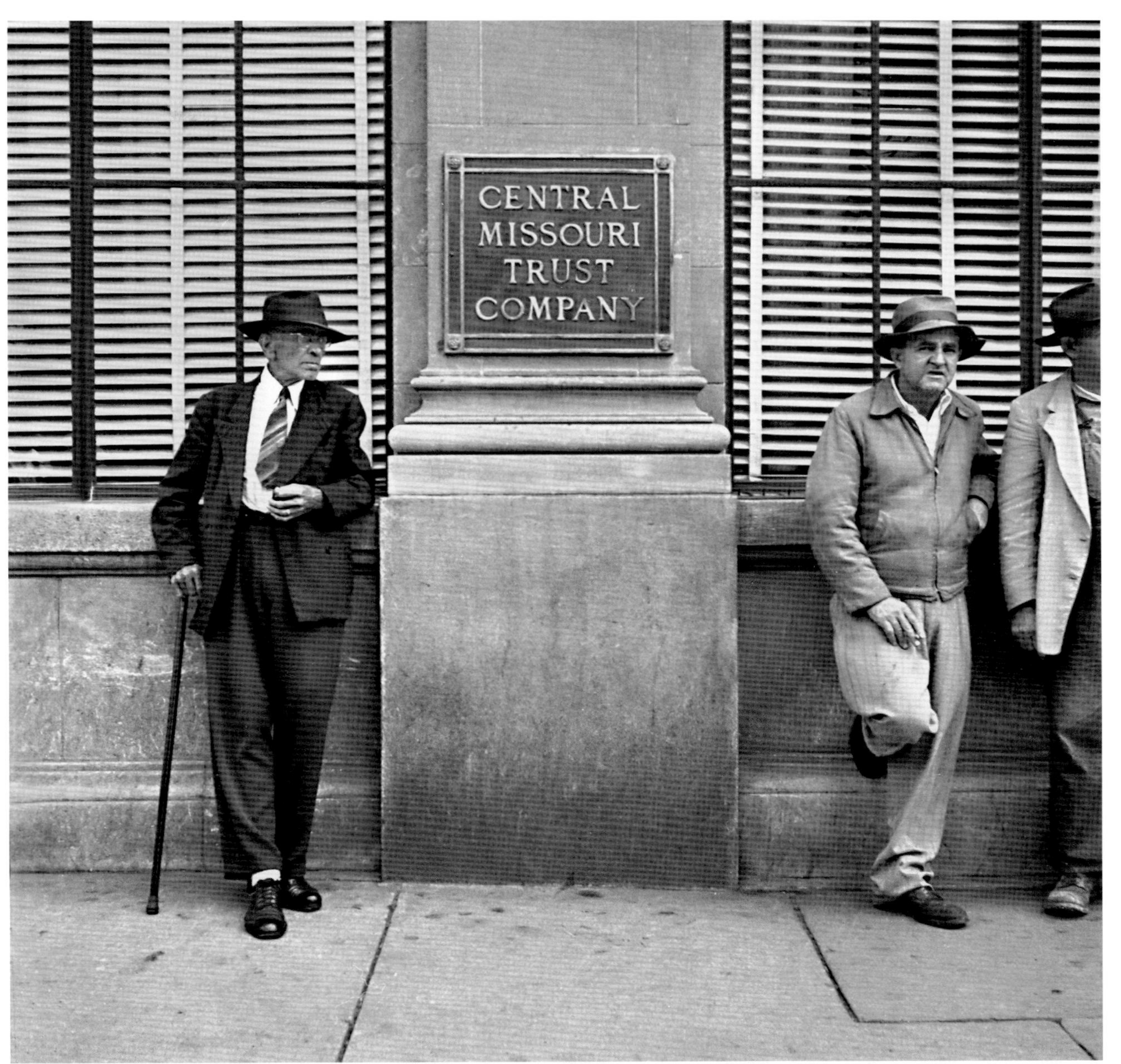

WAITING FOR THE BUS, MISSOURI WORKSHOP, 1952

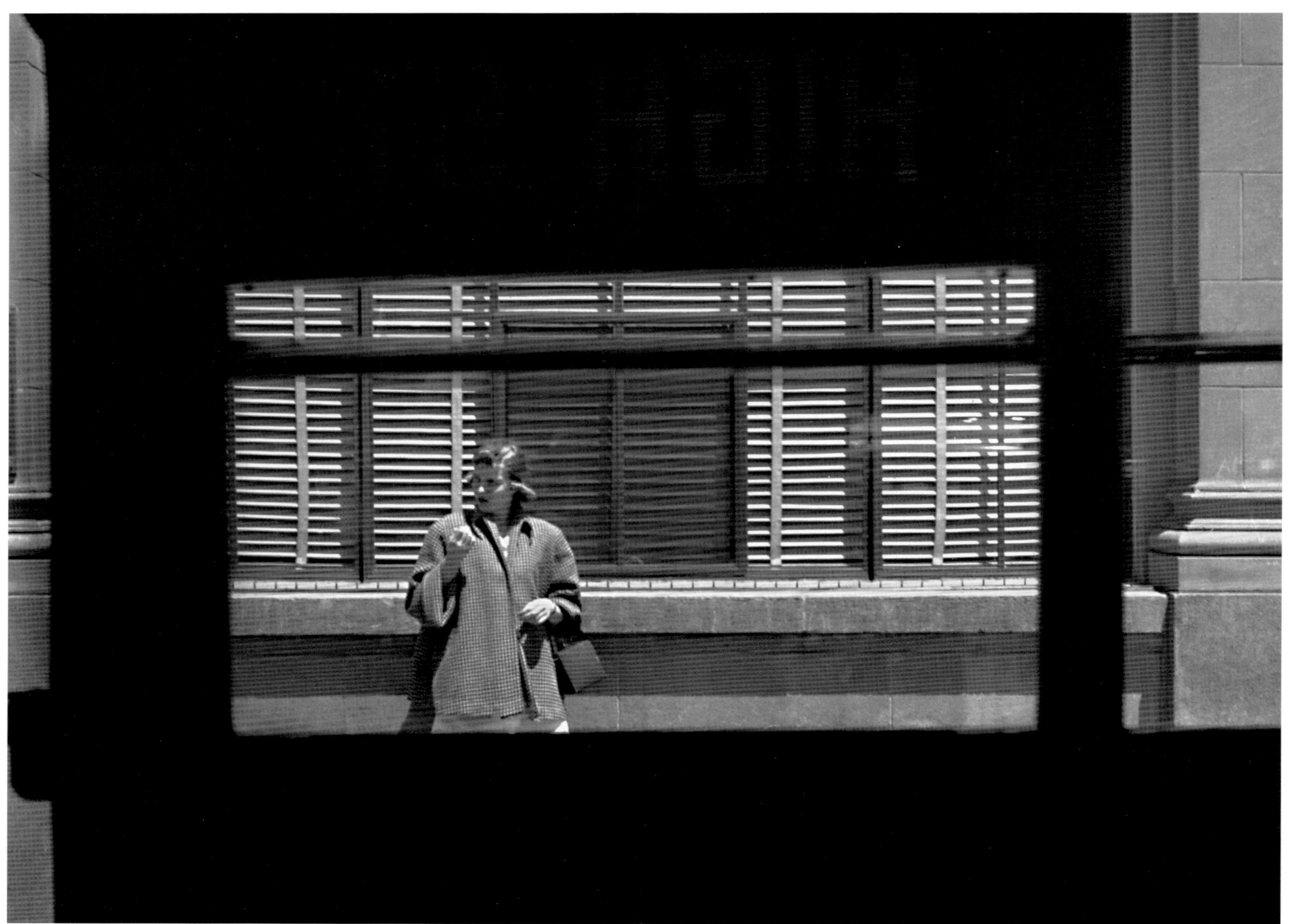

 | WAITING FOR THE BUS, MISSOURI WORKSHOP, 1952

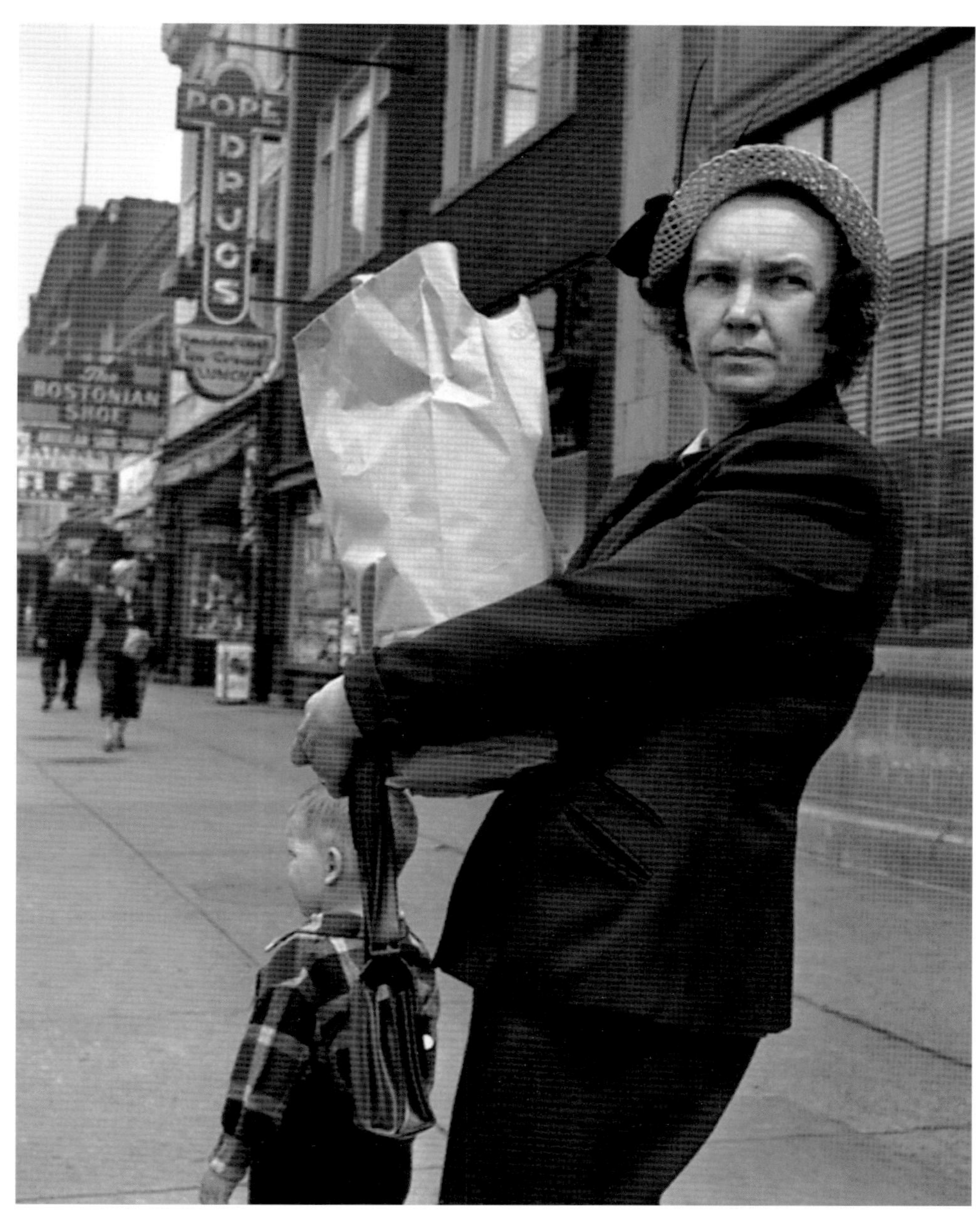

BRINGING HOME THE BACON, MISSOURI WORKSHOP, 1952

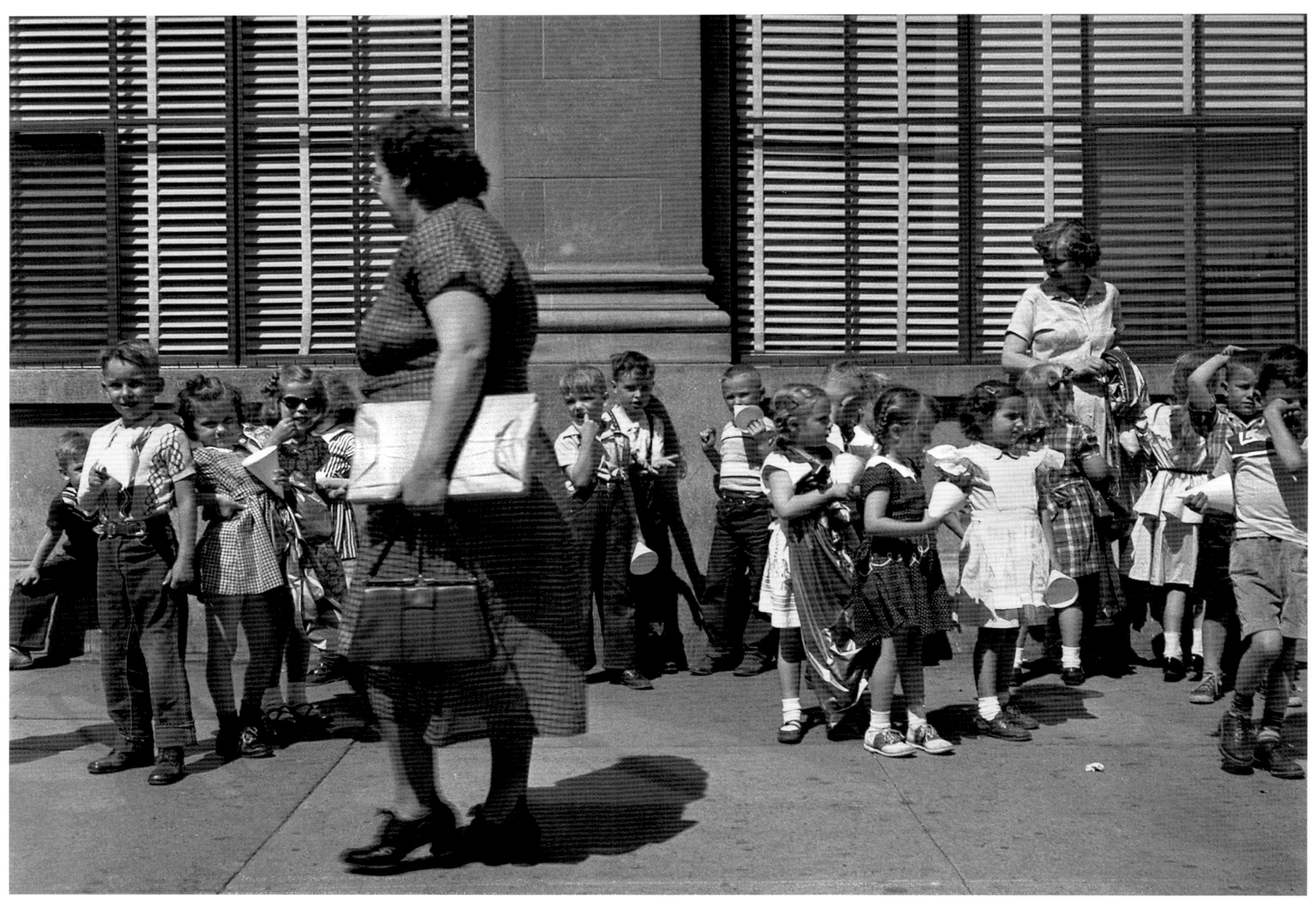

 | THE LINE UP, MISSOURI WORKSHOP, 1952

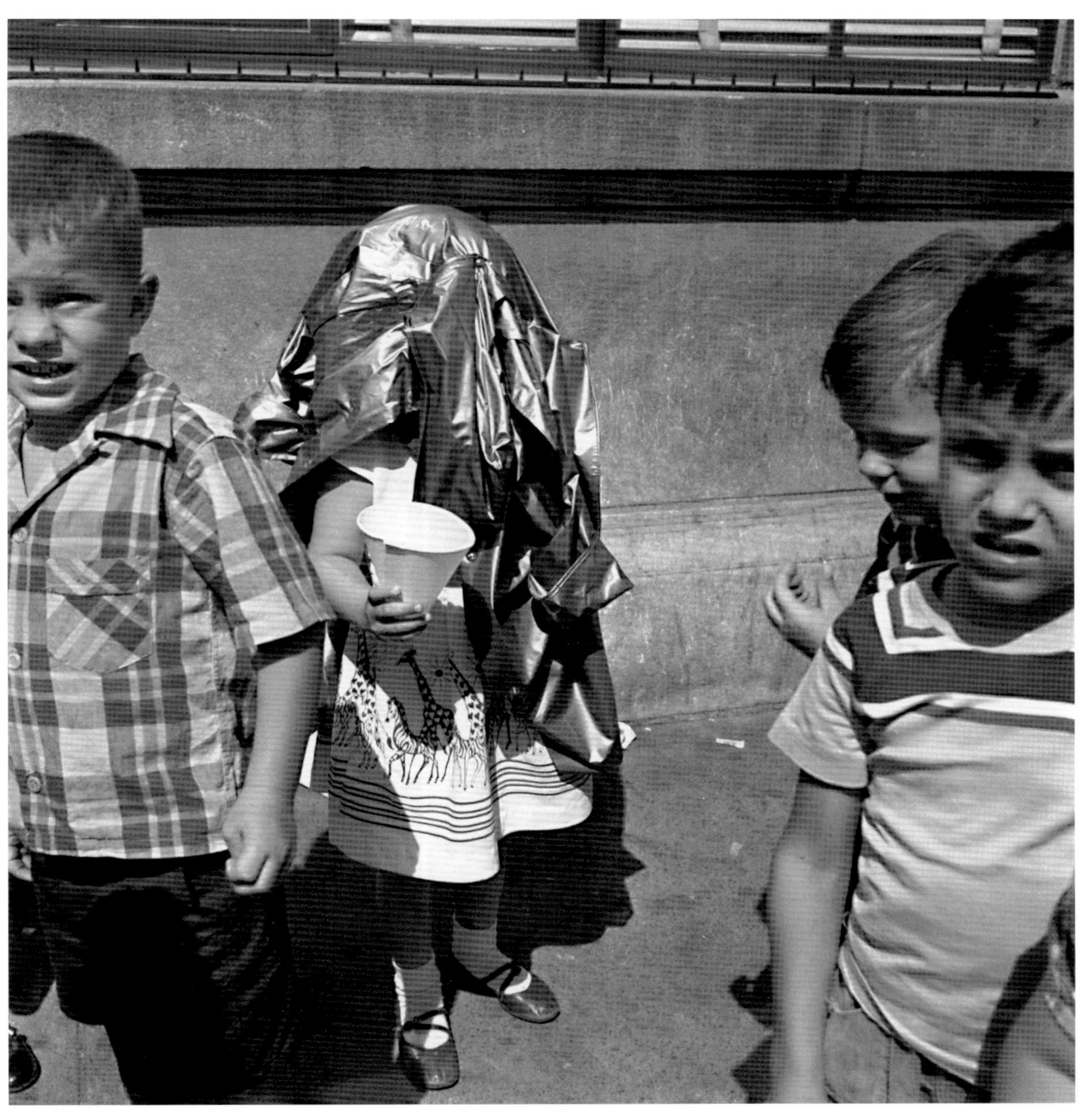

THE PANHANDLER, MISSOURI WORKSHOP, 1952

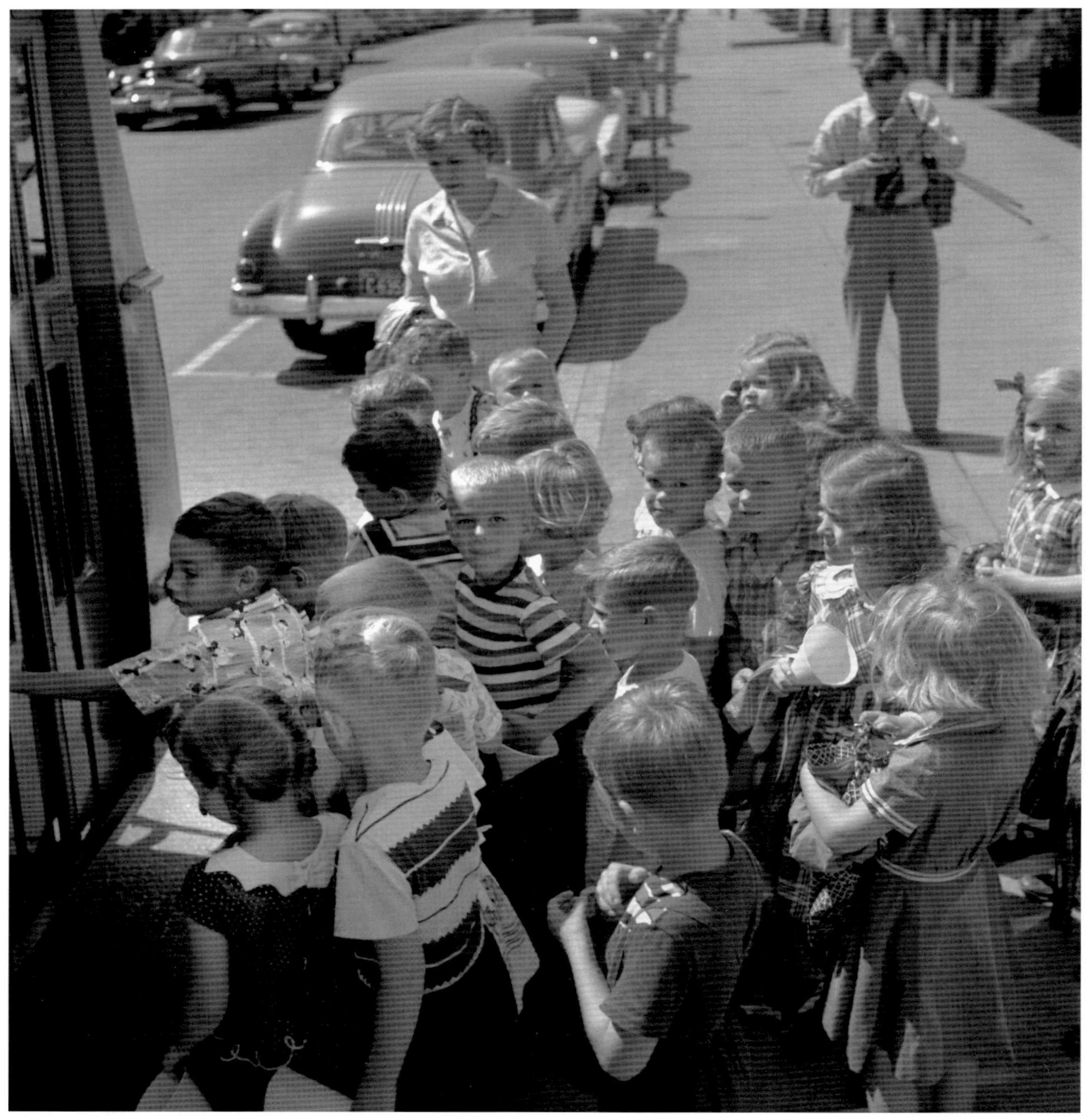

STAMPEDE, MISSOURI WORKSHOP, 1952

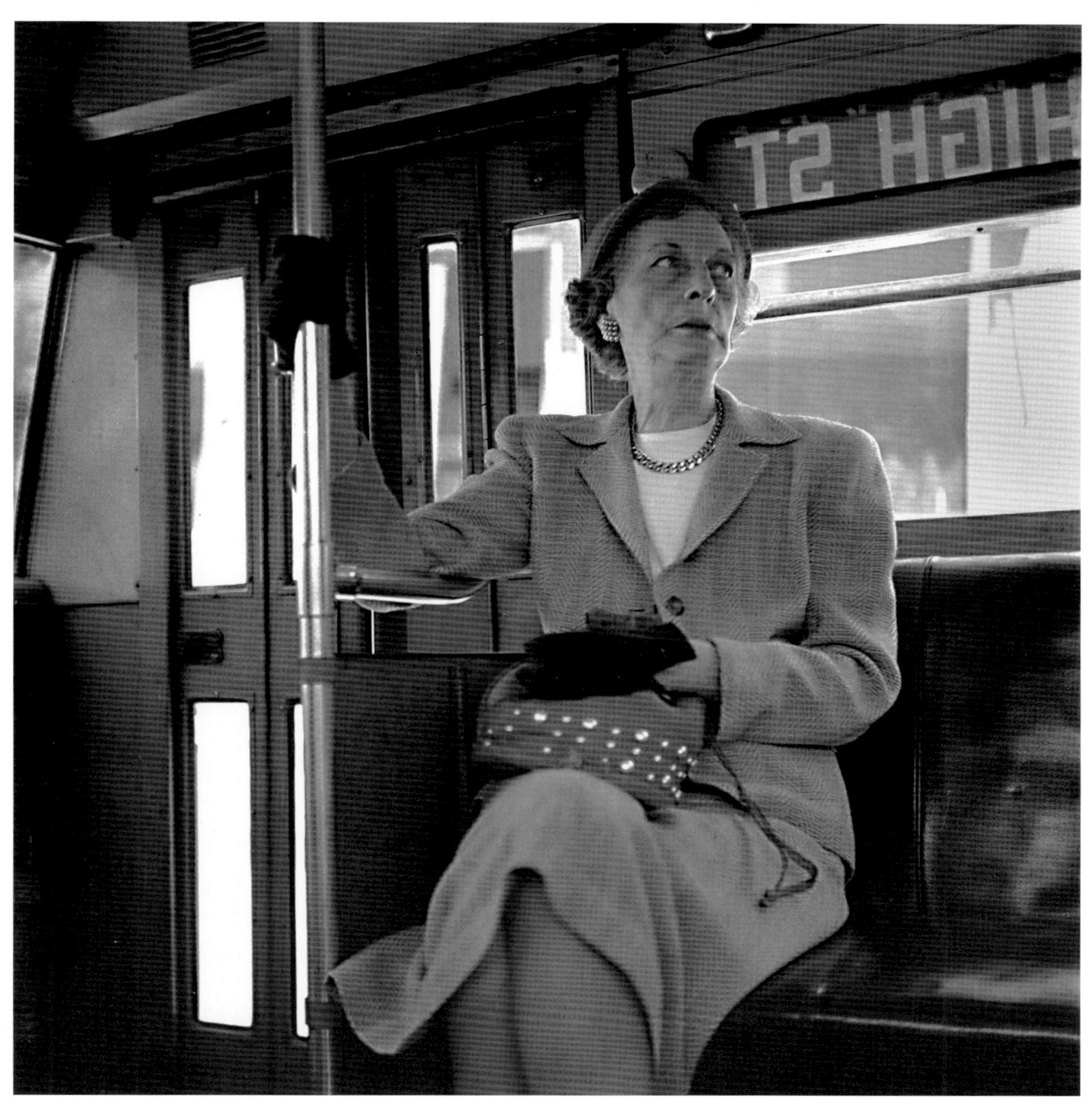

WOMAN ON THE BUS, MISSOURI WORKSHOP, 1952 |

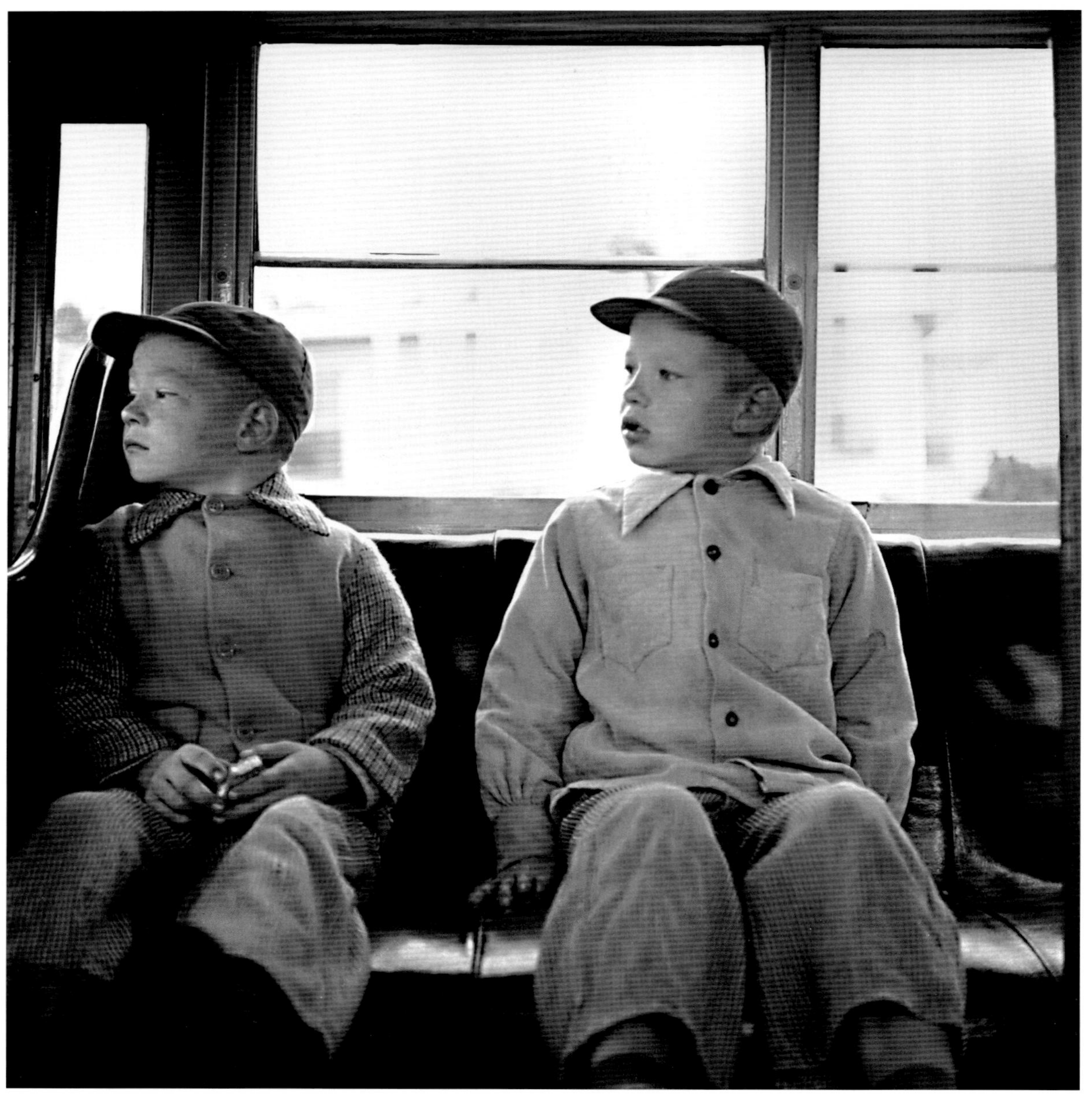

 | TWINS, MISSOURI WORKSHOP, 1952

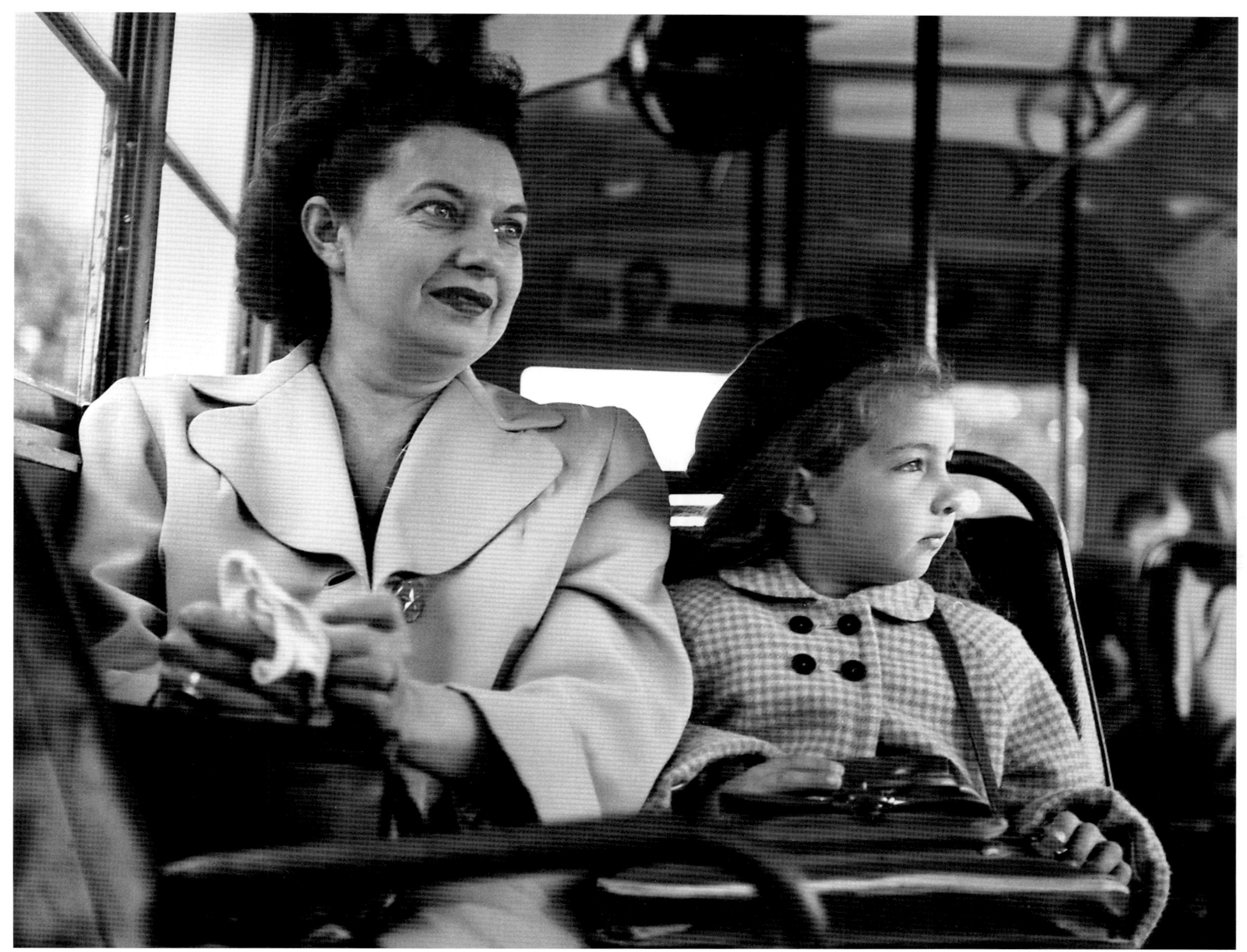

MOTHER AND DAUGHTER, MISSOURI WORKSHOP, 1952

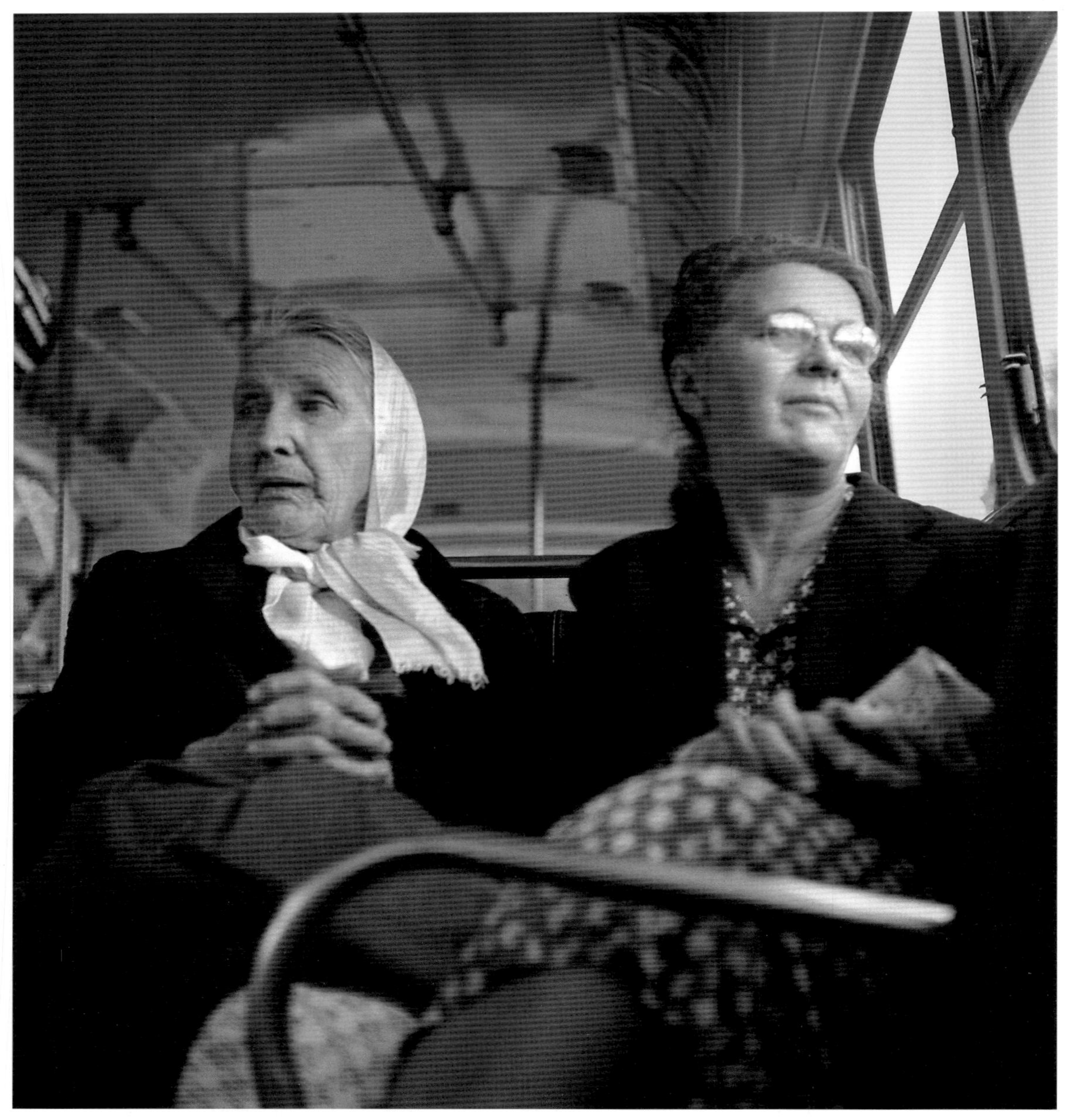

 | TWO GENERATIONS ON BUS, JEFFERSON CITY, MISSOURI, MISSOURI WORKSHOP, 1952

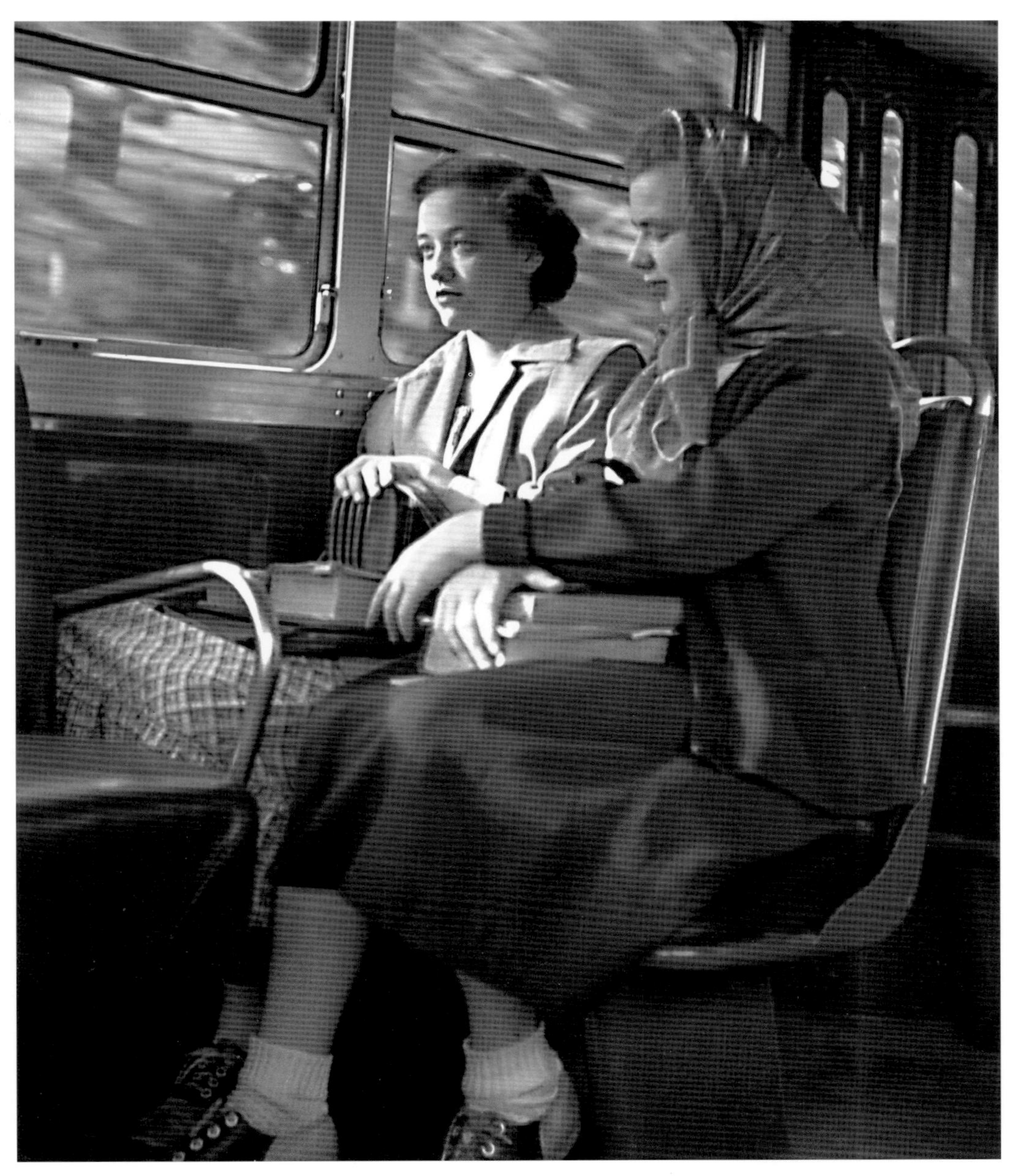

SCHOOL GIRLS ON BUS, MISSOURI WORKSHOP, 1952

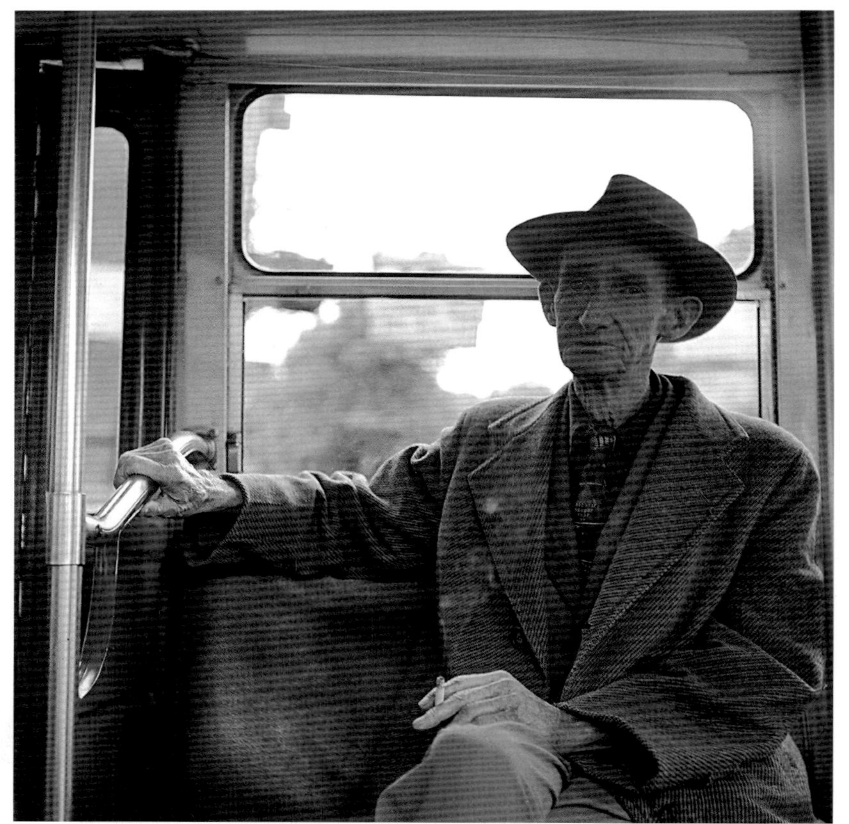

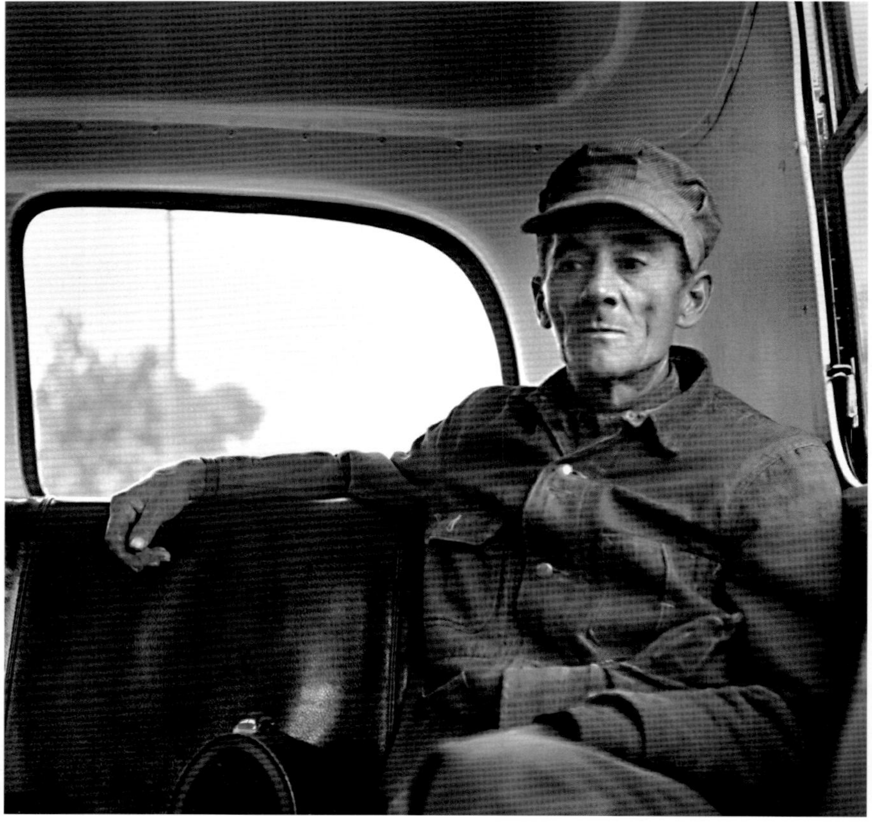

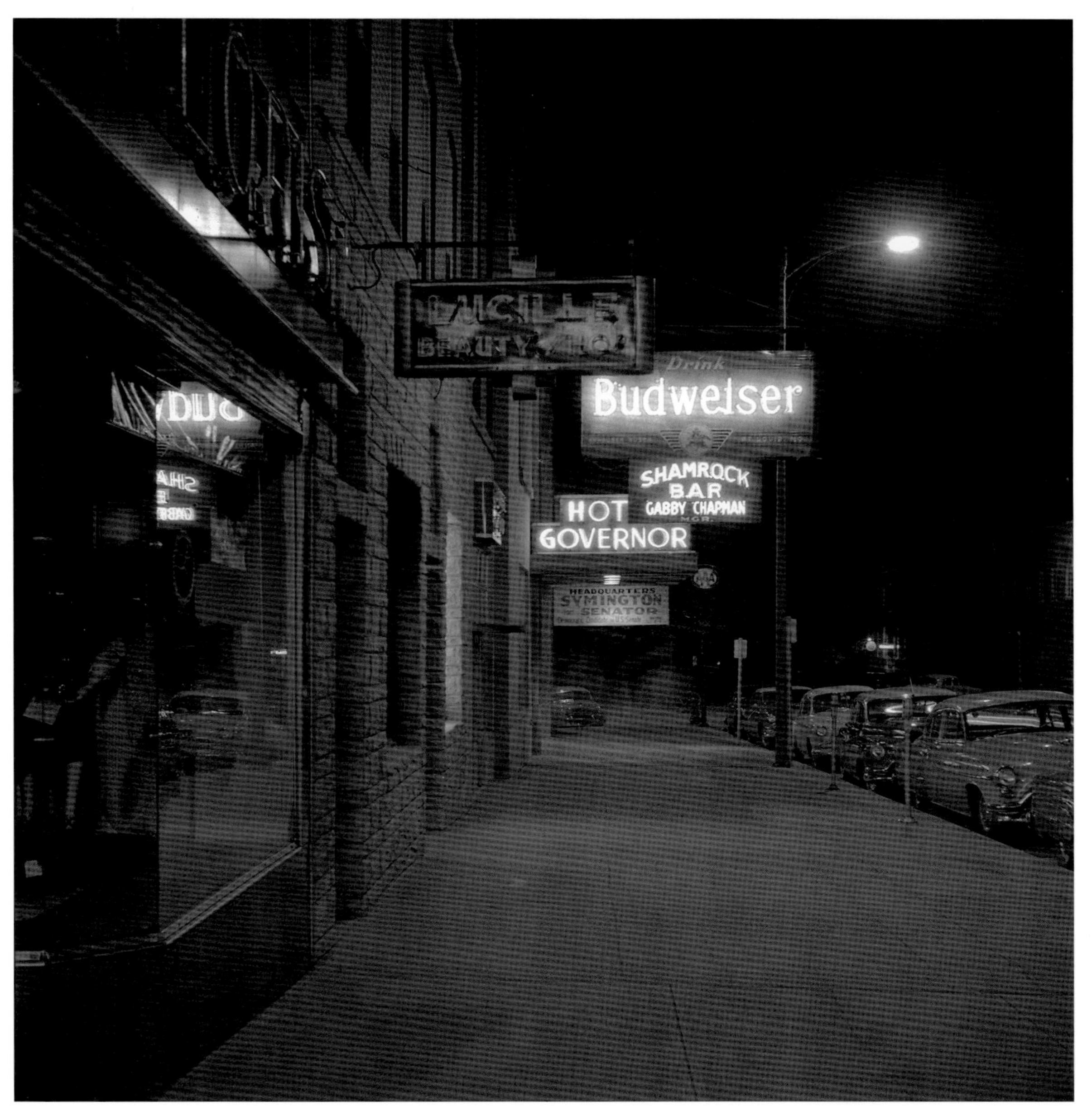
LUCILLE
Drink
Budweiser
SHAMROCK
BAR
GABBY CHAPMAN
HOT
GOVERNOR
HEADQUARTERS
SYMINGTON
SENATOR

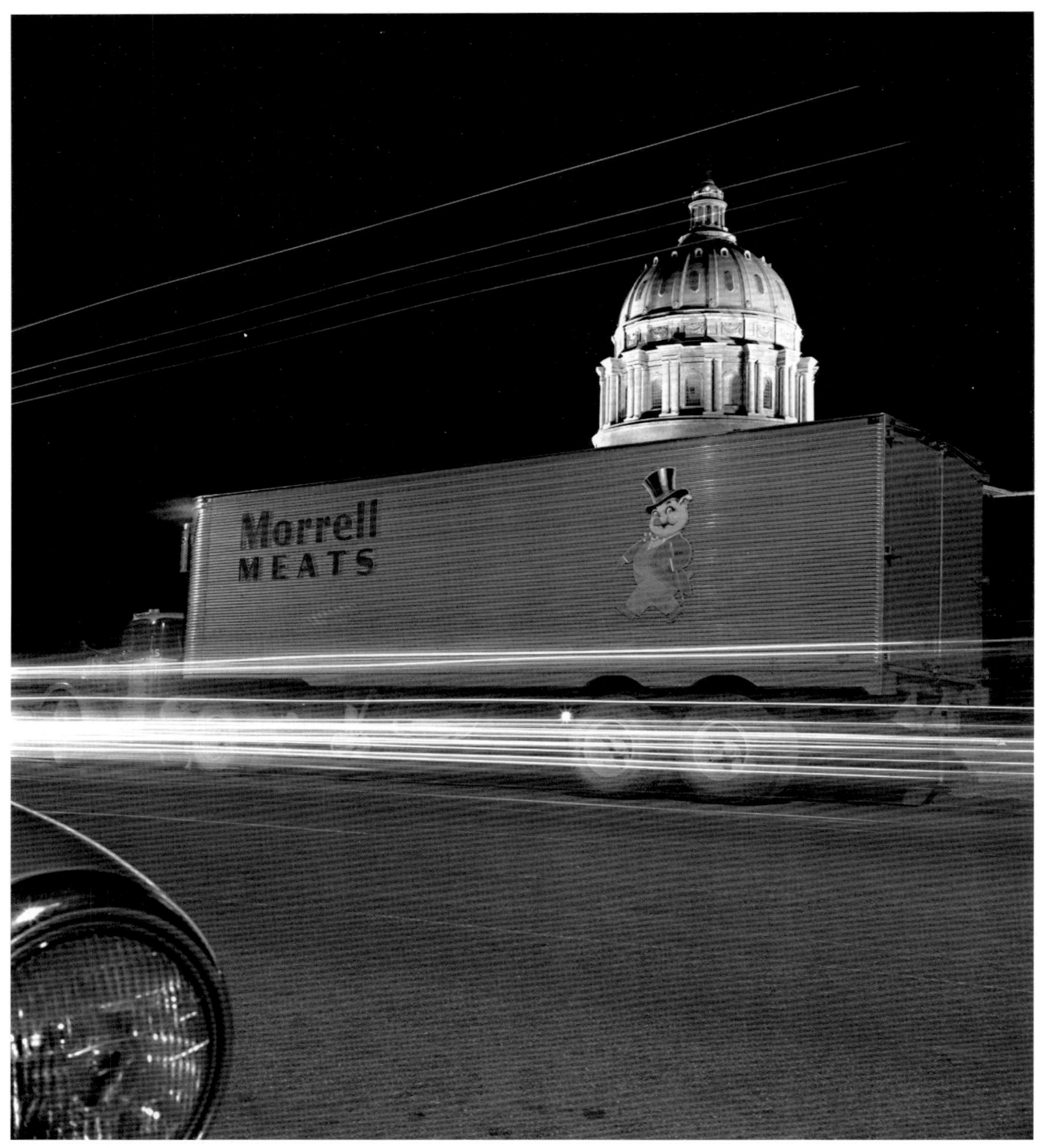

 | STATE CAPITOL, JEFFERSON CITY, MISSOURI, 1952

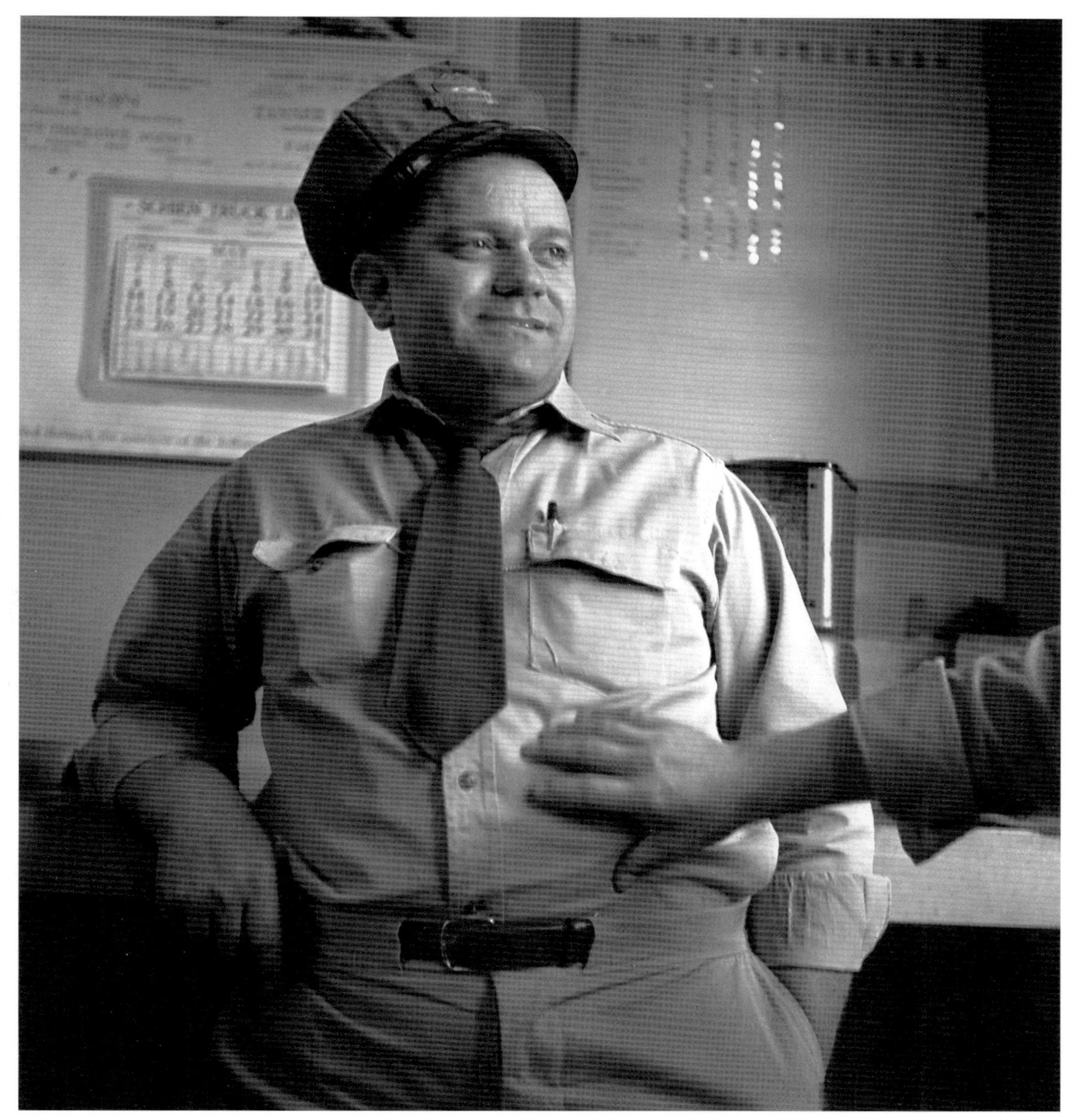

BUS DRIVER BEING KIDDED ABOUT HIS GIRTH, JEFFERSON CITY, MISSOURI

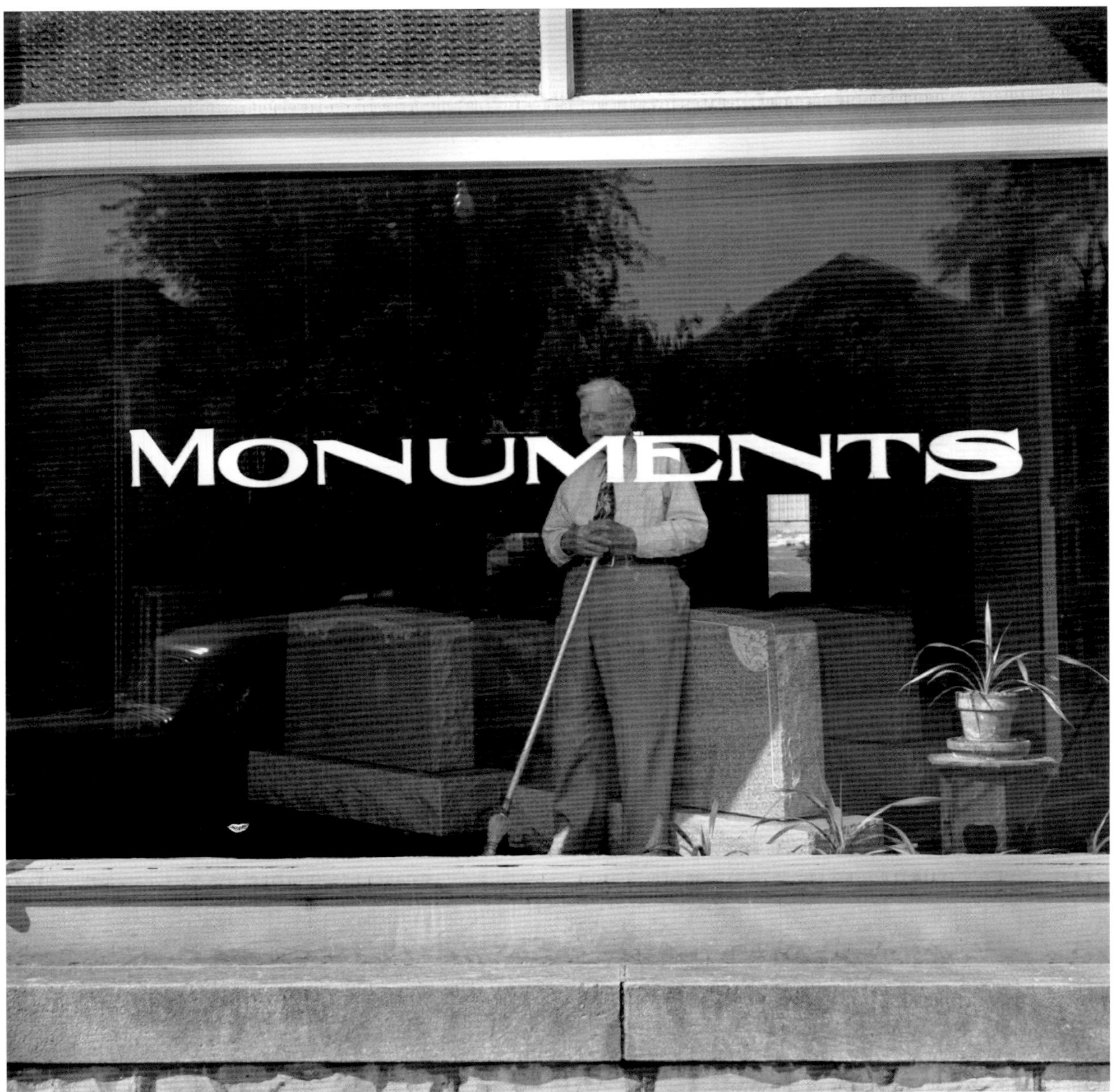

 | MONUMENT SALES, JEFFERSON CITY, MISSOURI

FIVE | Southern Indiana

It is fair to say that southern Indiana is smack in the middle of the Bible Belt. Communities of almost any size have churches. Sometimes there are more churches than the population can support. I have been in country churches where the whole congregation consisted of only two families. Sometimes feuds erupt and folks abandon their church. There exists what one might call "The Church of the Rock." It consists of the teachings of Jesus and is unassailable. Then there is the "Temporal Church," which consists of people with all of their faults. The churches become intense rallying points for worship, and, sometimes, for conflict.

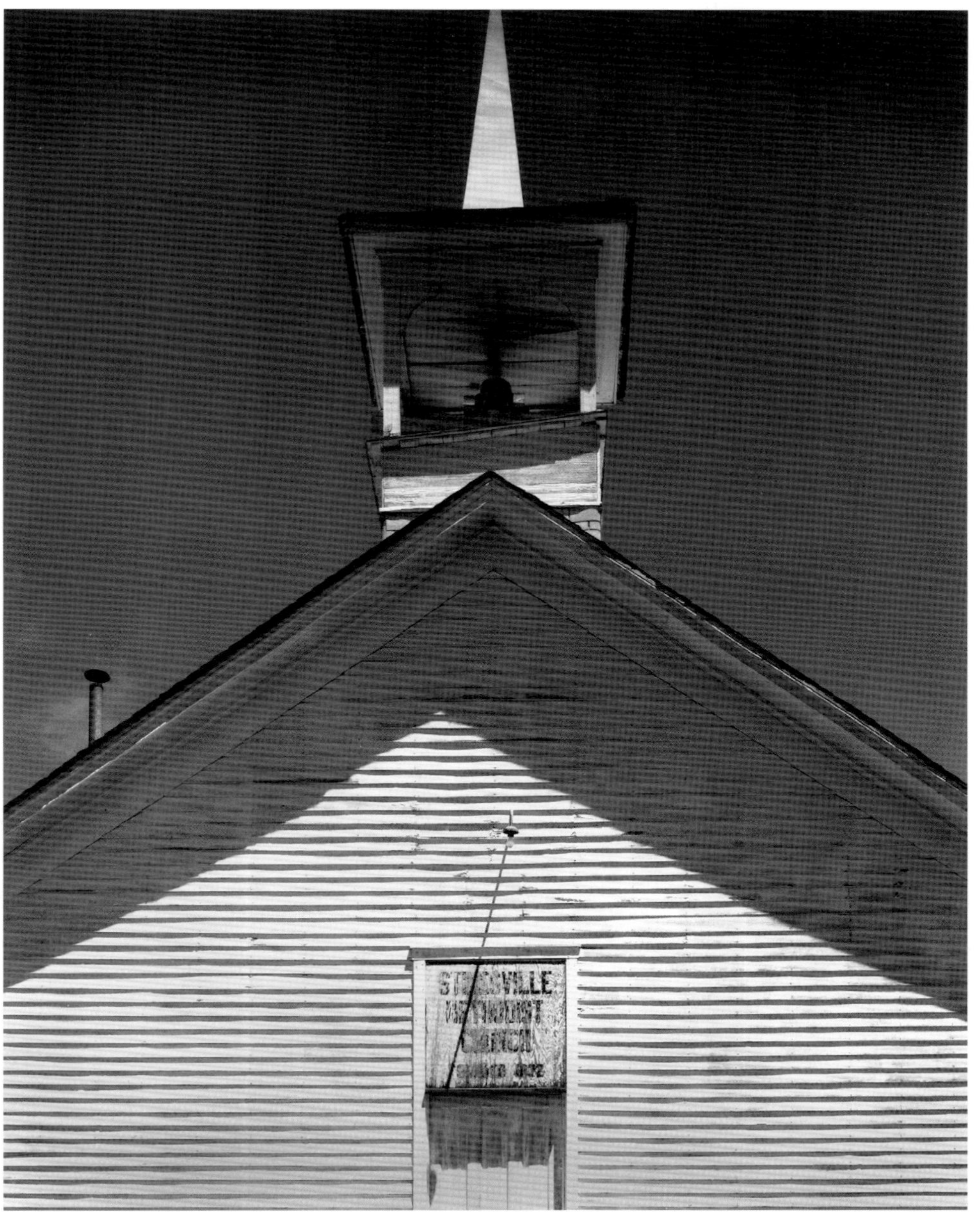

STINESVILLE, INDIANA, CHURCH, c. 1959

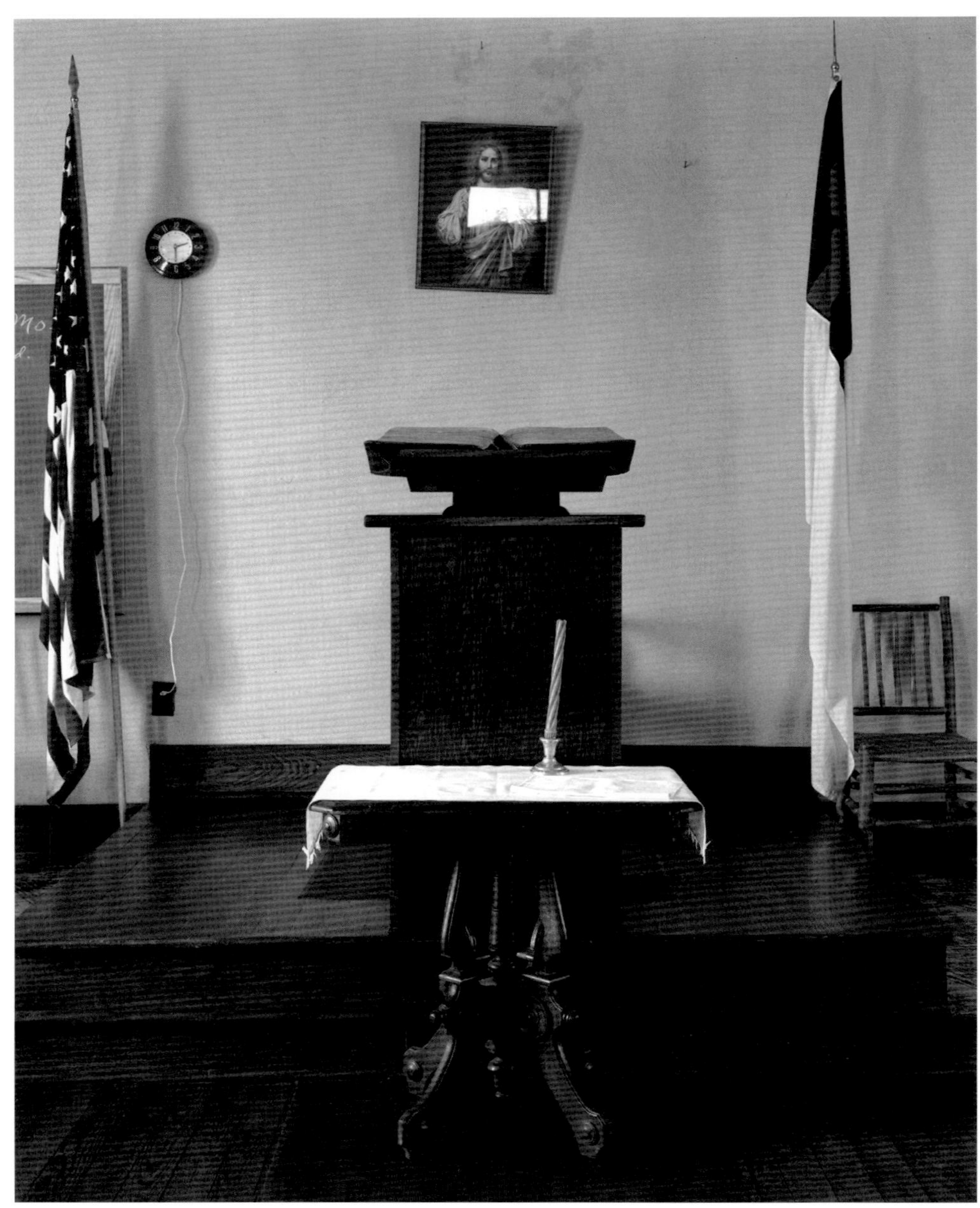

 | CHURCH PULPIT, c. 1959

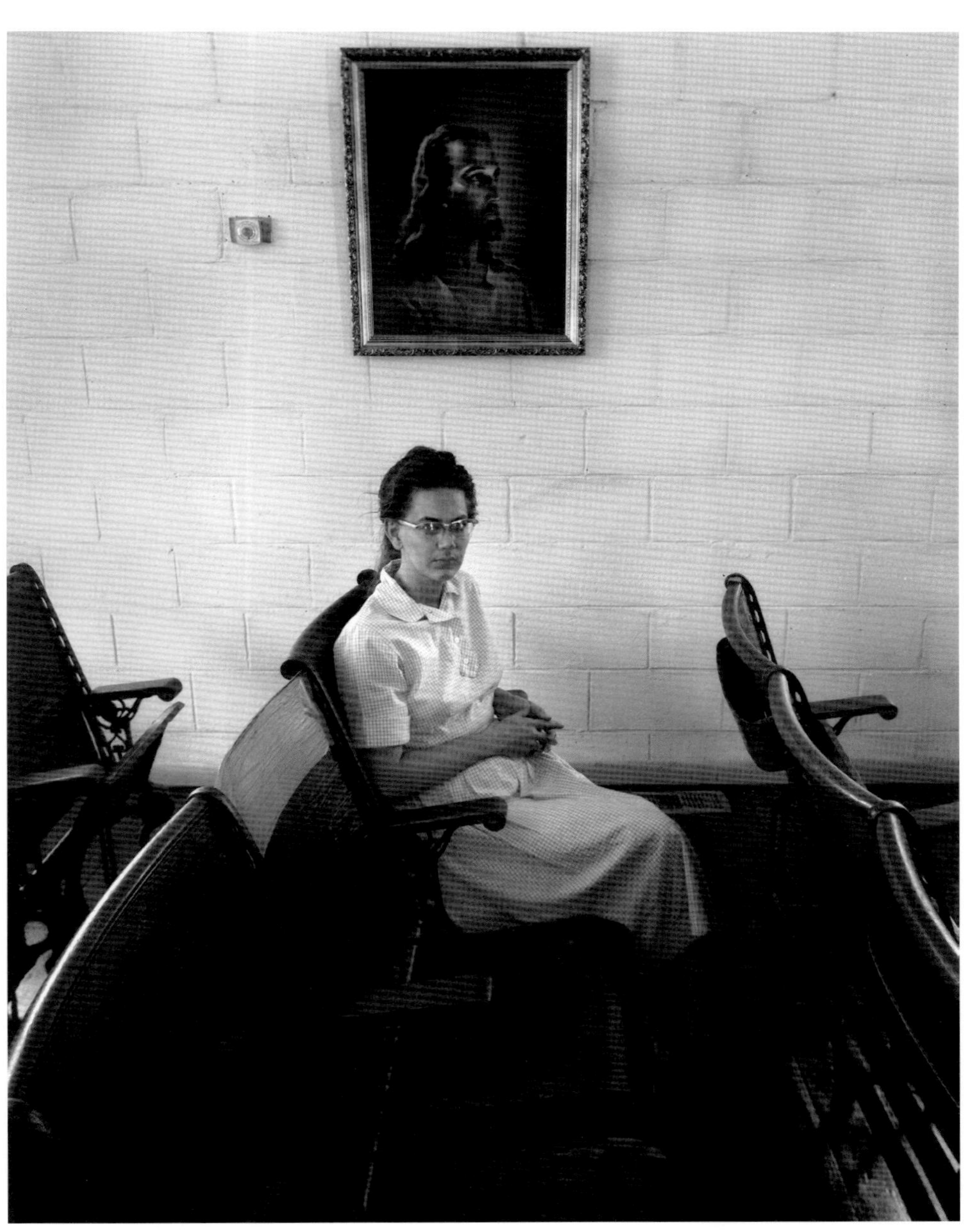

THE PREACHER'S WIFE, c. 1959

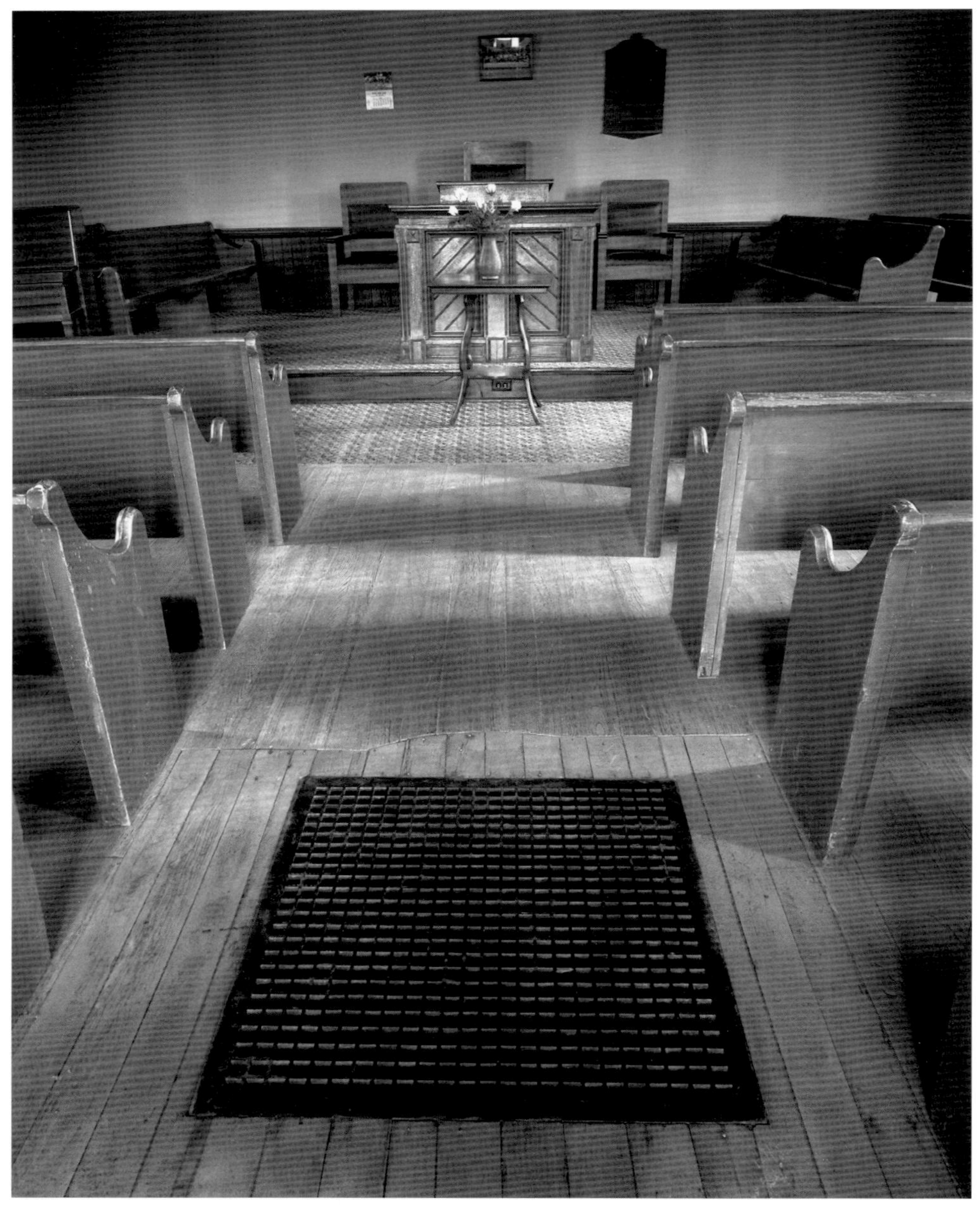

 | STINESVILLE METHODIST CHURCH INTERIOR, c. 1959

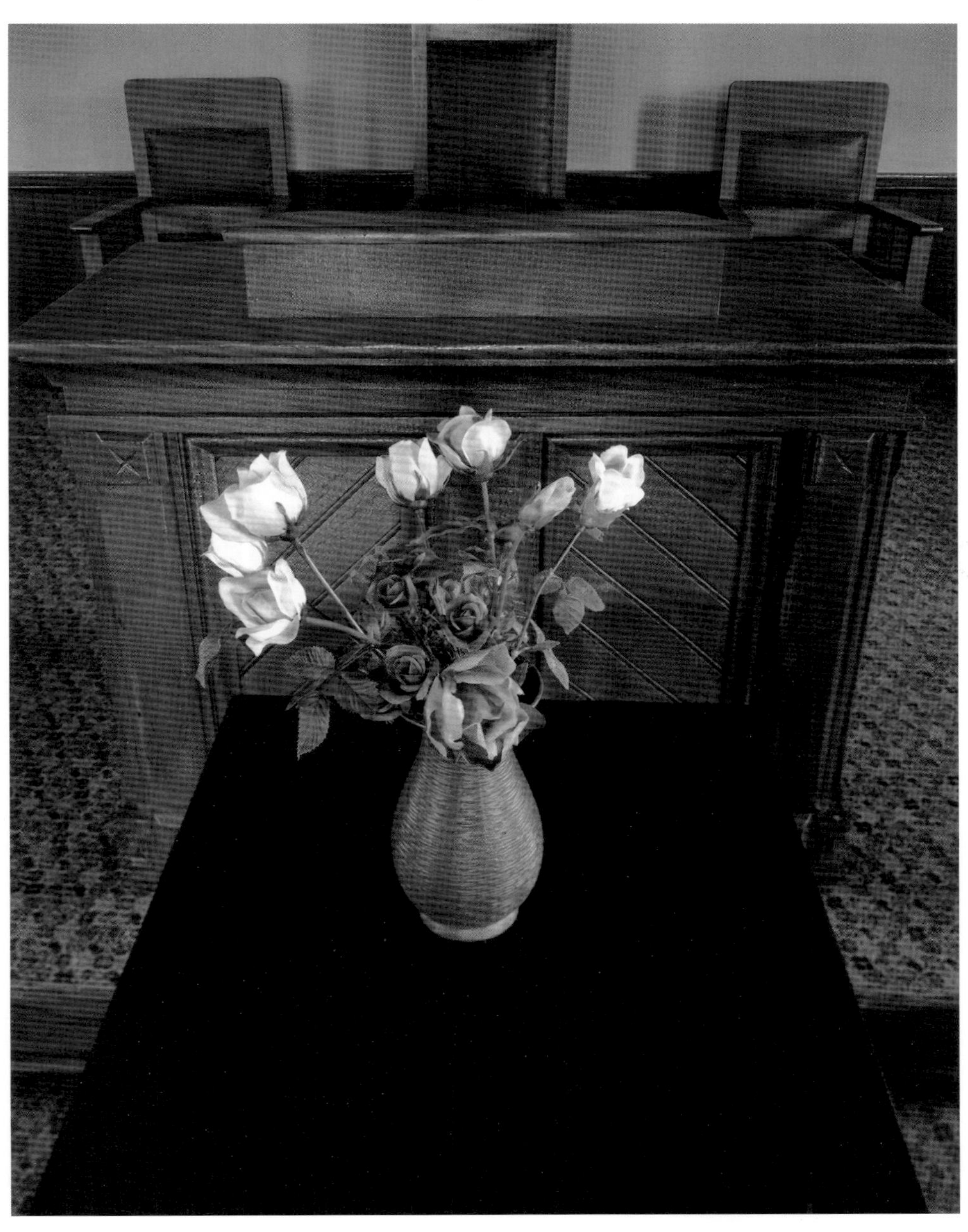

STINESVILLE METHODIST CHURCH INTERIOR, c. 1959

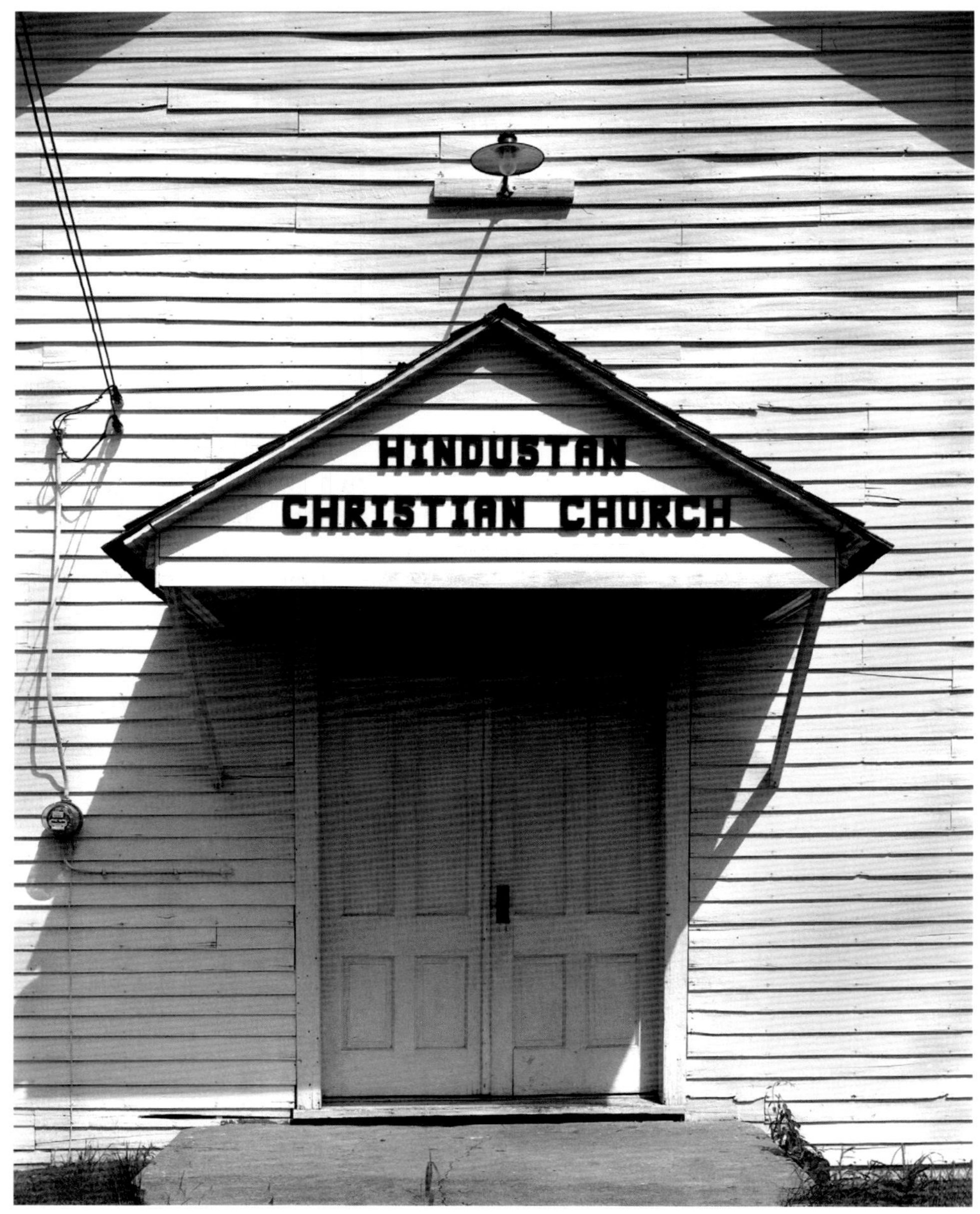

 | HINDUSTAN CHRISTIAN CHURCH, 1958

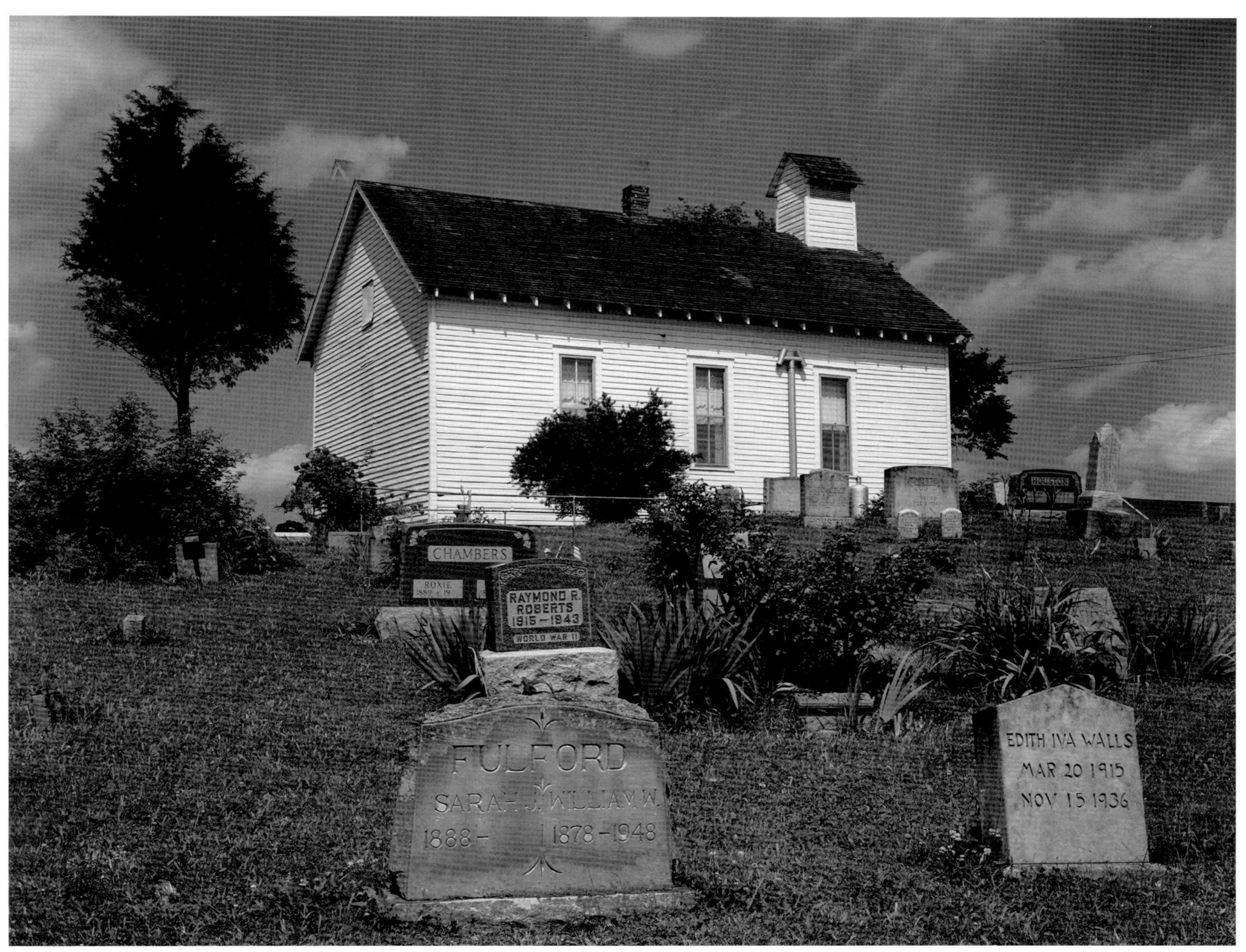

CHURCH CEMETERY, c. 1959

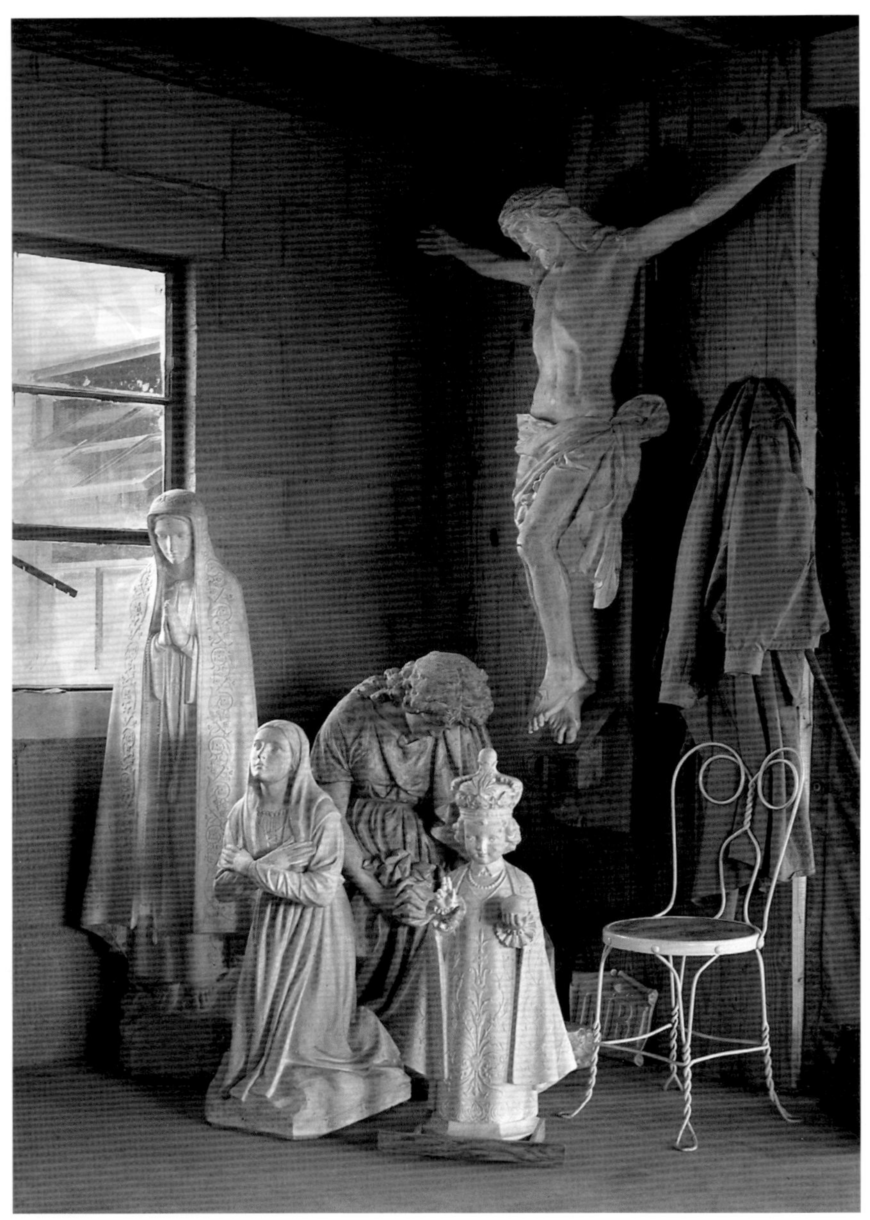

 | CHURCH STOREROOM, c. 1955

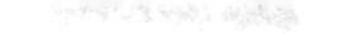

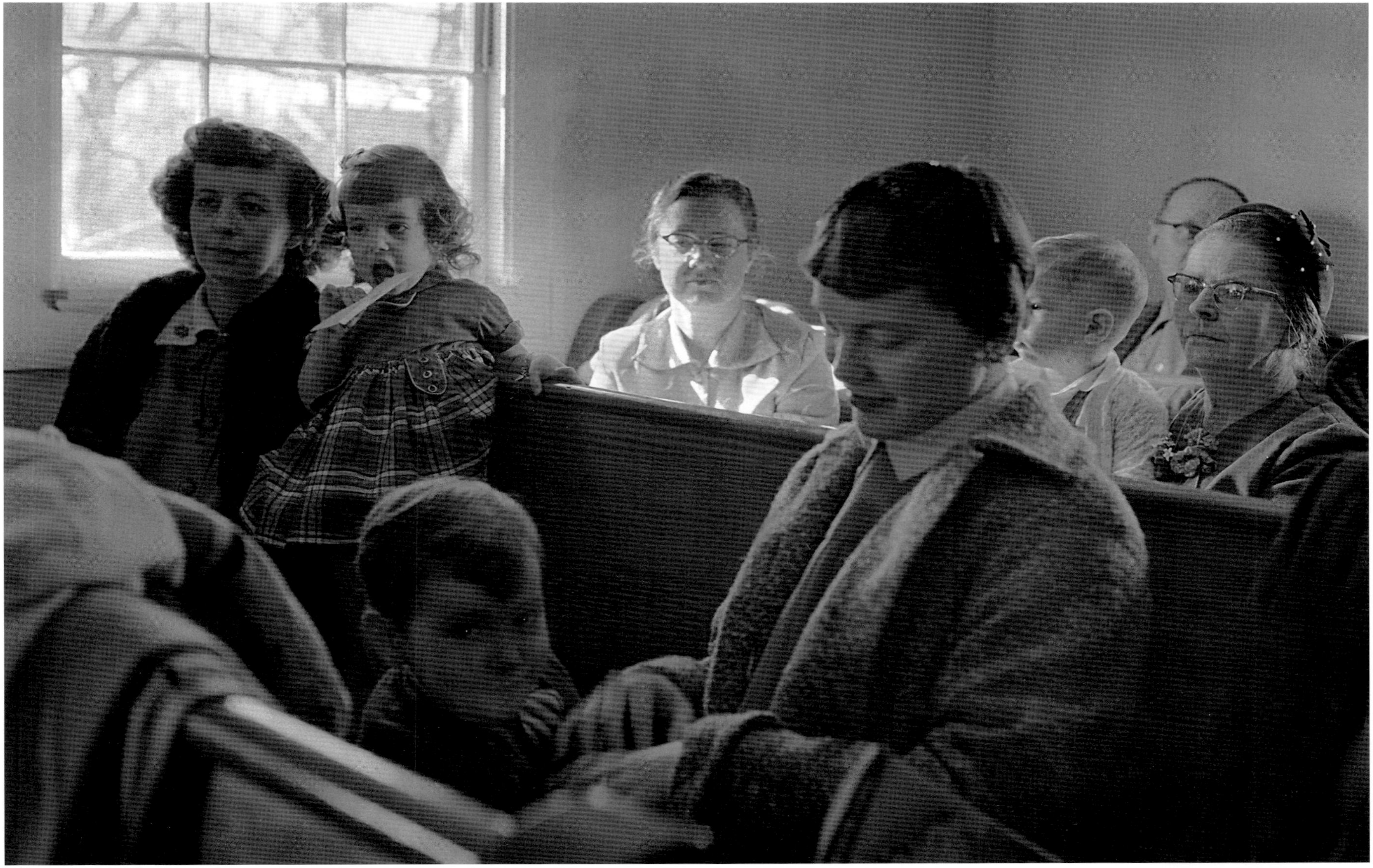

PEOPLE IN CHURCH, c. 1957

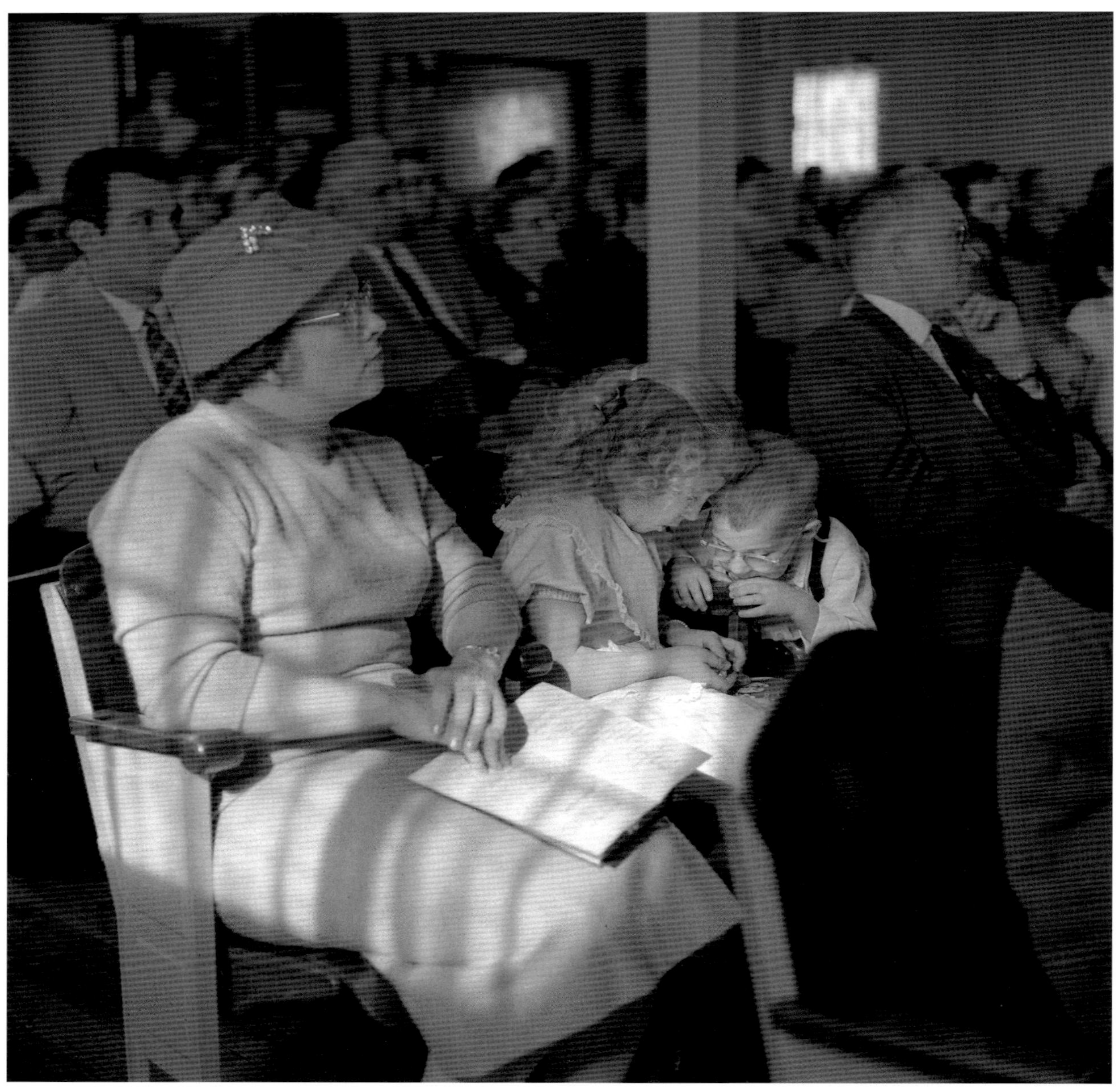

 | MOTHER AND KIDS IN CHURCH, c. 1958

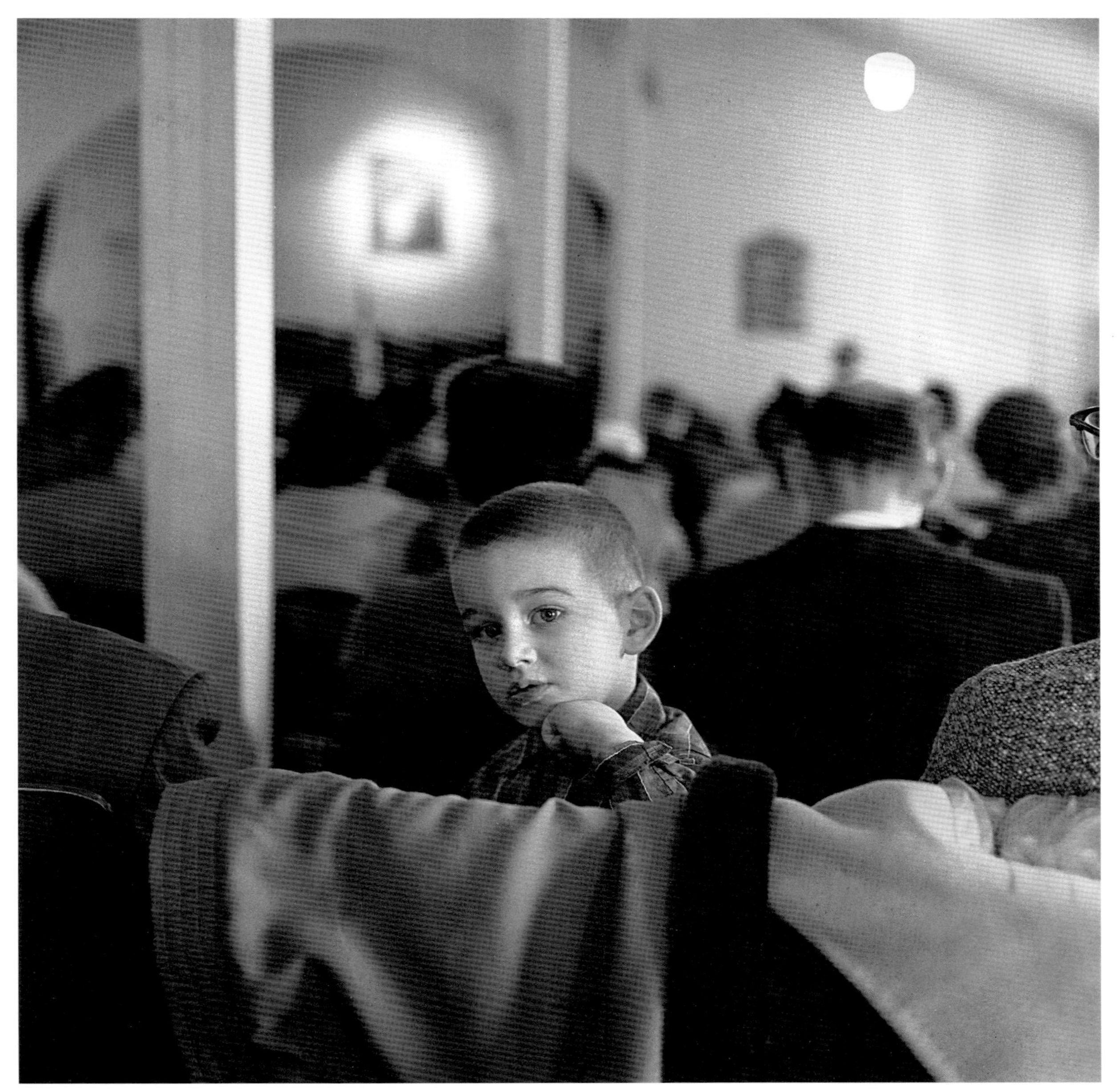

BOY IN CHURCH OF GOD, BLOOMINGTON, INDIANA, 1958

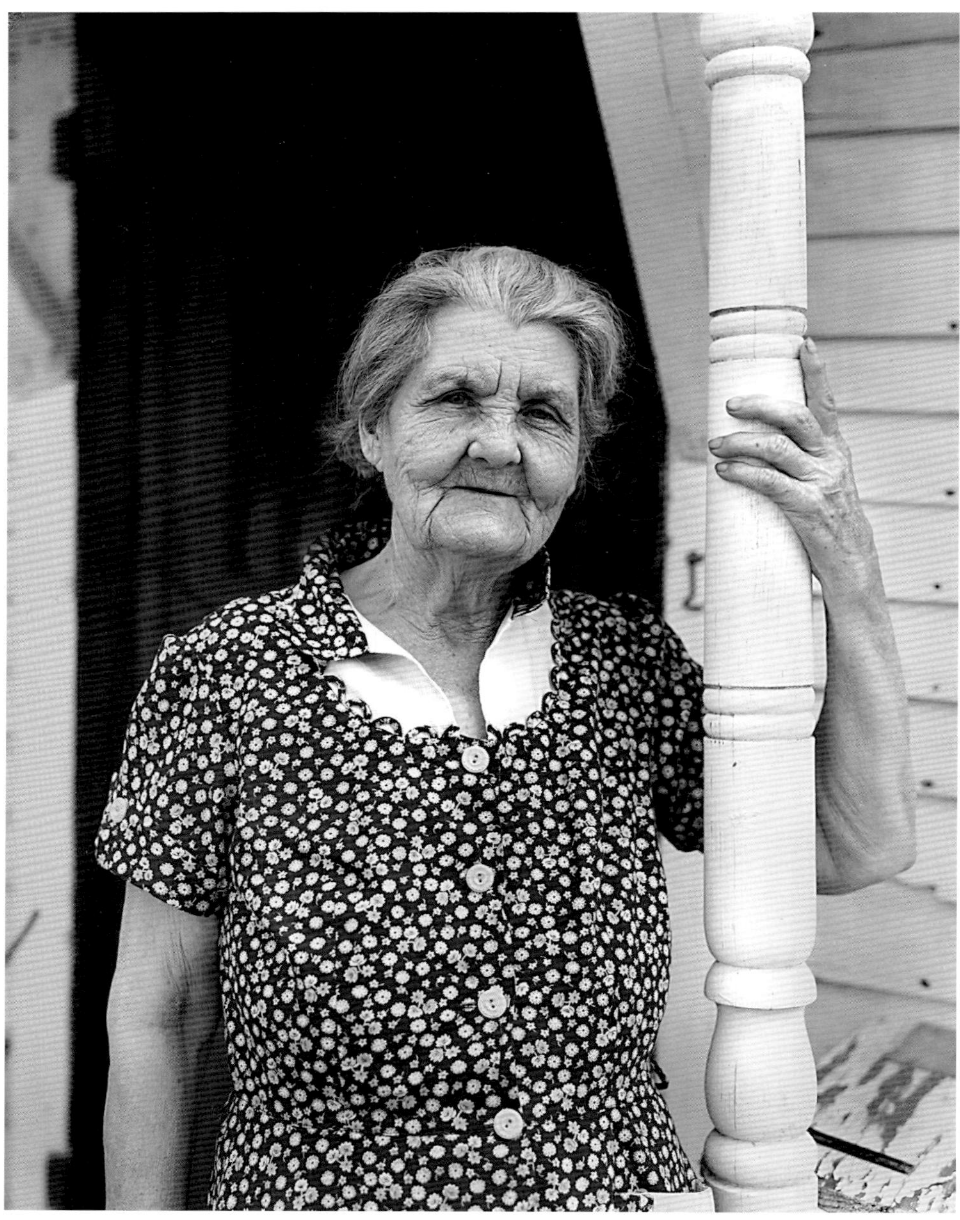

There is a place in southern Indiana called Hindustan. The folks who live there pronounce it Hin-DOO-stun. I chanced onto a country church there, a small, one-room kind of place. It had no electricity, just a few scattered chairs, some funeral home fans strewn about, and the pulpit. The place seemed abandoned.

Close by there was a house. It was there that I met Aunt Addie. I asked her about the church. She told me that the congregation consisted of only about a dozen or so people. One night they had a big fight and everyone left and never came back.

 | AUNT ADDIE, HINDUSTAN, INDIANA, c. 1958

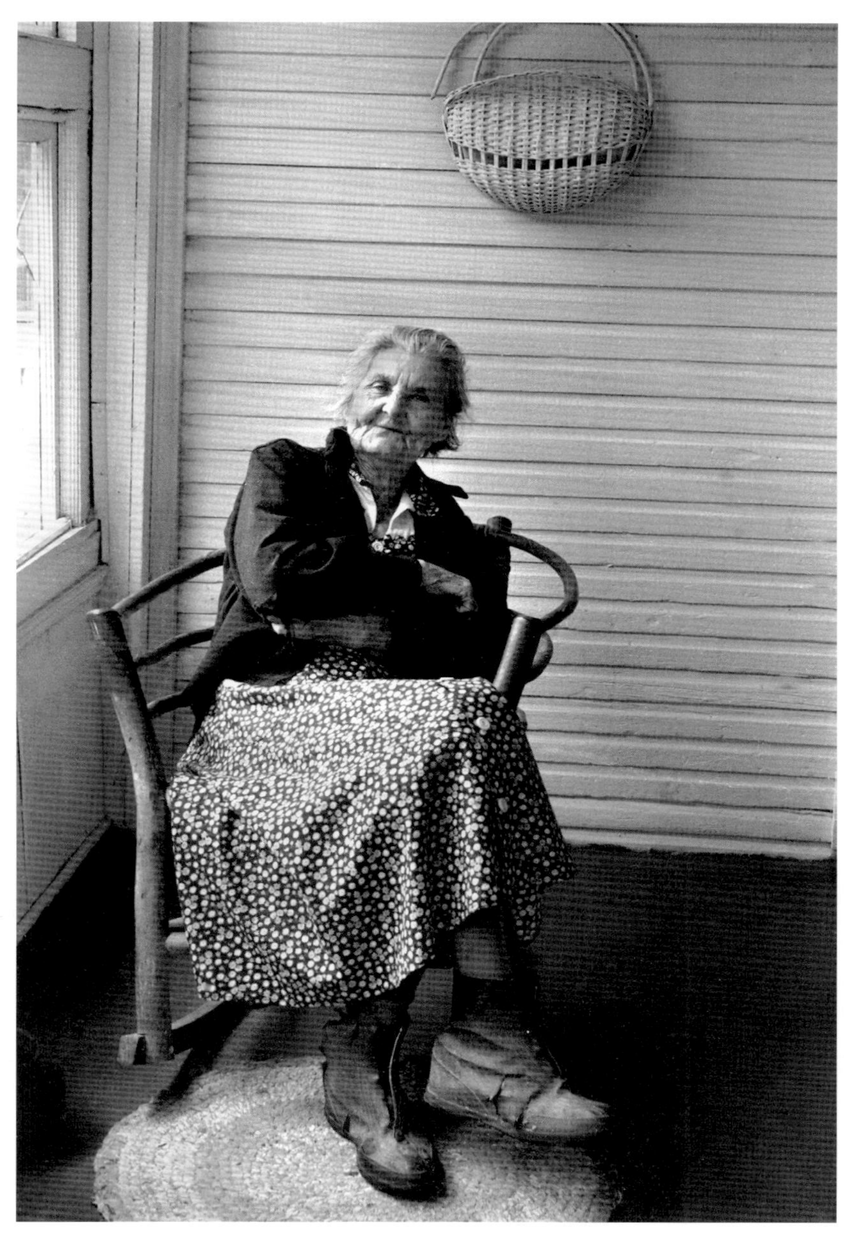

AUNT ADDIE, HINDUSTAN, INDIANA, c. 1958

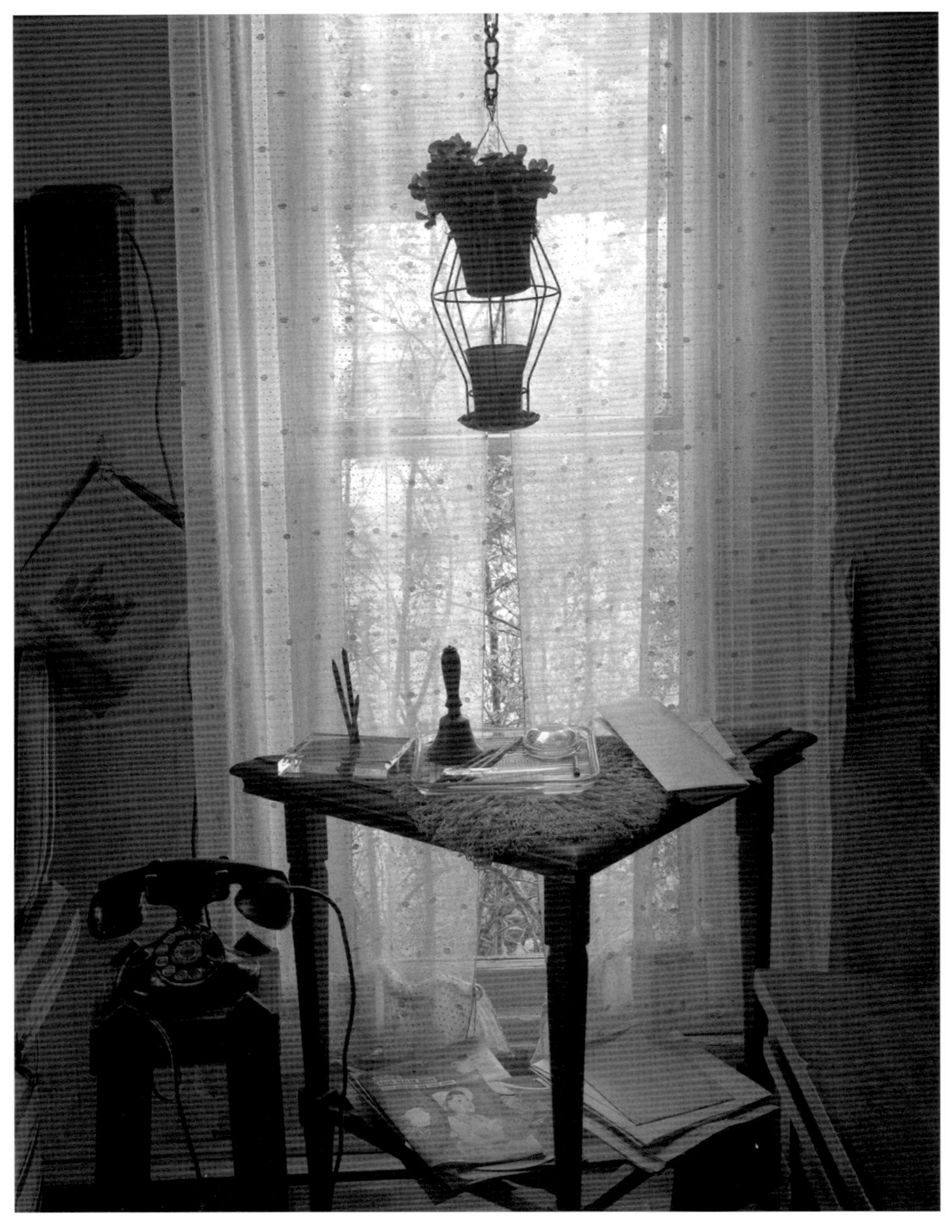

 | AUNT ADDIE'S TABLE, c. 1958

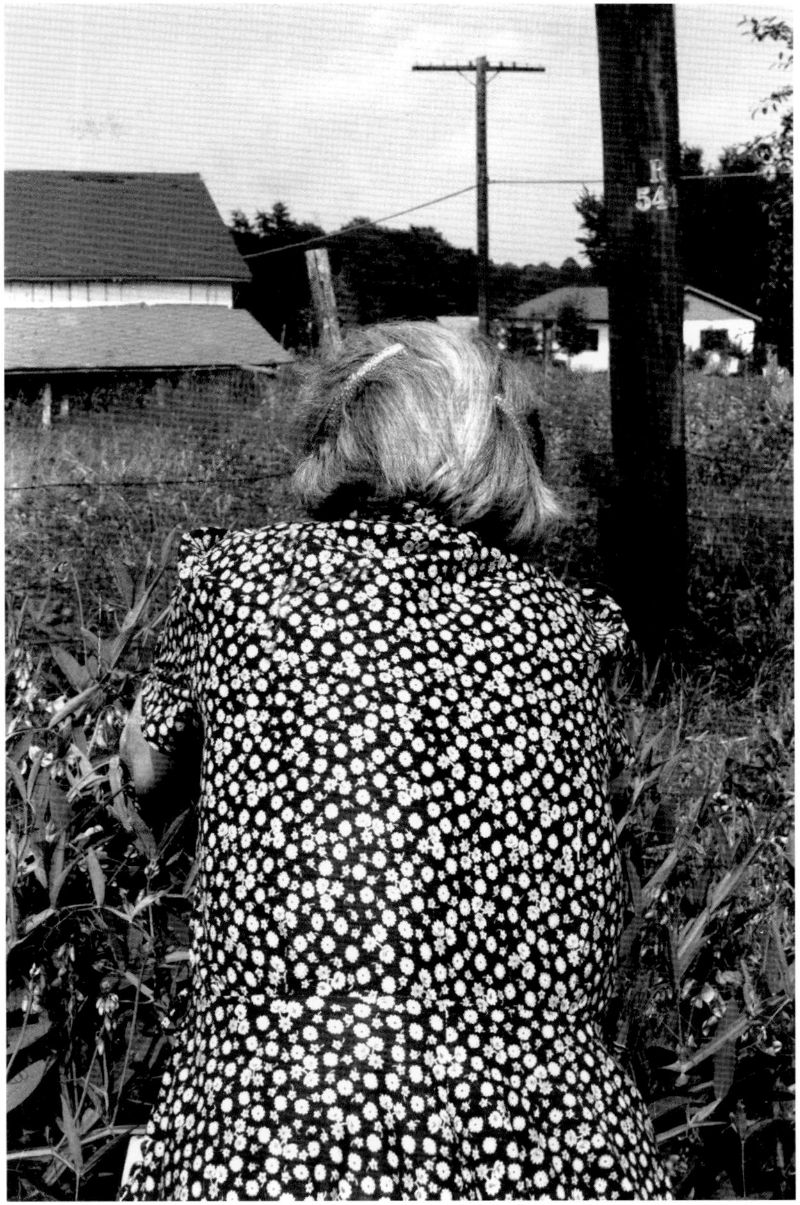

AUNT ADDIE, HINDUSTAN, INDIANA, c. 1958

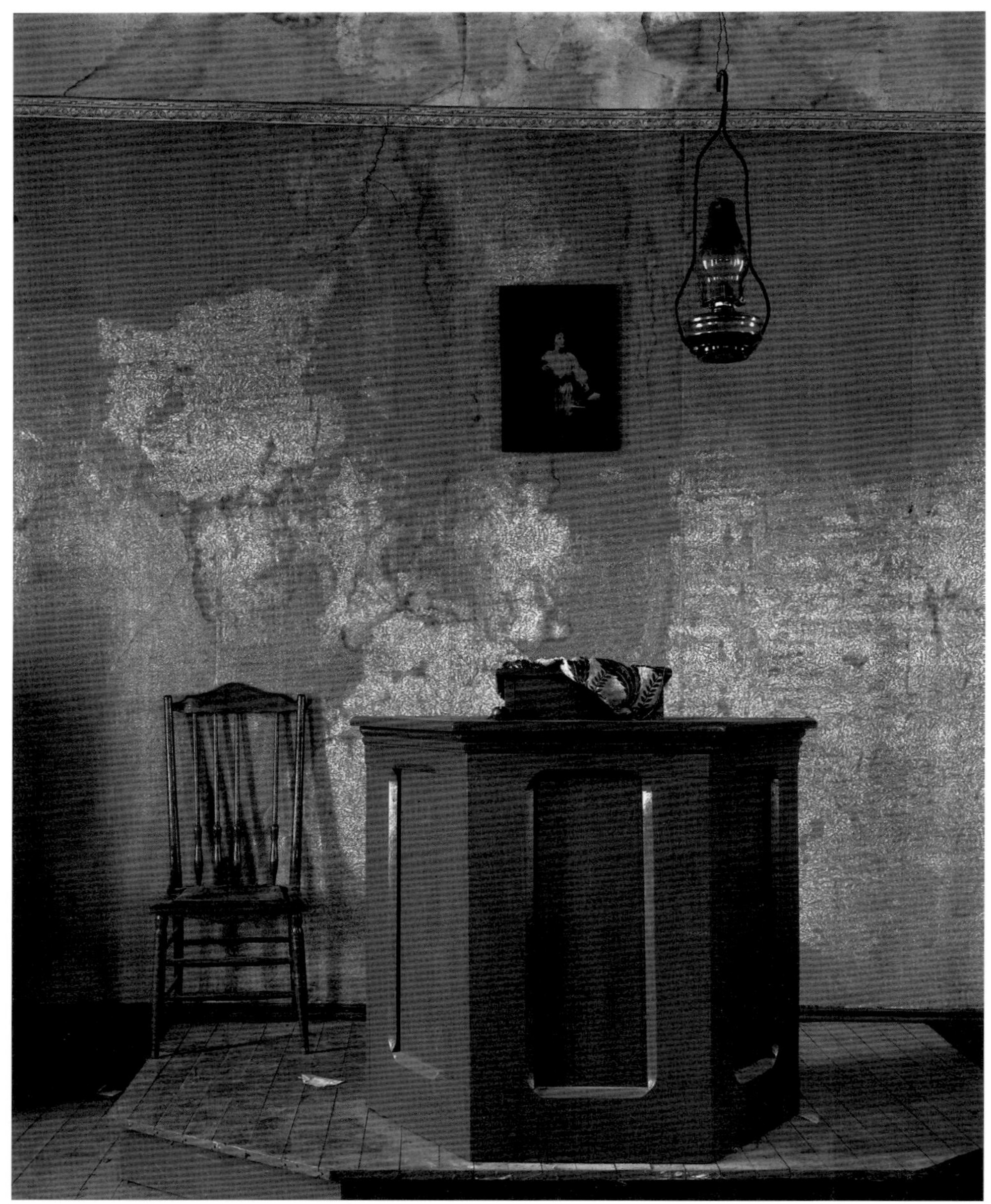

 | ABANDONED CHURCH, HINDUSTAN, INDIANA, c. 1958

Stone Head was a crossroads with a general store and a few houses. It was there I met Mr. Penrose, who told me how the place got its name. One dark night, one of the country boys came barreling down the road in his pickup truck. When he came to the intersection, rather than turning left or right, he plowed ahead into the side of a house.

This fellow (let's call him Charlie) was hauled before the judge, who said, "What am I going to do with you, Charlie? You caused a lot of property damage." He replied, "Well, if you will let me off, I'll make a big stone head from limestone and put it there and the next son of a bitch that comes barreling down that road will kill hisself." The judge, being a reasonable man, thought it was a good idea and the bargain was struck.

Mr. Penrose lived four miles from the general store. Each morning he walked there to hang out with the old guys who liked to sit on barrels inside. After an hour or so he would walk home and then repeat that trip in the late afternoon. All together he walked sixteen miles a day.

I once took him for a ride in my car. We passed a lady who was building a bridge over a creek by herself. I remarked on how unusual that was. Mr. Penrose told me that she lived alone in a cabin across the creek. When winter came she was snowbound and no one

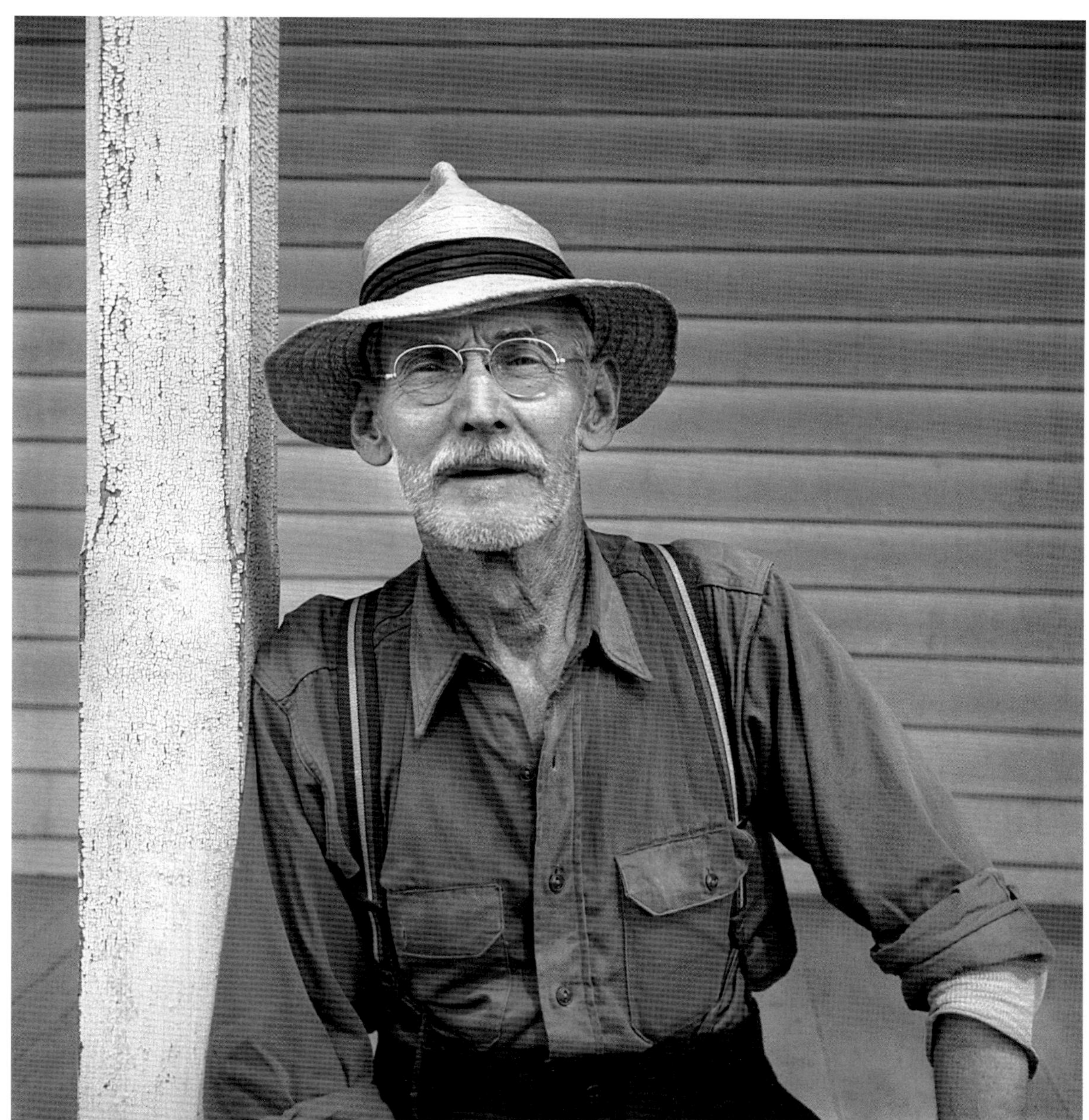

MR. PENROSE, STONE HEAD, INDIANA, c. 1955

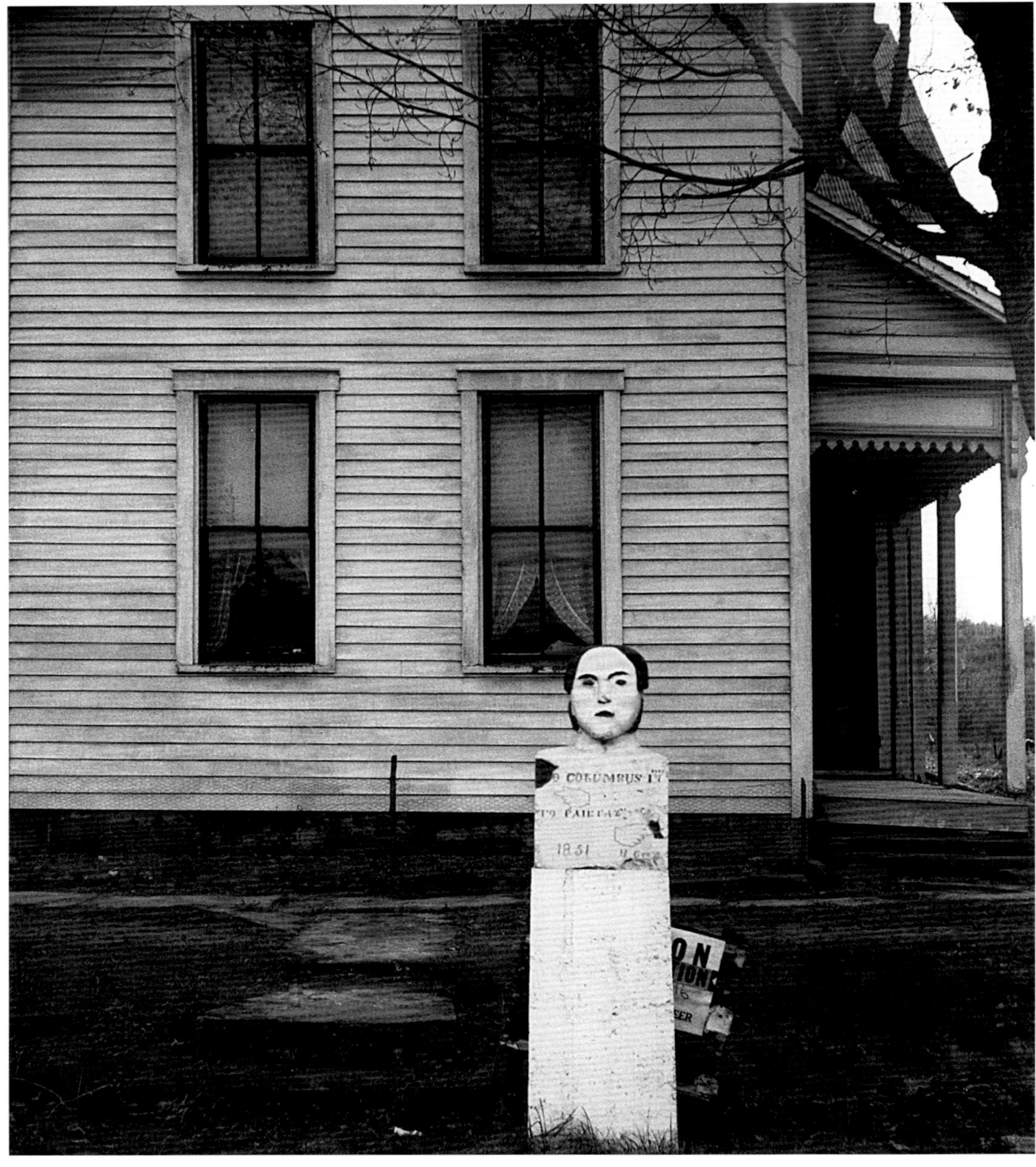

saw her until spring. One spring she showed up at the general store with a baby in her arms. The old guys began kidding her. One said, "I didn't know you had a husband." She replied, "I didn't want a husband, I wanted a baby."

Mr. Penrose took me to the top of a hill and showed me where the boys assembled to march off to war—the Civil War.

 | STONE HEAD, INDIANA, c. 1955

SIX | Friends and Relations

The impulse to make photographs of friends and family was no less strong in me than was the case with my father. The difference was that I had progressed in my understanding of photography beyond the snapshot and wanted to make finer images. It seems in retrospect that I usually had a camera handy and would attempt now and then to take what I hoped were meaningful portraits of these people who were such an important part of my life.

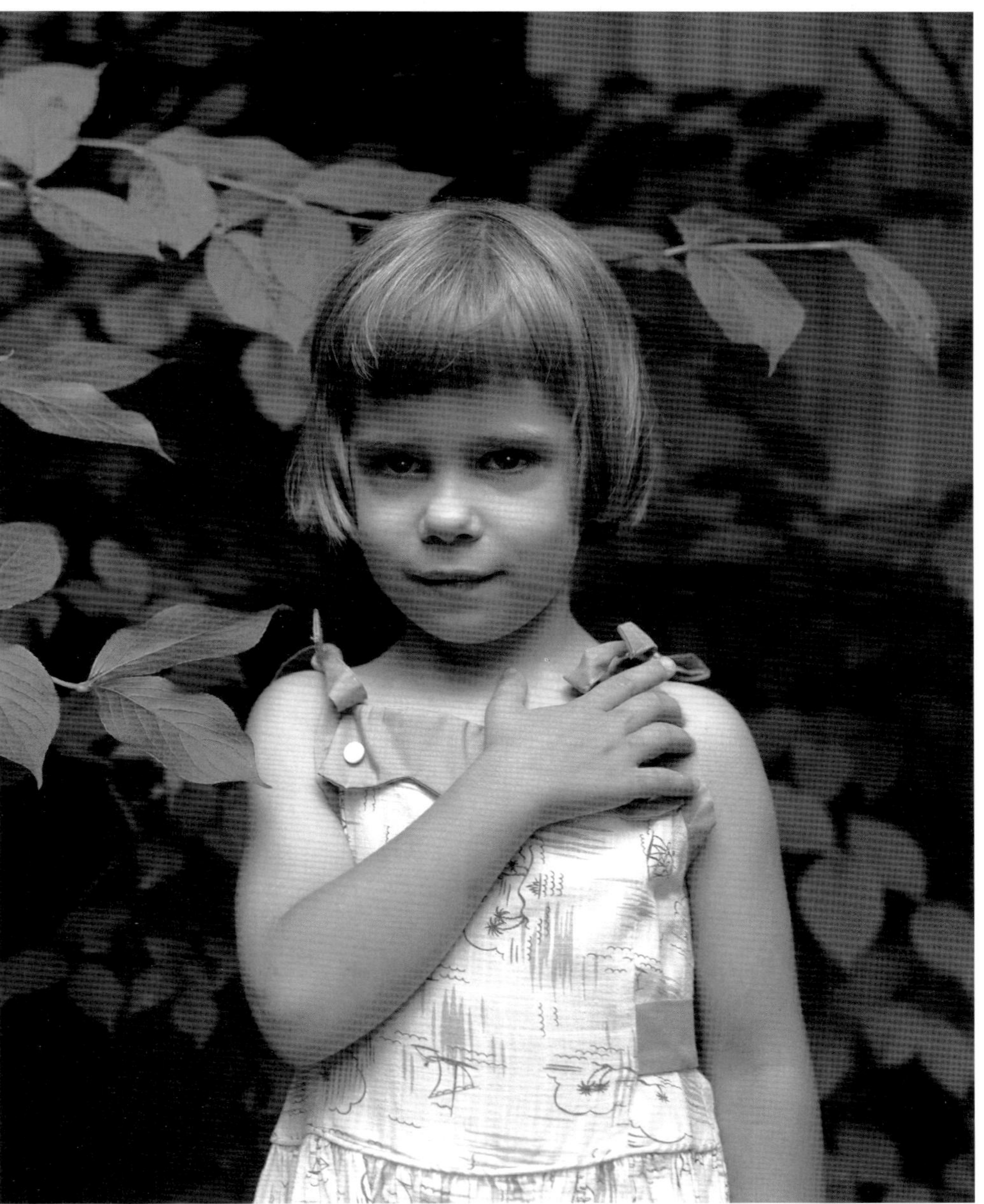

MY DAUGHTER, JAN MARIE WELPOTT, c. 1958 |

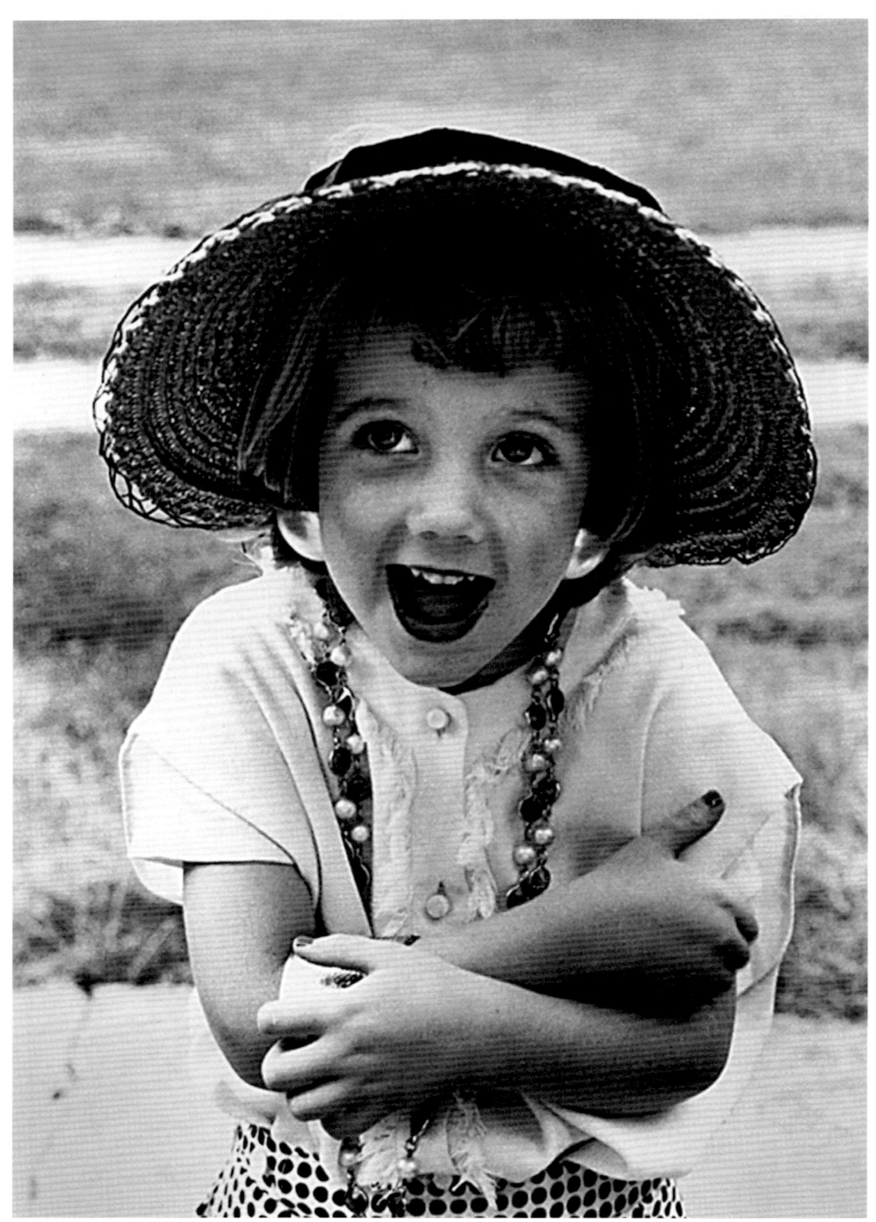

 | DAUGHTER JAN MARIE PLAYS DRESS UP

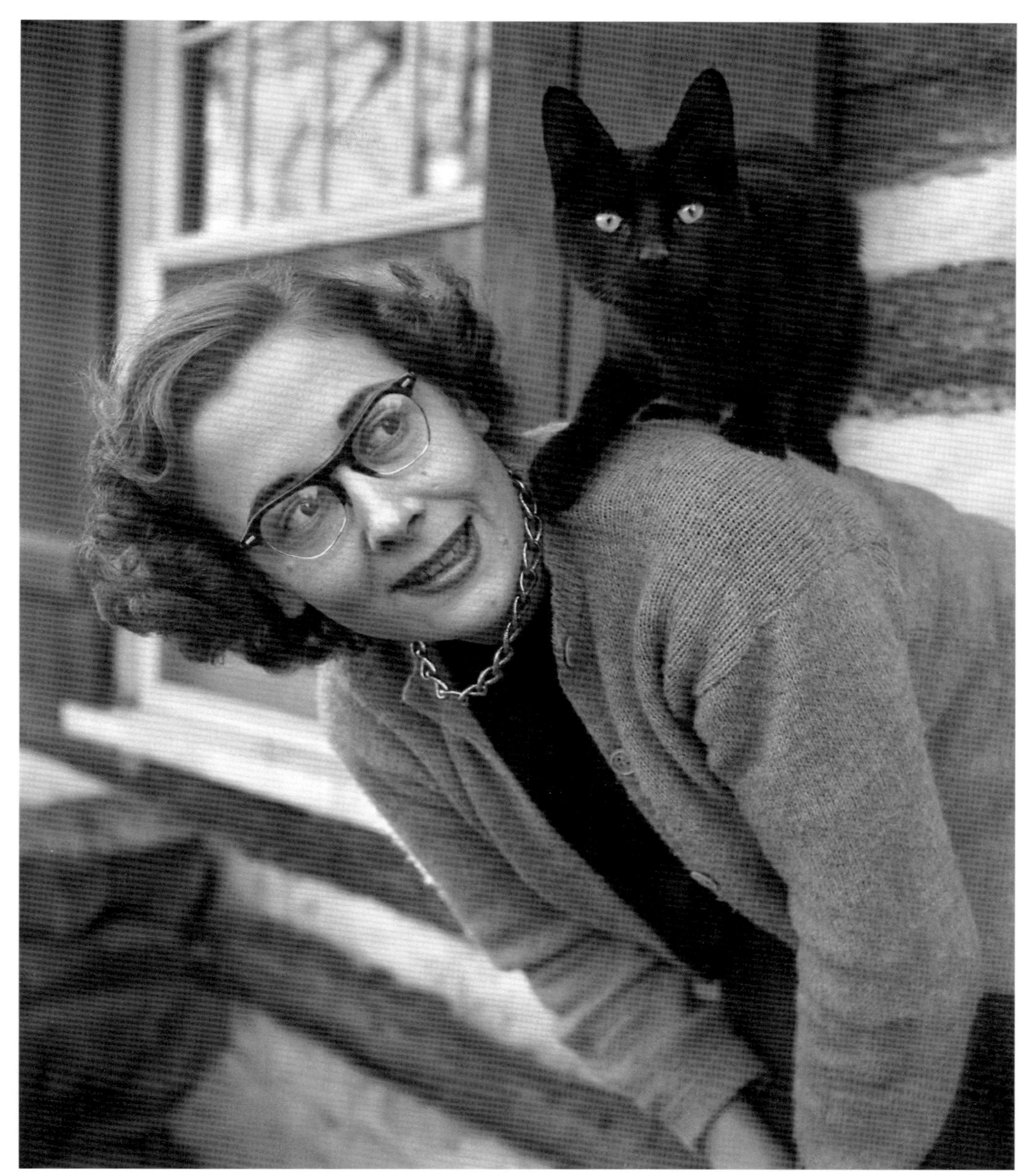

JEAN FRANKLIN WELPOTT, c. 1956

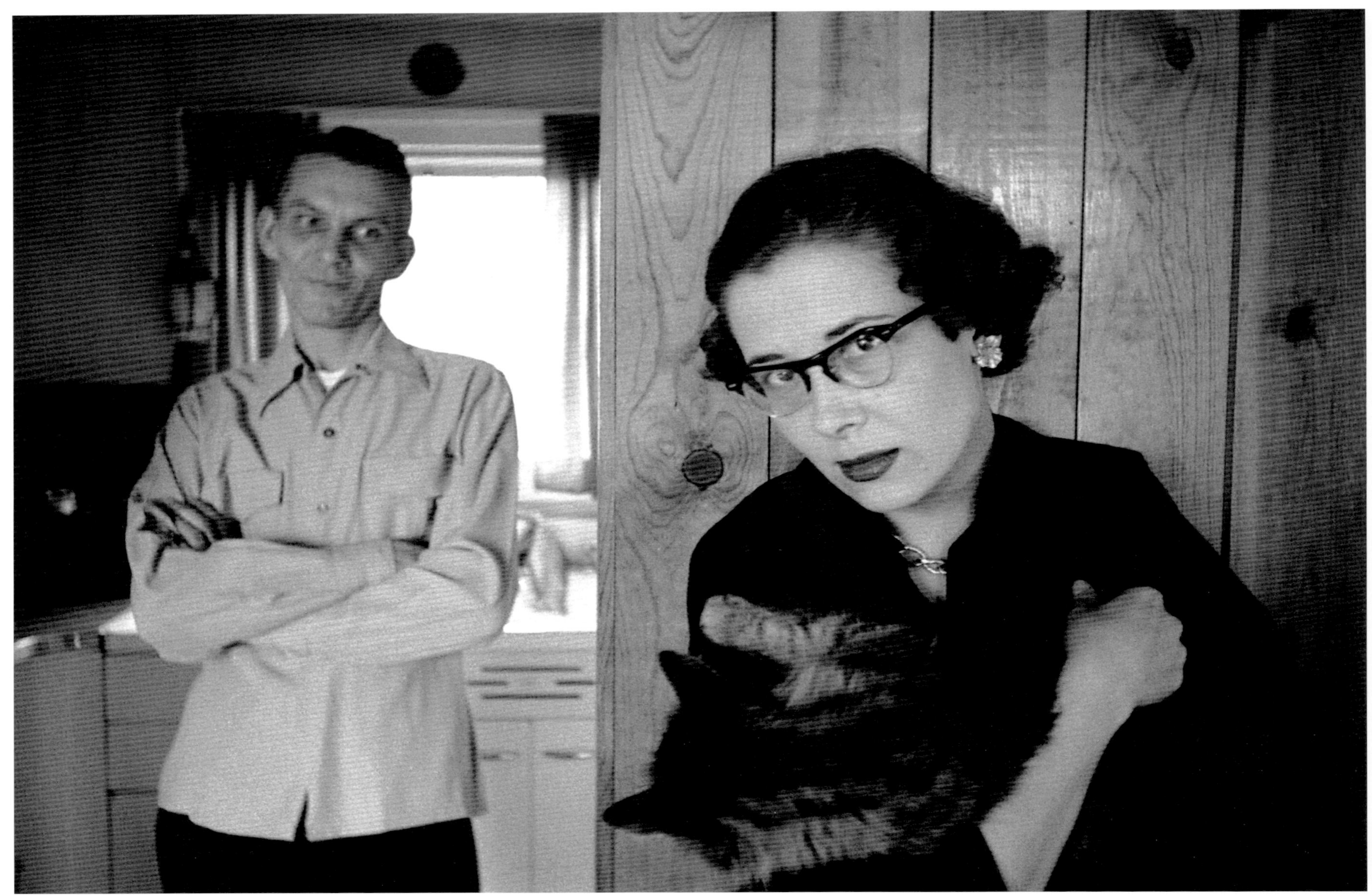

 | REED FRANKLIN AND JEAN FRANKLIN WELPOTT, c. 1951

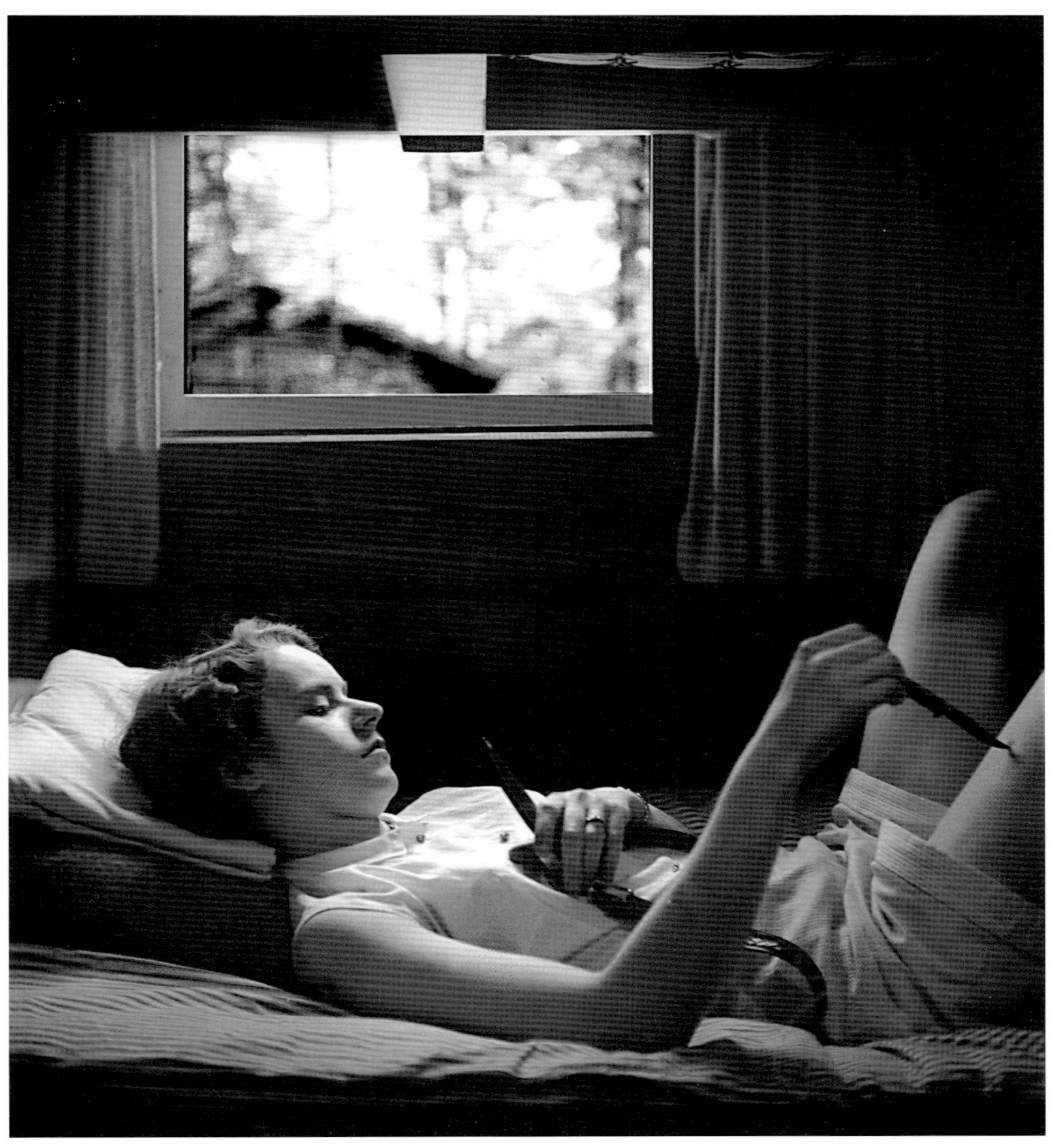

JO HUNTINGTON, c. 1953

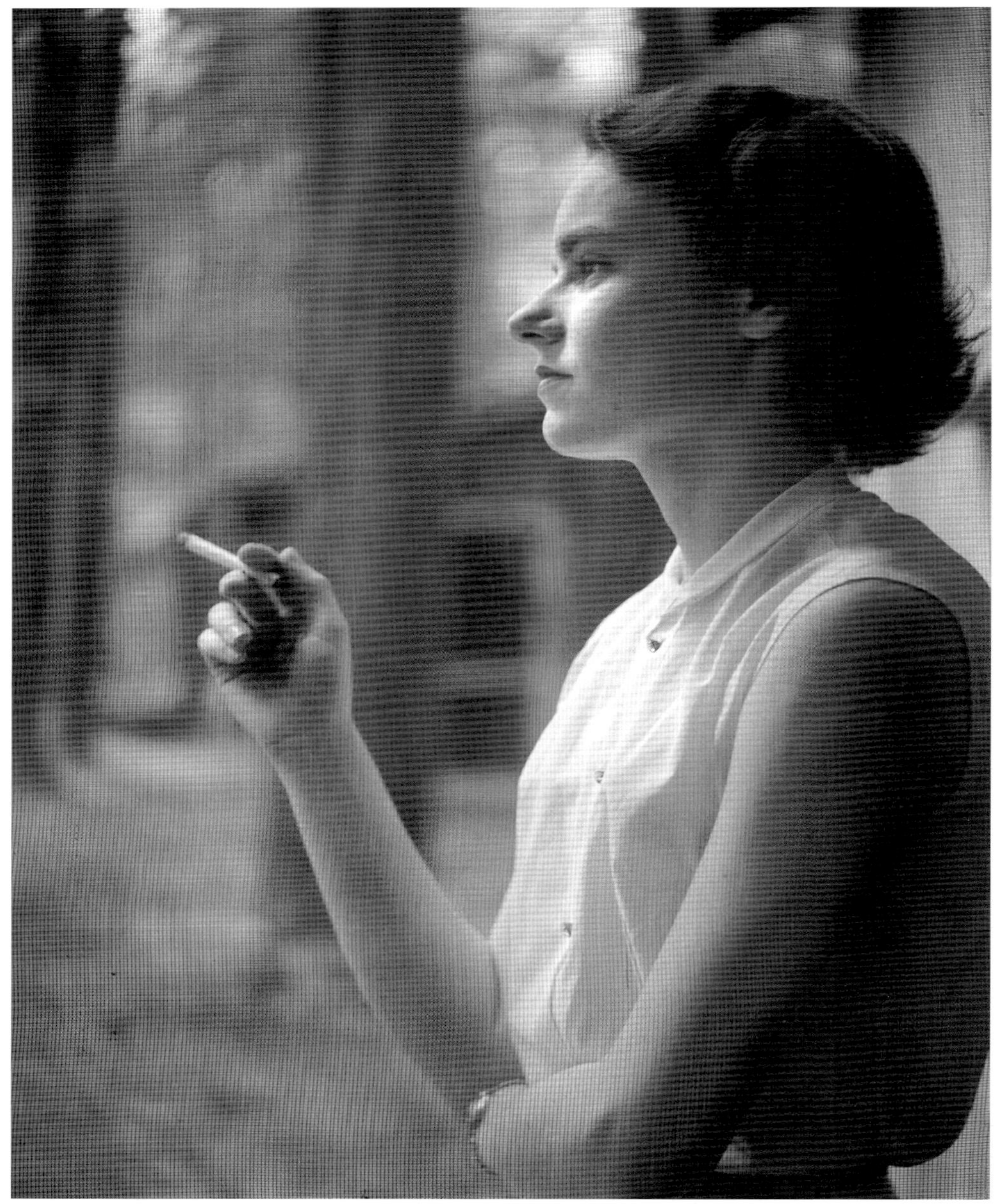

 | JO HUNTINGTON, c. 1953

George Disborough was a graphic artist with whom I worked on many projects at Indiana University. He and I became good friends. George held a degree from Indiana University in art. He went on to a distinguished career with Upjohn Corporation where he served as art director for many years.

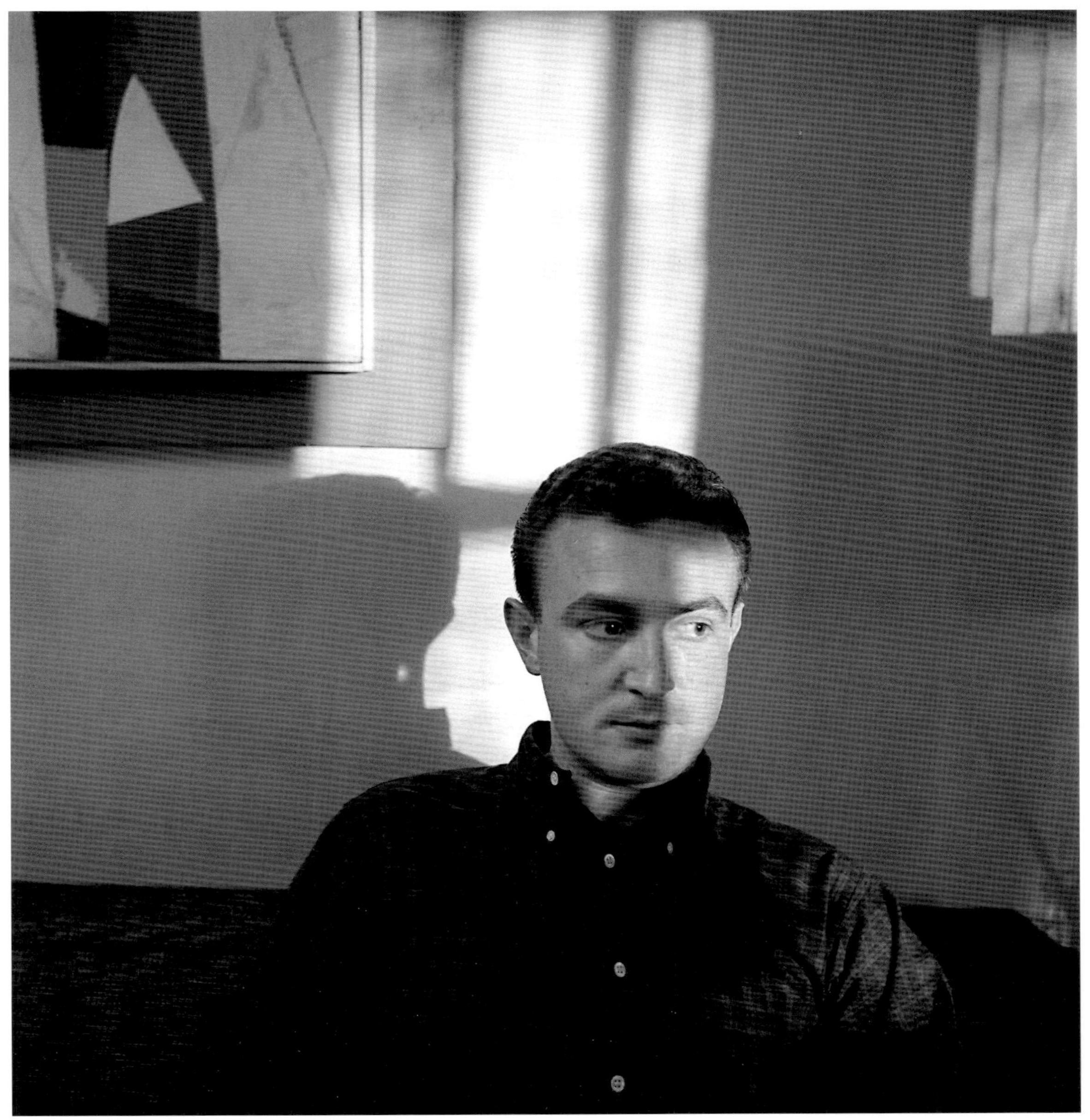

GEORGE DISBOROUGH, GRAPHIC ARTIST, c. 1955

There were two layers of survivors of war in the fifties, those from World War II and those from the Korean War. We did seem to have a lot of parties. In retrospect, it was all about survival. There was much boozing and hilarity. This photograph is of my brother-in-law, Bill Franklin, who was a survivor of the Korean War. He is with Jo Huntington, who was a close family friend.

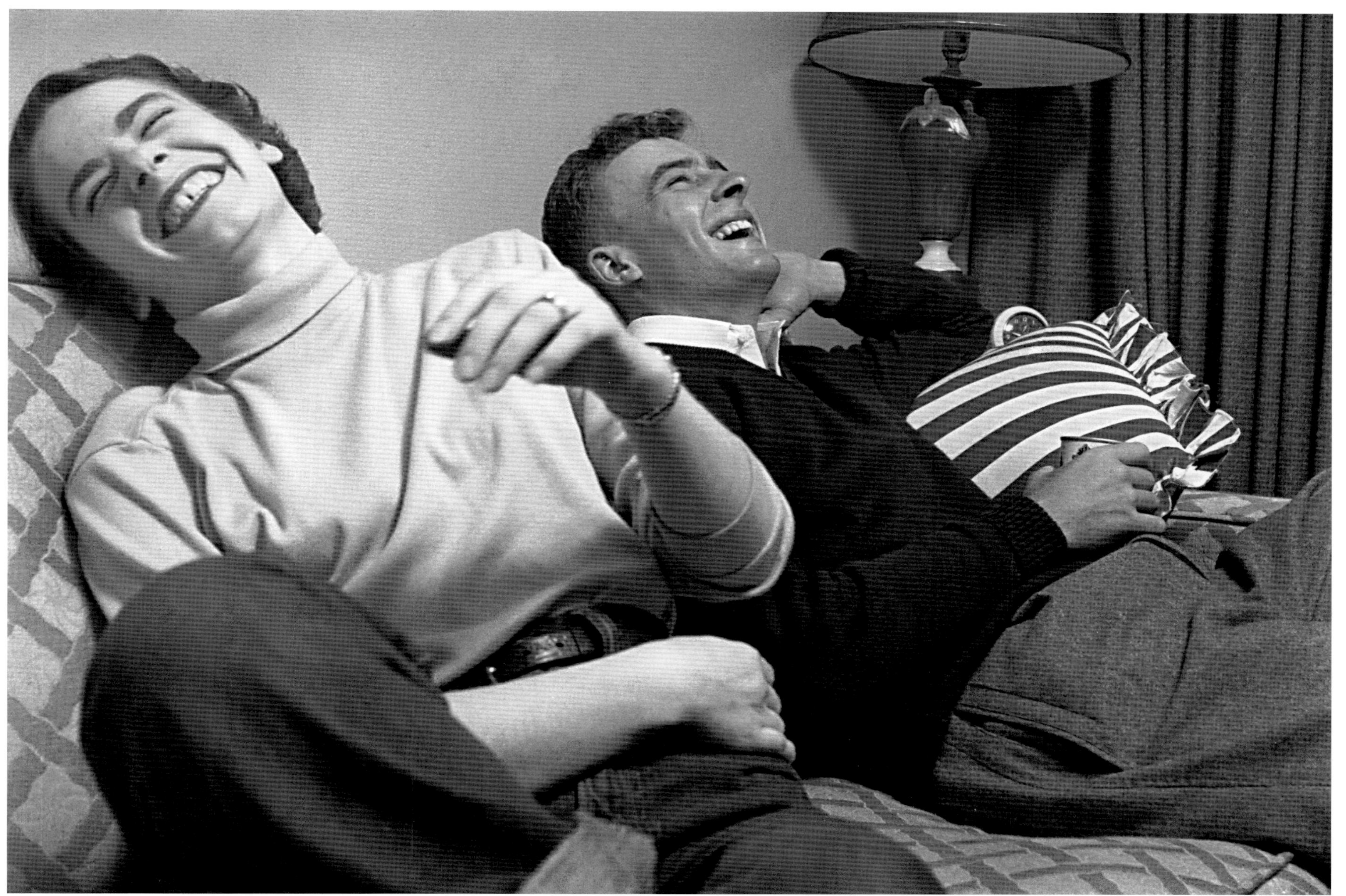

CRACKING UP, JO HUNTINGTON AND BILL FRANKLIN, c. 1955

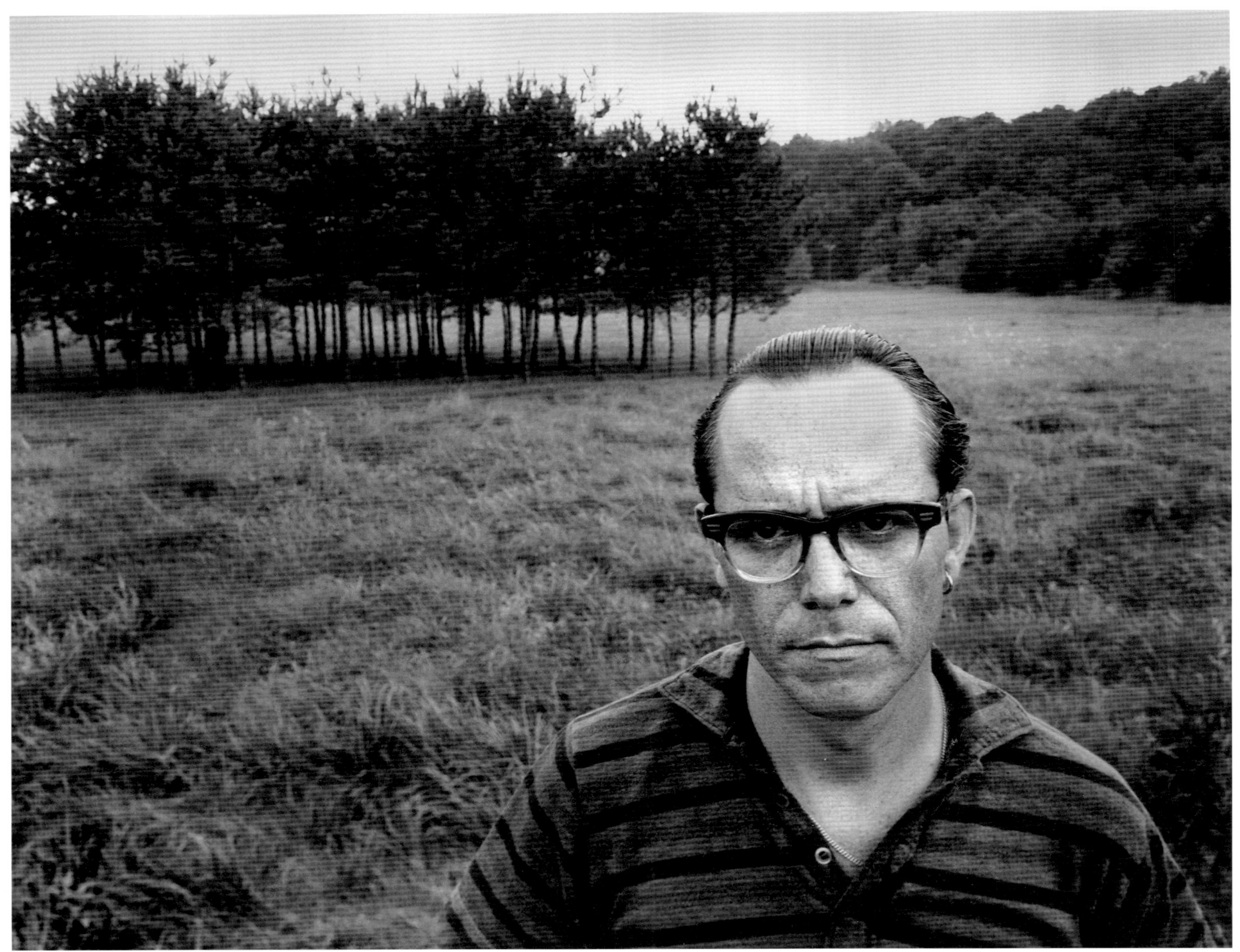

 | BILL MIETZLER, PHOTOGRAPHER, c. 1957

(at right) The artist as a young man. Jerry Uelsmann came to work for Indiana University as a photographer. I was the chief photographer at the time and became his boss. In 1959, I was the first person to get an MFA with a concentration in photography at Indiana University. Jerry followed and became the second photographer to receive an MFA.

Jerry has had a distinguished career in photography and is acknowledged as a major American artist. He is now a retired research professor from the University of Florida and continues his creative work.

(opposite) Bill Mietzler was a friend and co-worker, one of the photographers who worked at the Indiana University photo lab.

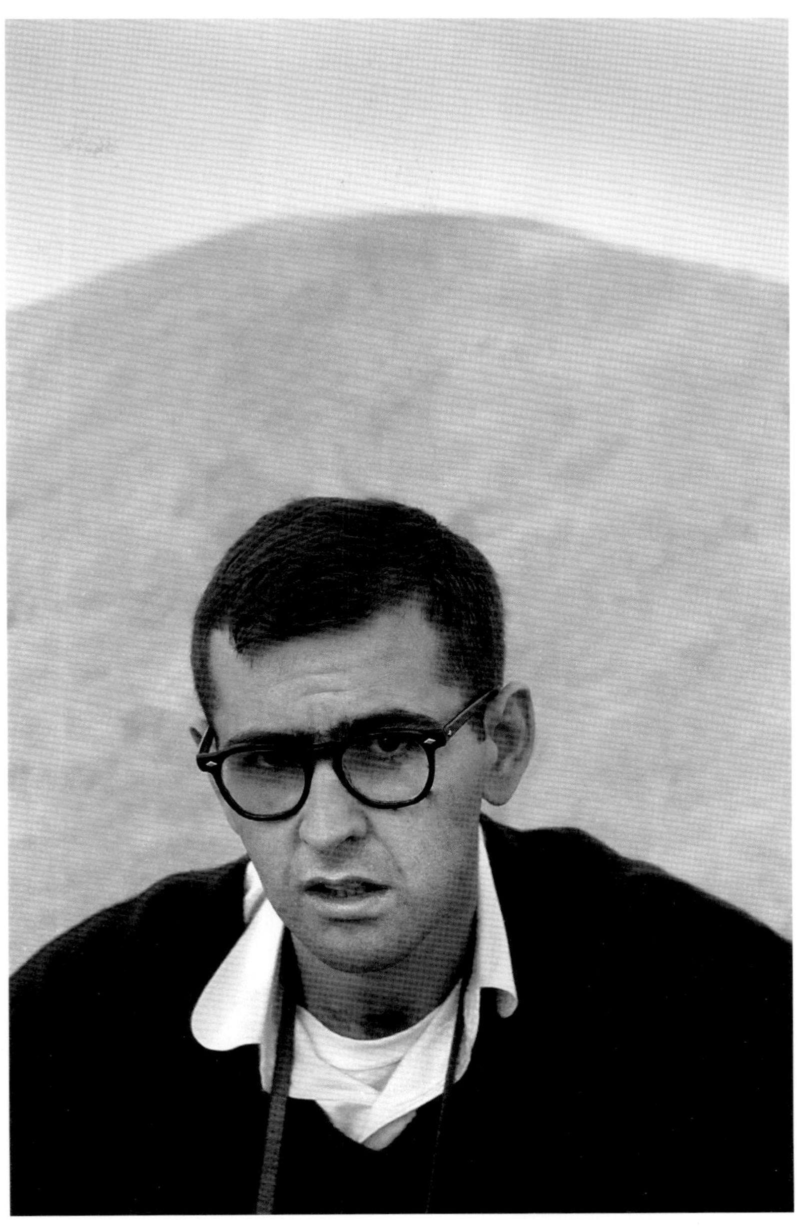

JERRY UELSMANN, PHOTOGRAPHER, c. 1957

Dr. Jo Ann Fineman is a graduate of Indiana University School of Medicine. She has had a distinguished career in psychiatry, having received analytic training in Boston and served in faculty positions at Harvard, UCLA, University of New Mexico, and University of Arizona, and is, at present, in private practice in Santa Fe, New Mexico. She has written with distinction about the arts. This is all very well and good; but I came to know Jo Ann when she was just fourteen and was the girl down the block named Jo Ann Booze. Jo has been a real presence in my life ever since. As luck would have it, the many incarnations of the girl-next-door that populated my teenage years were remarkable women. Almost without exception they became doctors, actors, or artists. One can only speculate on the effect this had on my nascent manhood.

Jo has graciously written about my life and work for this book.

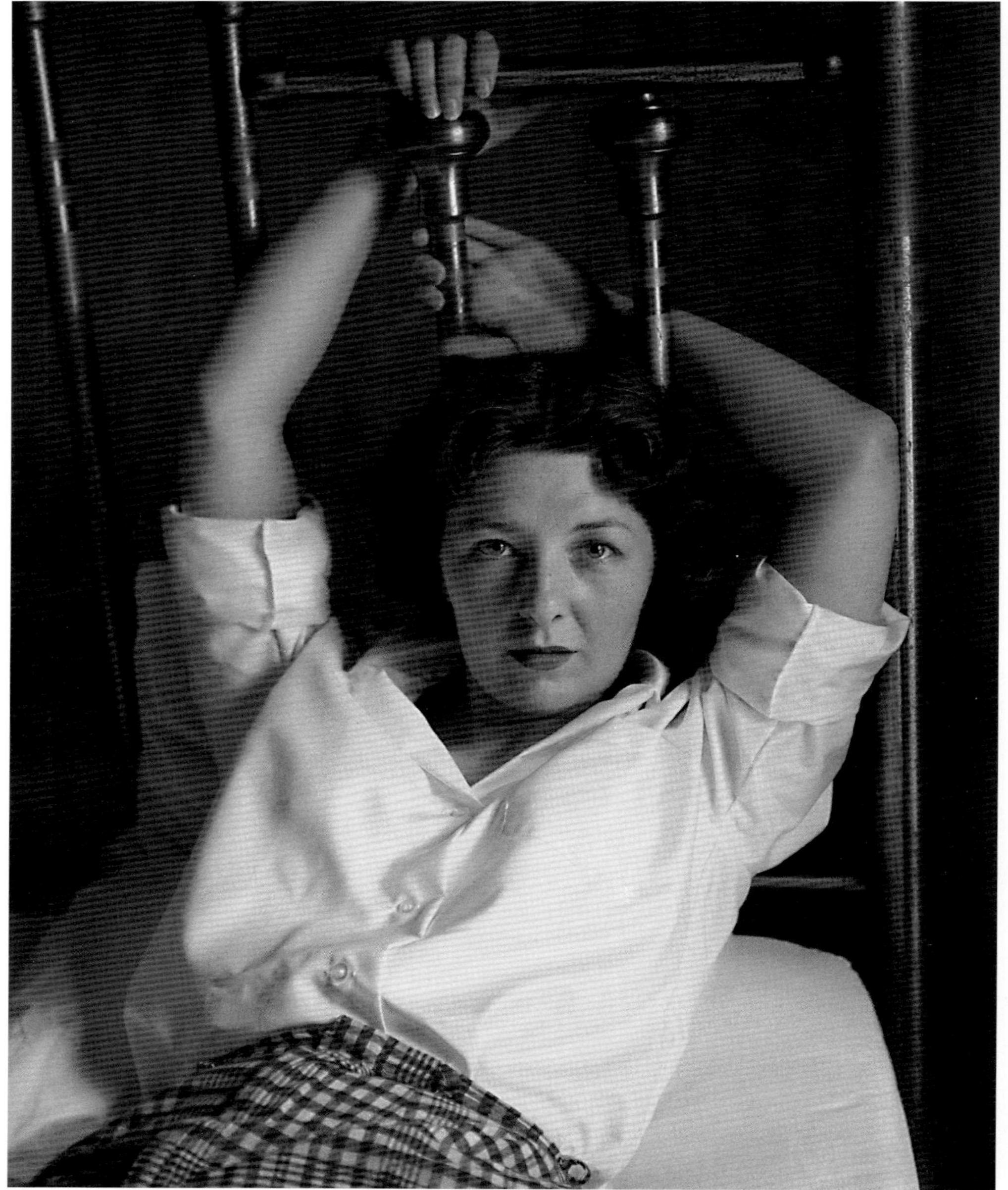

 | JO ANN FINEMAN, c. 1957

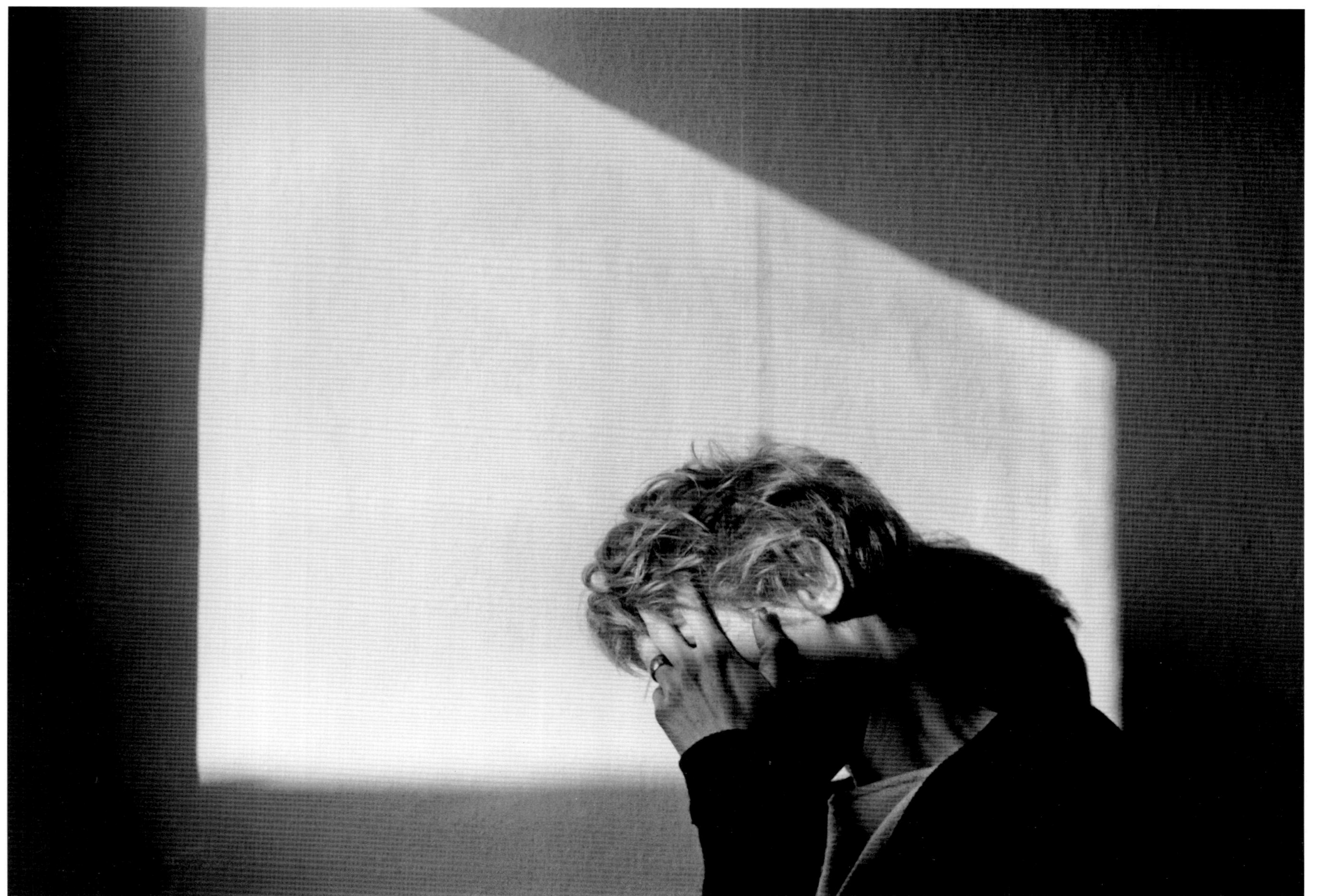

NANCY SPERO, ARTIST, c. 1958

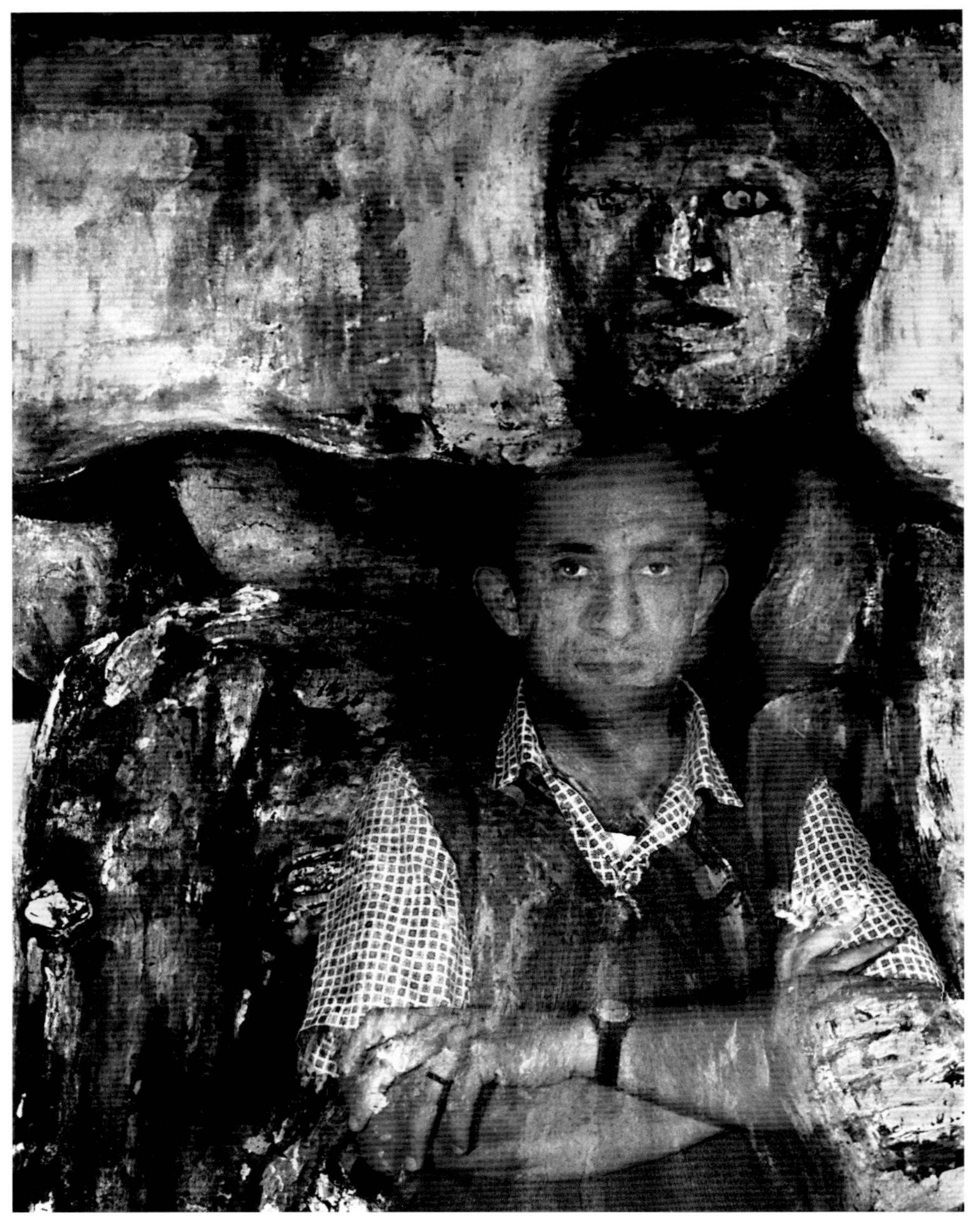

 | LEON GOLUB, PAINTER, c. 1958

When I applied for admission to the art department to earn an MFA, Henry Holmes Smith was unsure if I would be accepted. No one had ever applied with a major in photography. I had taken a lot of painting courses and he suggested that a split major would be more likely to gain acceptance. It was a fortuitous choice. It provided the opportunity to study with Leon Golub. Through this association, I came to photograph both Leon and his wife, Nancy.

Nancy Spero and Leon Golub have become major figures in the American visual arts. It was a rare privilege to get to know these people and to study with Leon.

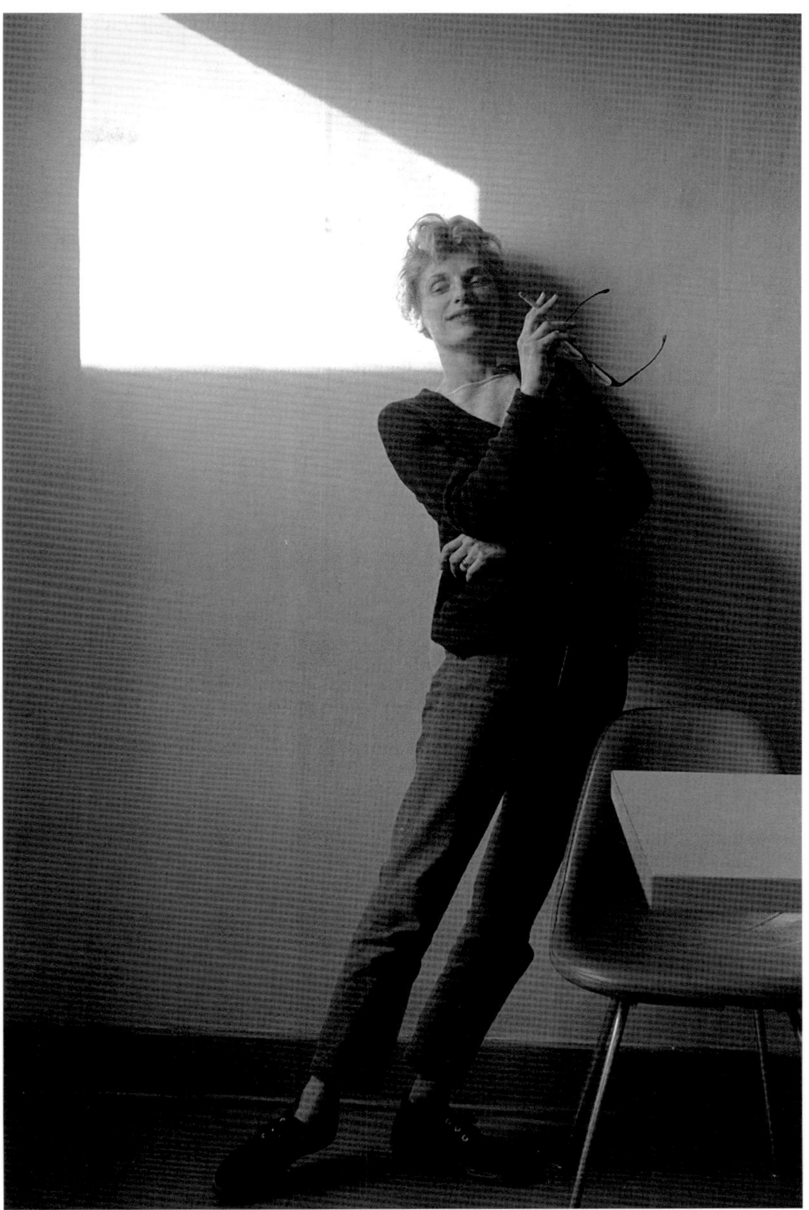

NANCY SPERO, ARTIST, c. 1958

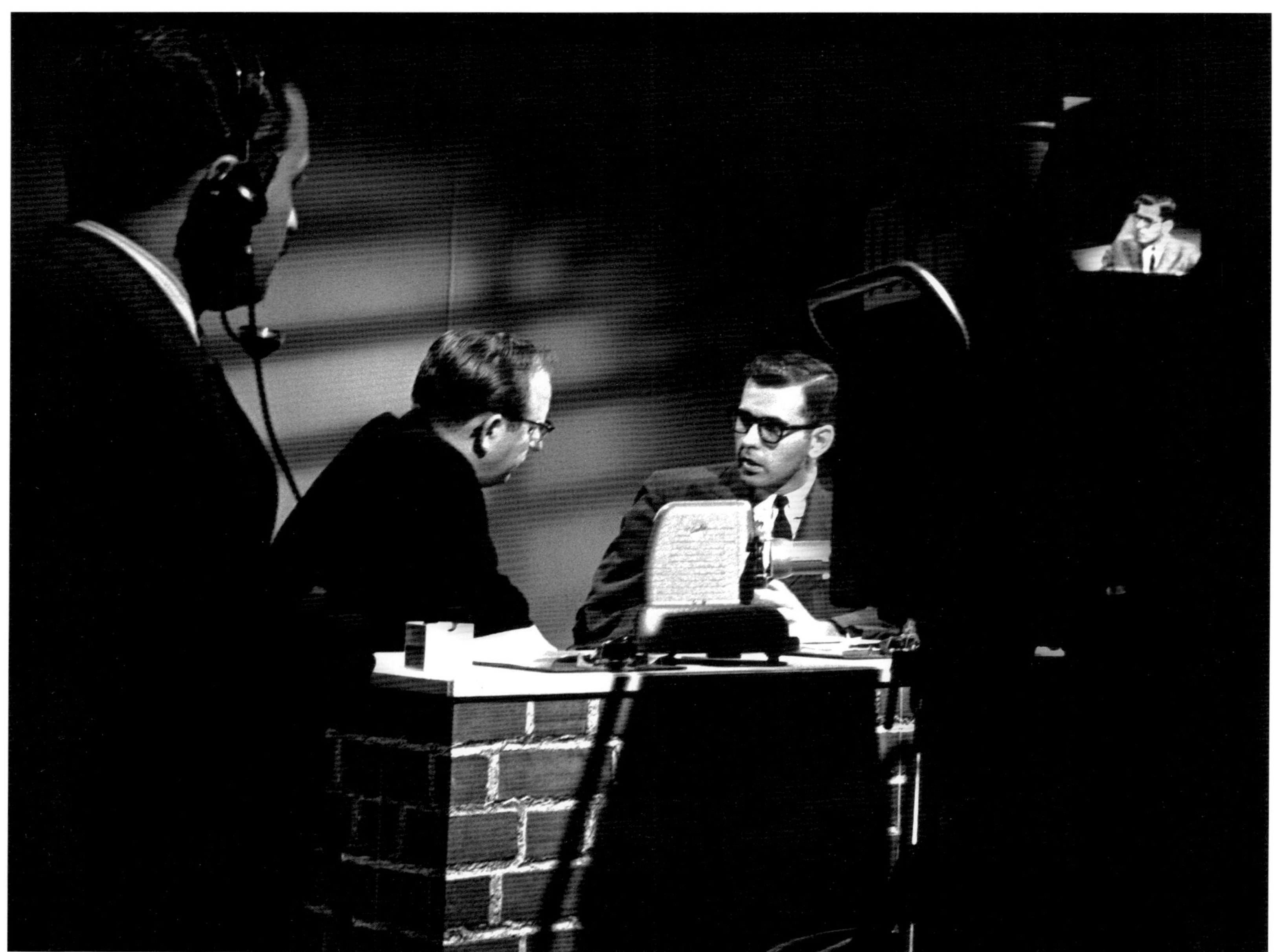

 | JACK WELPOTT AND JERRY UELSMANN, IU TELEVISION SHOW

Jerry Uelsmann and I did a series of television shows for the Indiana University television station. For one show the producer had the idea that we should both photograph the same girl and see what the differences were. The girl with the big eyes was provided as our model. For the life of me, I can't remember her name. It was such a long time ago.

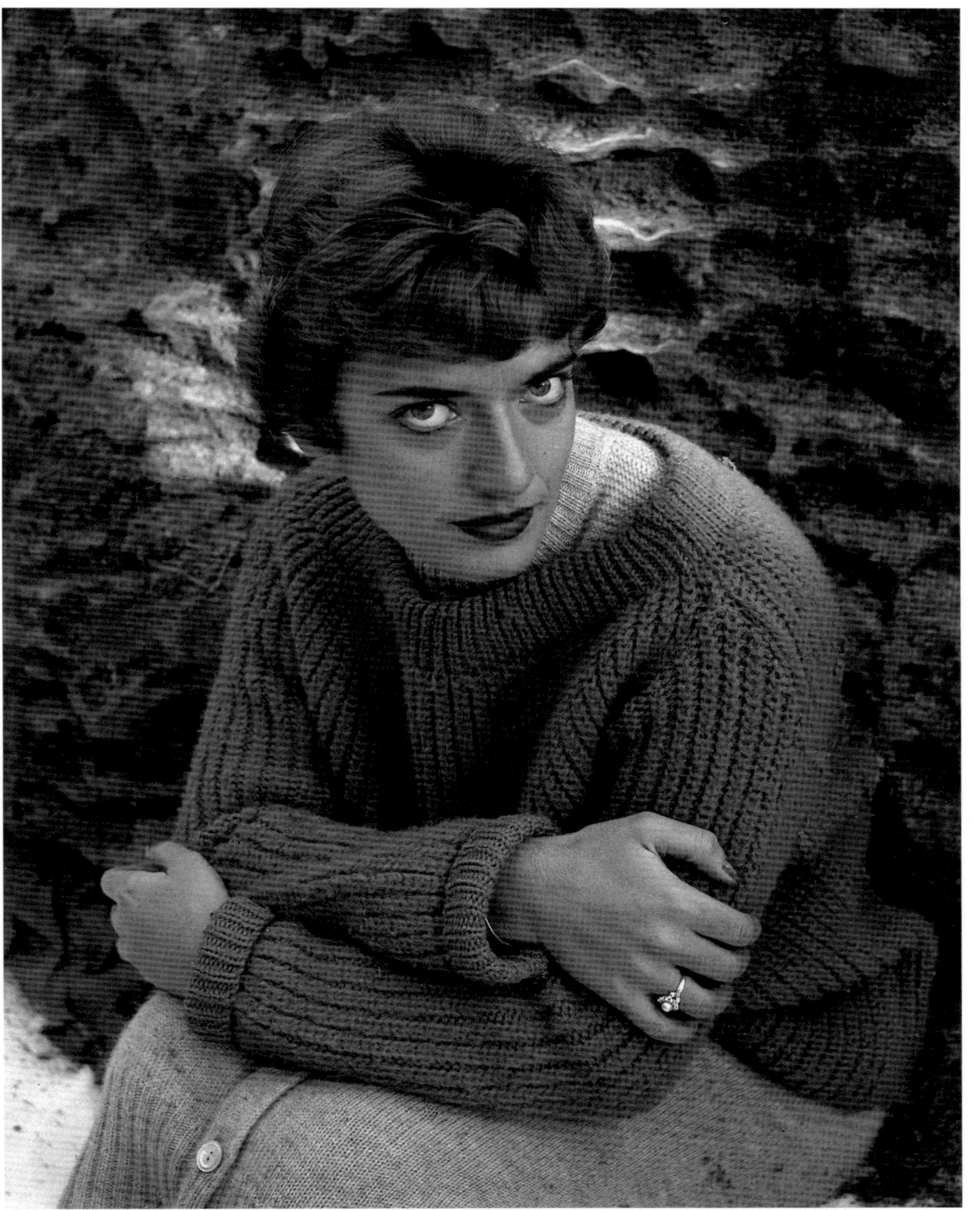

(opposite) Jerry and I fancied ourselves the Huntley-Brinkley of photography. Photographer unknown.

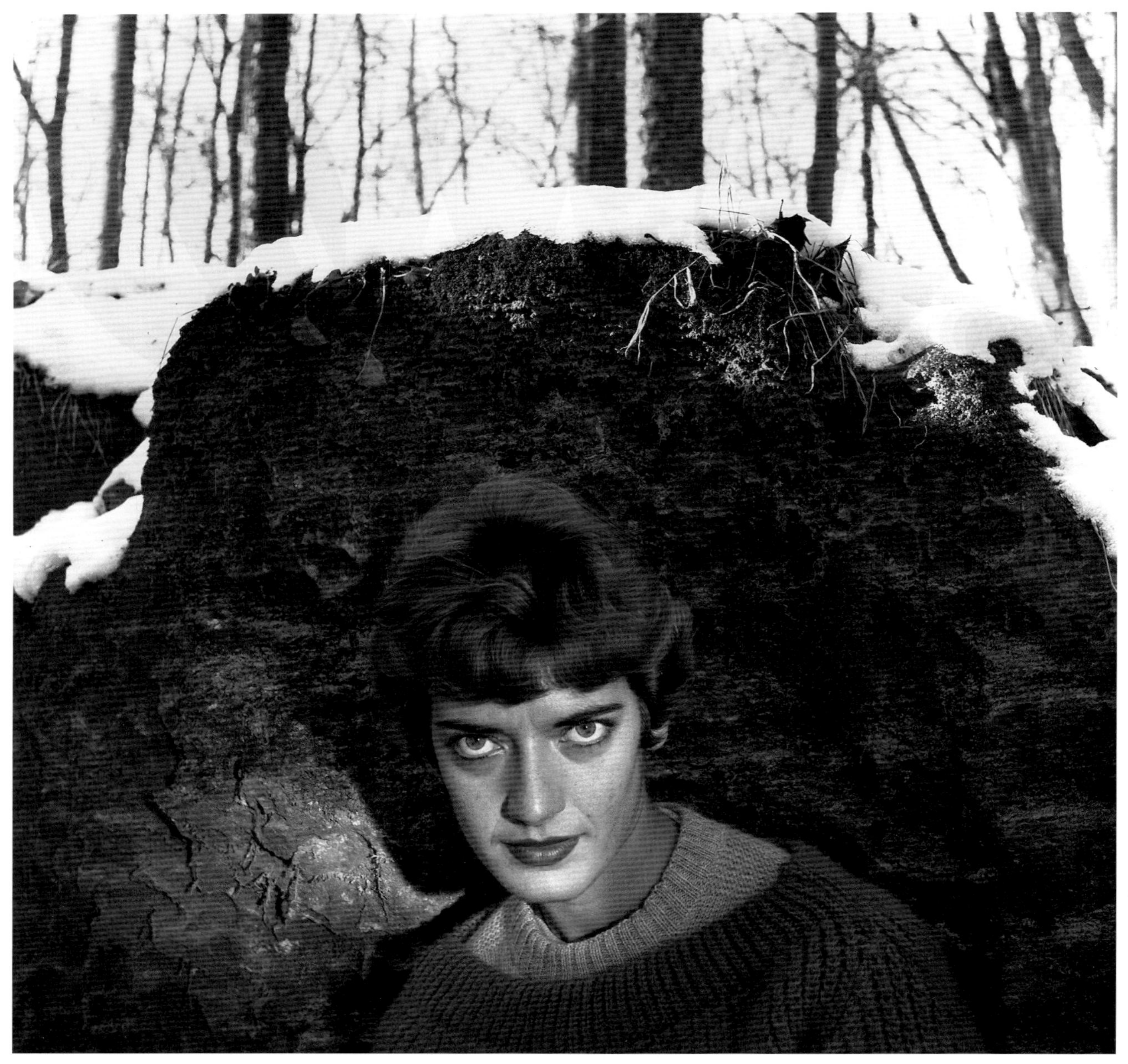

 | GIRL WITH BIG EYES, 1957

SEVEN | People and Places

I was what you might call a peripatetic cameraman. Sounds like a rare and incurable disease. I usually went forth armed with a camera; sometimes it was a little, old 35mm and sometimes 40 pounds of hardware slung from my shoulder on a strap. Socrates walked around the Agora spouting his philosophy to any who would listen. I walked around in the most improbable places, poking around in alleys, on the streets, to fairs and carnivals, to neighboring towns and villages, photographing buildings, people, kids; I hung out along the Monon, in junk yards, cemeteries, alleys. You name it. If it was off the beaten path I would be there chasing my obsession.

There was a particular fascination with walls and windows. Crazy windows—What did they imply? Leaning chimneys on old houses—What was at the bottom? What was behind all these façades? Now and then I found my way inside. In retrospect I wish I had done it more often. I can't say I was searching for an honest man but I was sure searching for something. The truth?

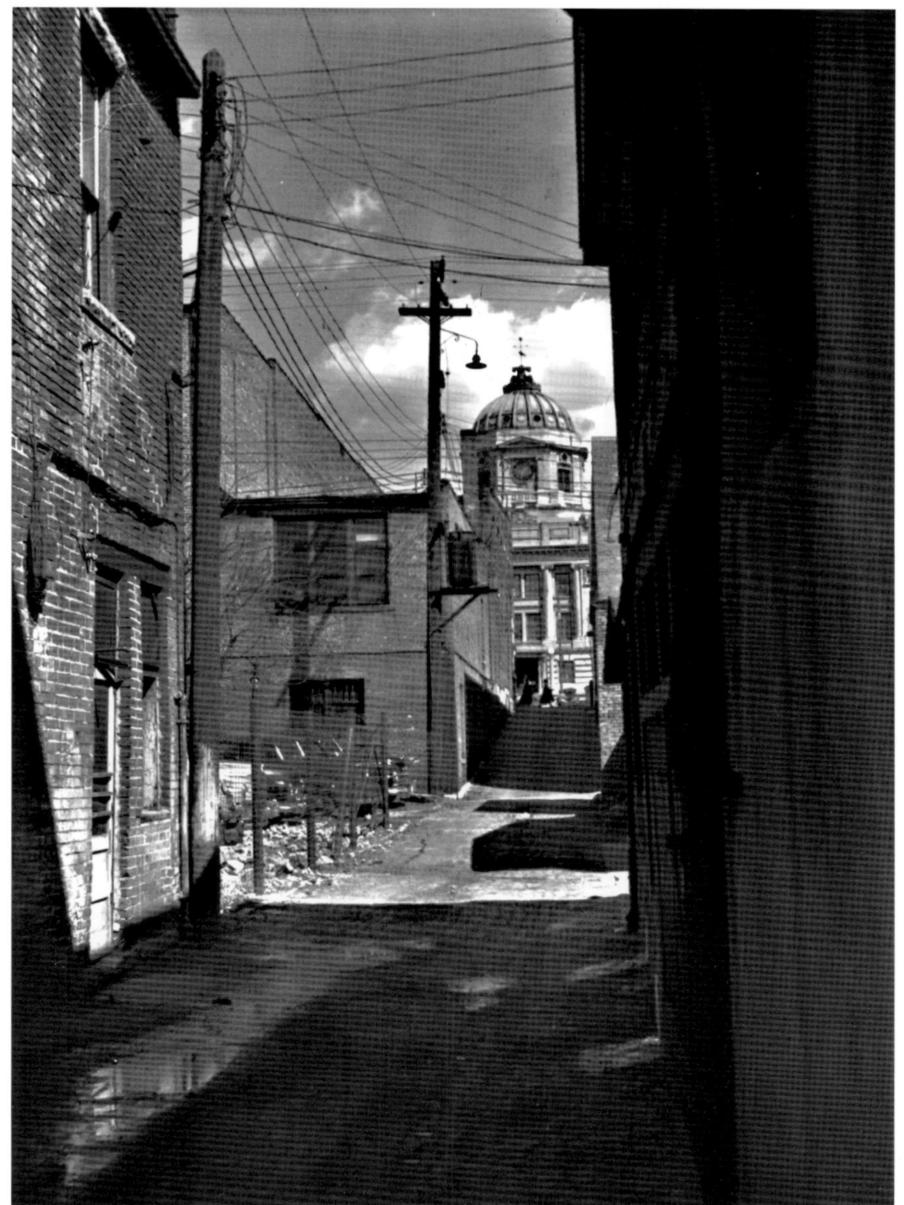

MONROE COUNTY COURT HOUSE, 1948

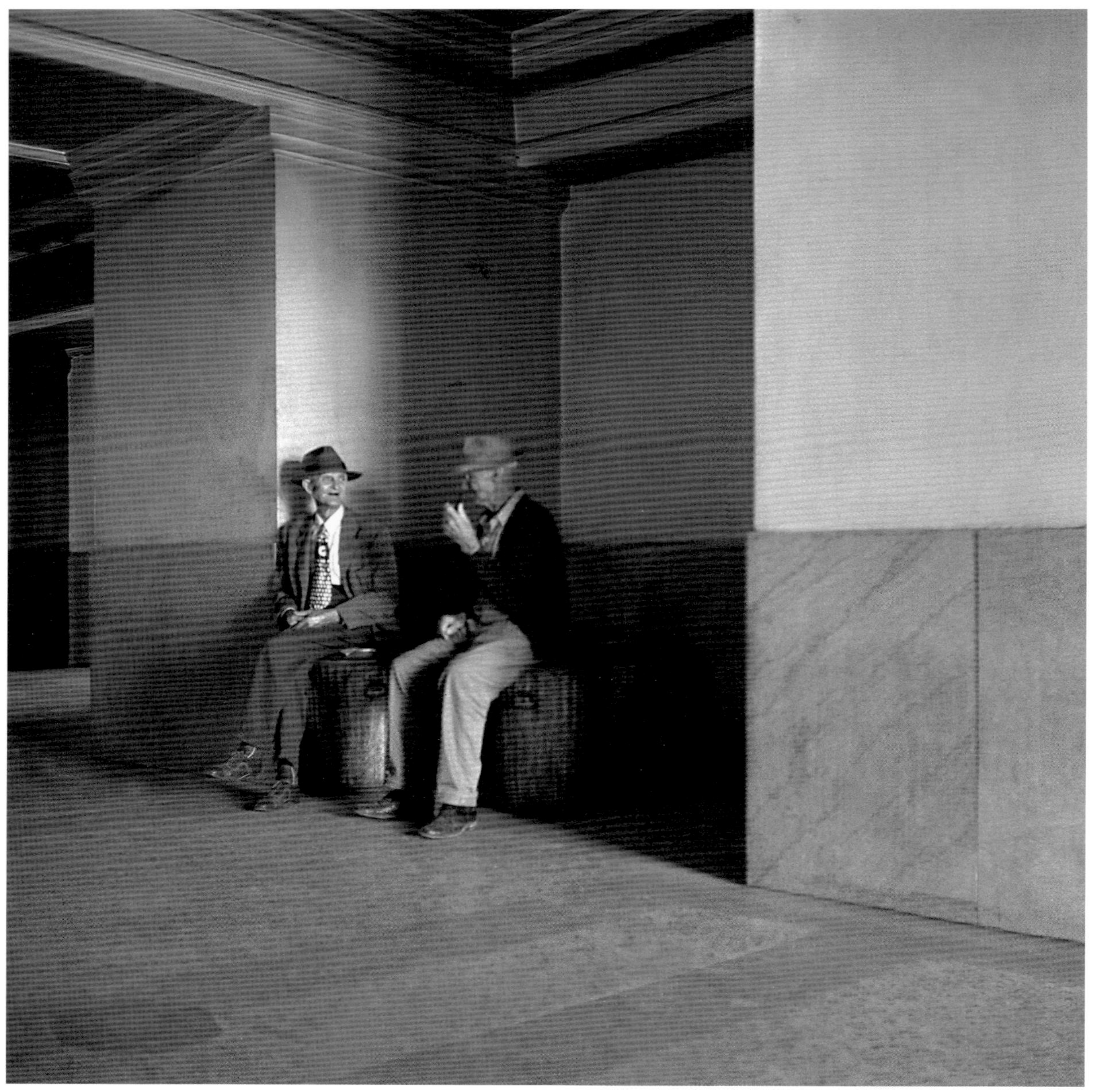

 MONROE COUNTY COURT HOUSE, c. 1950

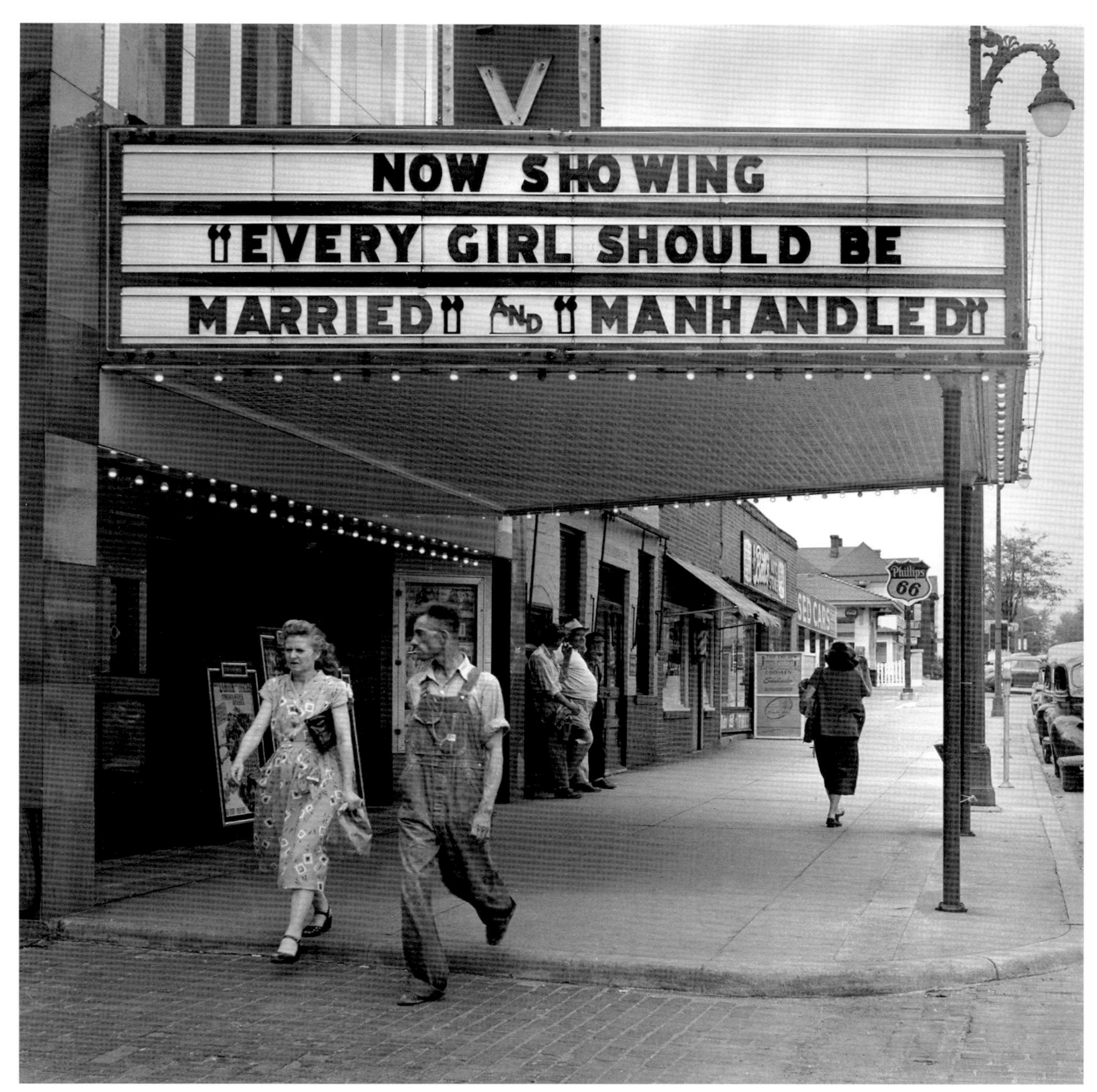

ROXY THEATER, BLOOMINGTON, INDIANA, c. 1950

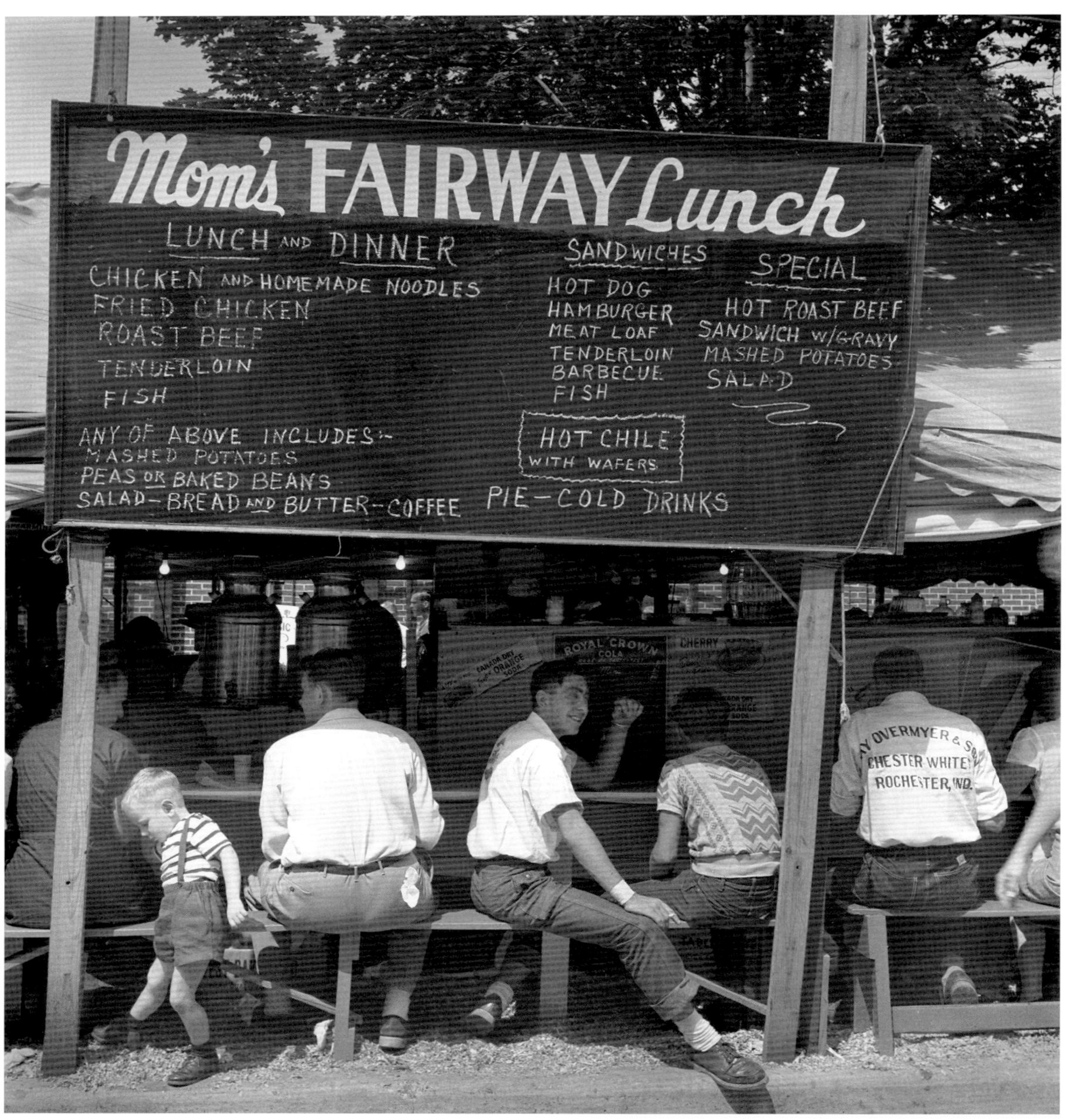

 | INDIANA STATE FAIR, c. 1953

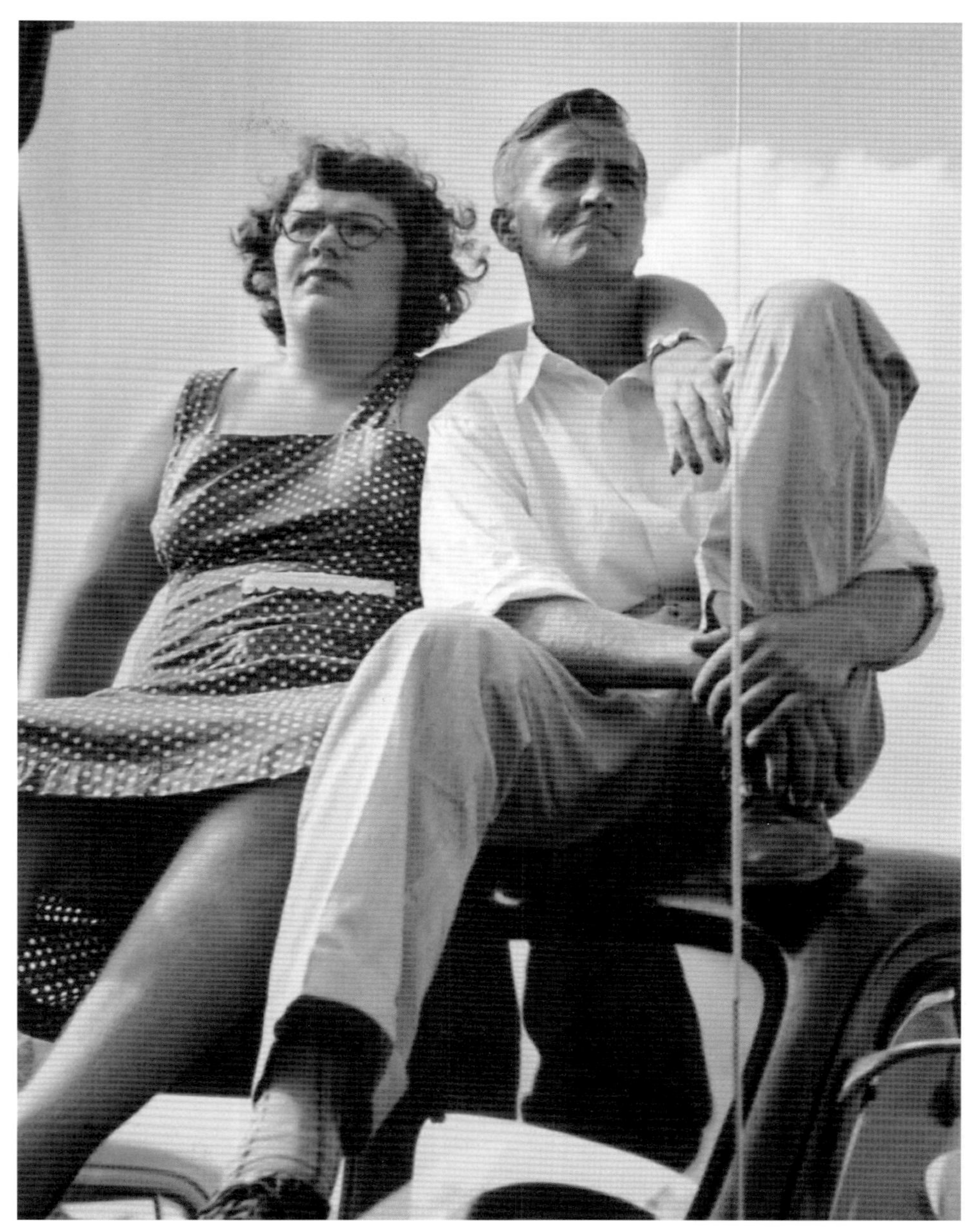

WATCHING THE TROTTERS, INDIANA STATE FAIR, c. 1953

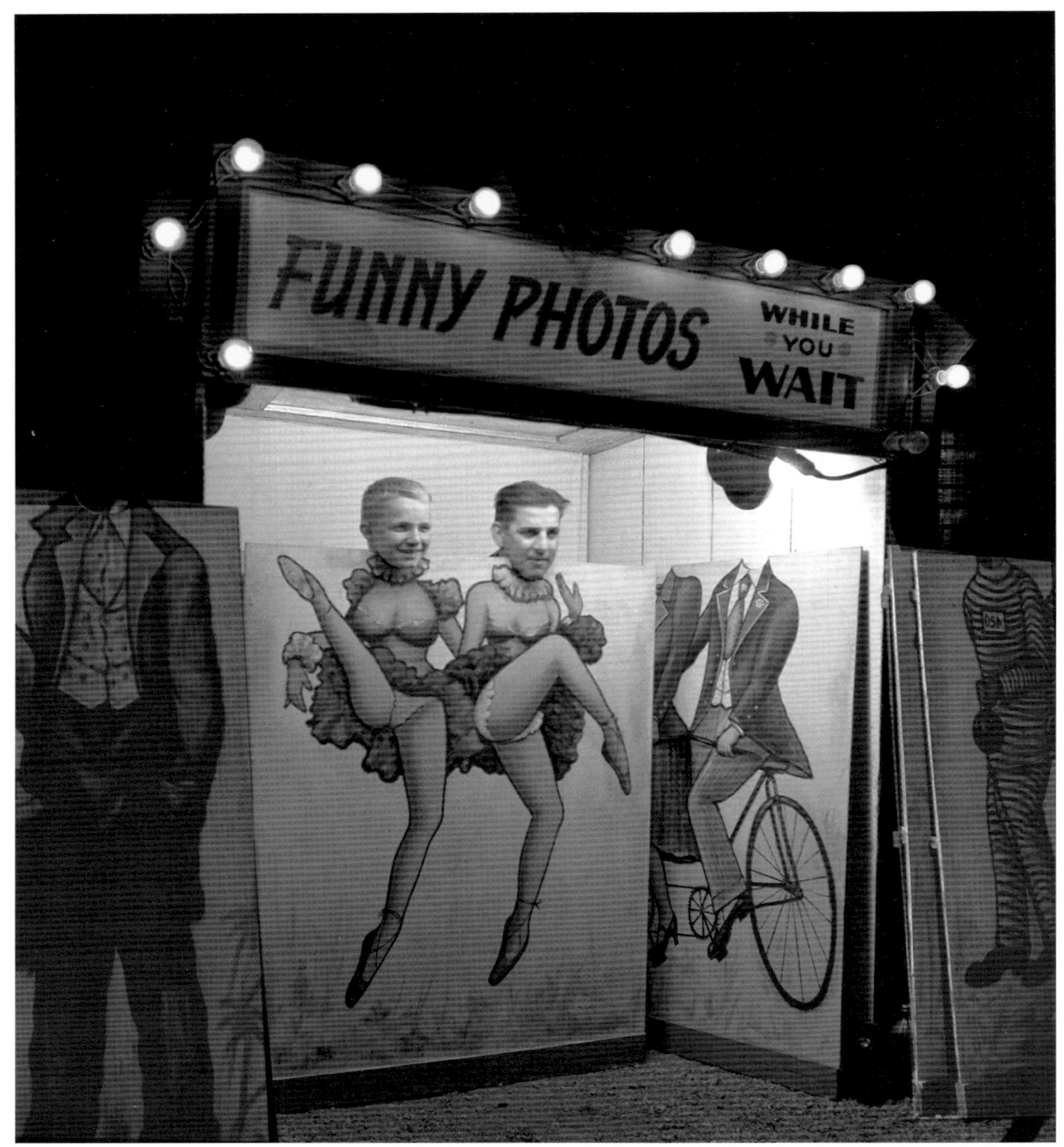

 | FUNNY PHOTOS, INDIANA STATE FAIR, c. 1953

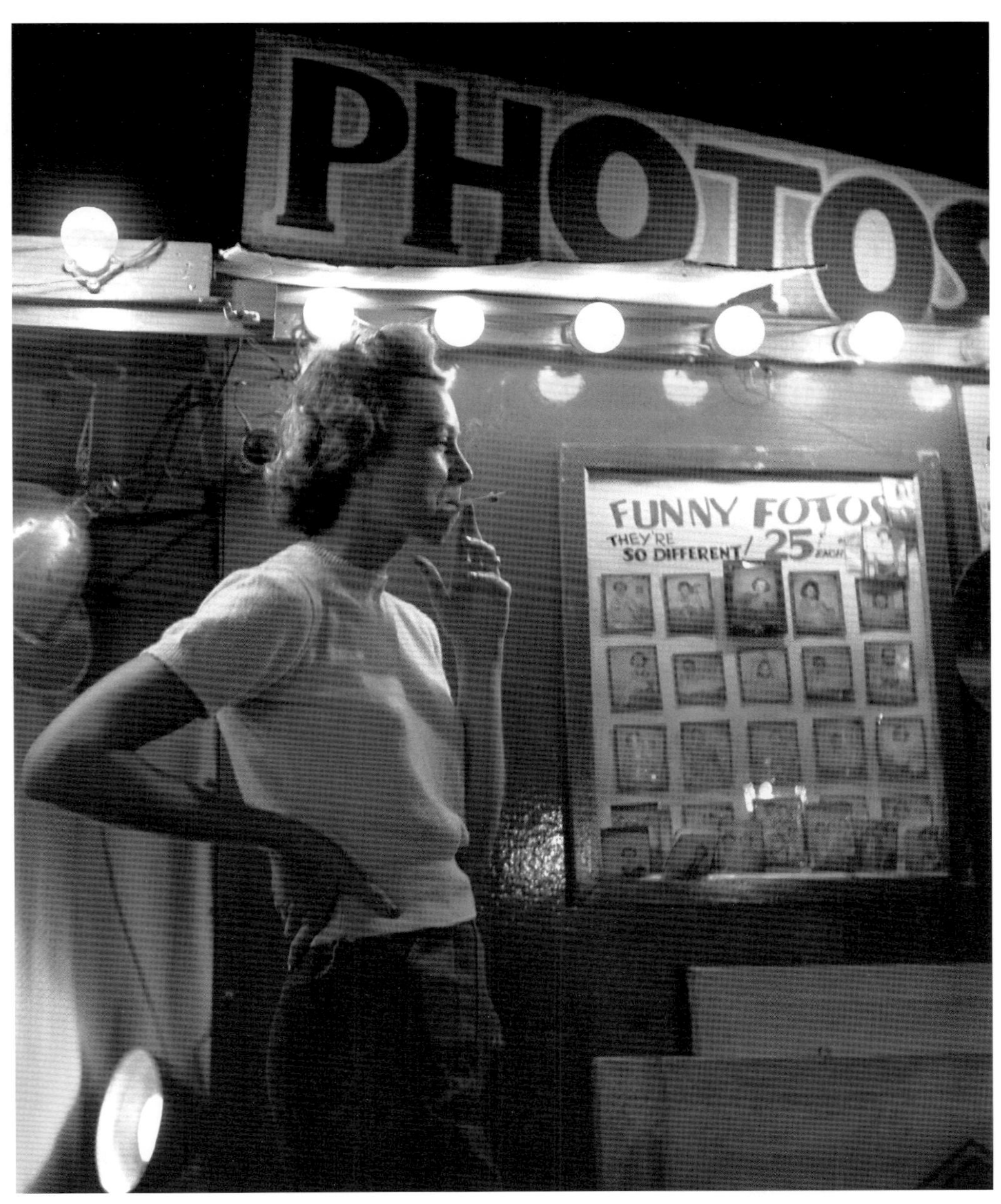

CARNIVAL WOMAN, INDIANA STATE FAIR, c. 1953

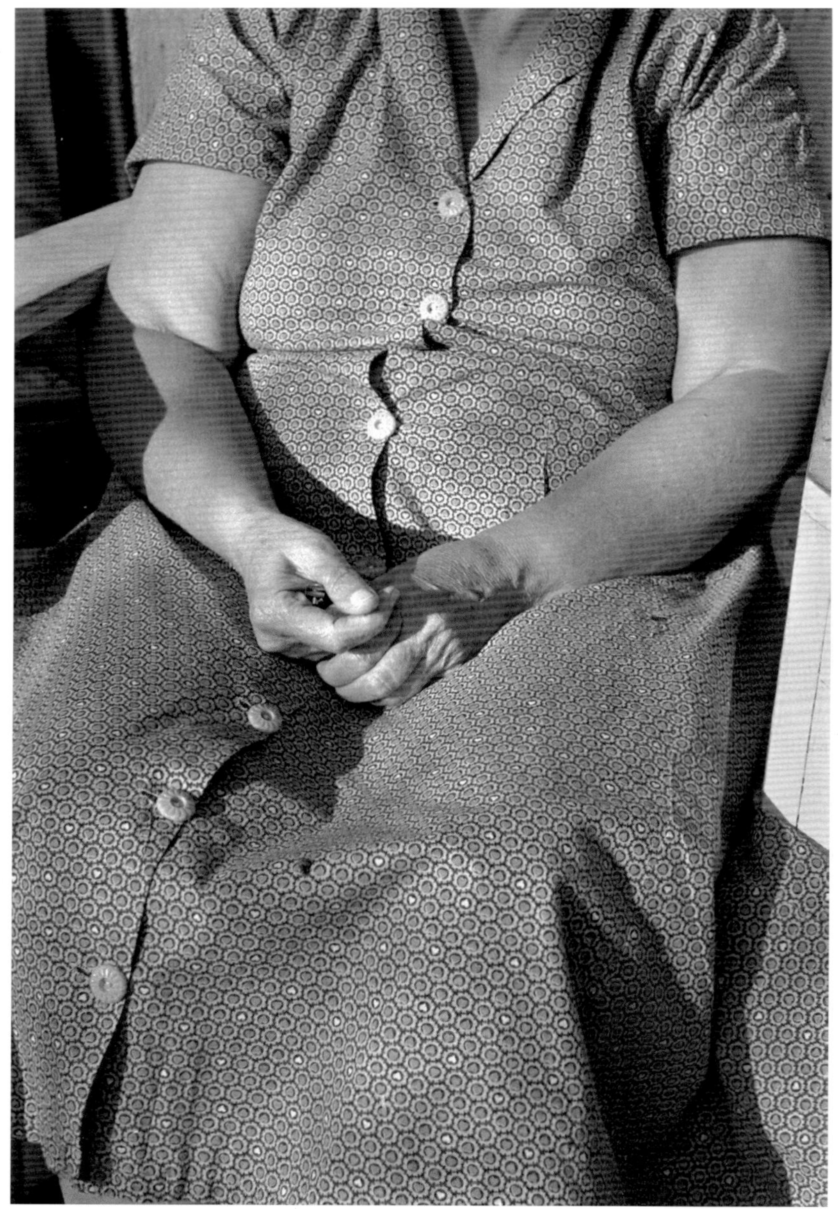

 | “MA JOAD’S HANDS LAY IN HER LAP LIKE TIRED LOVERS.” —JOHN STEINBECK. c. 1955

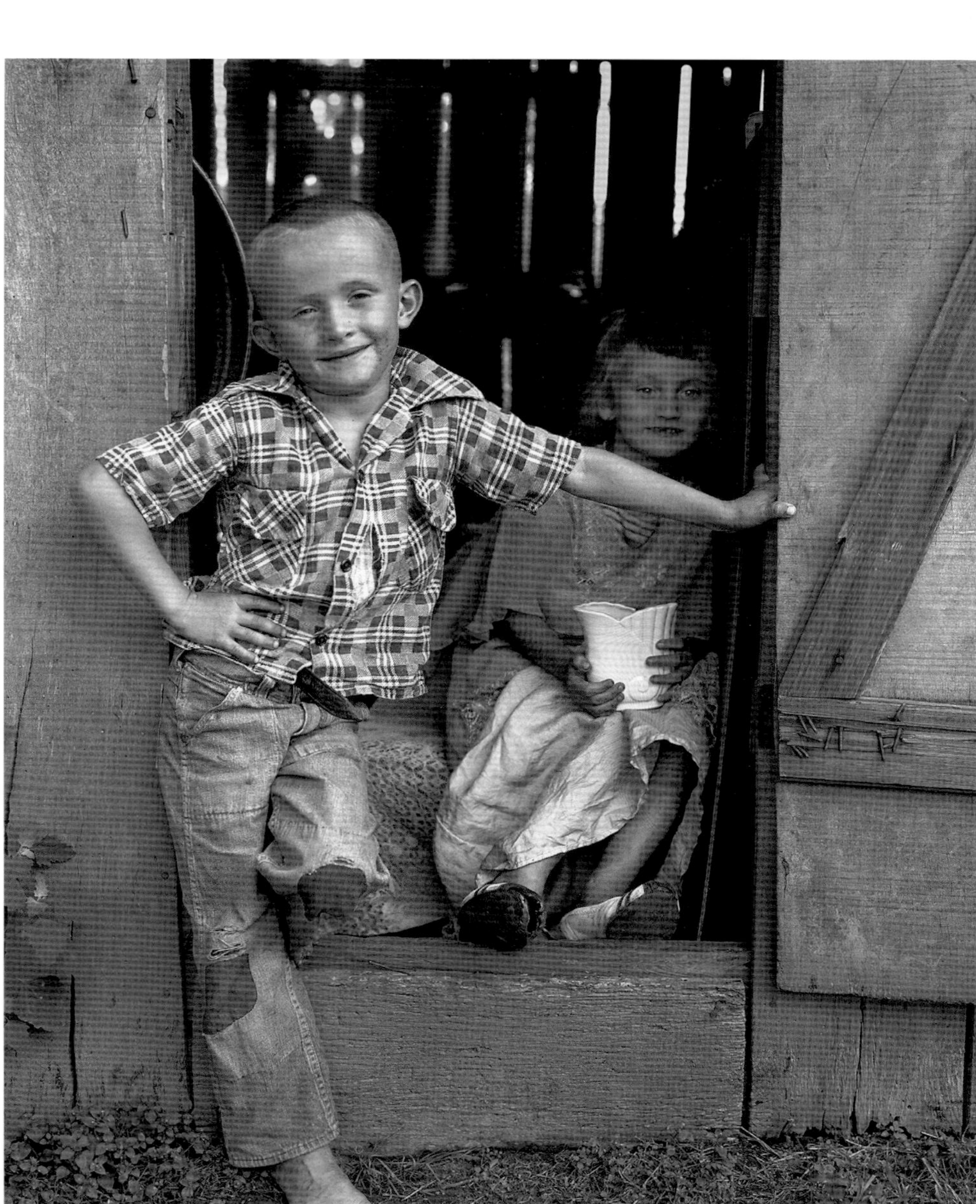

STINESVILLE, INDIANA, KIDS, c. 1958

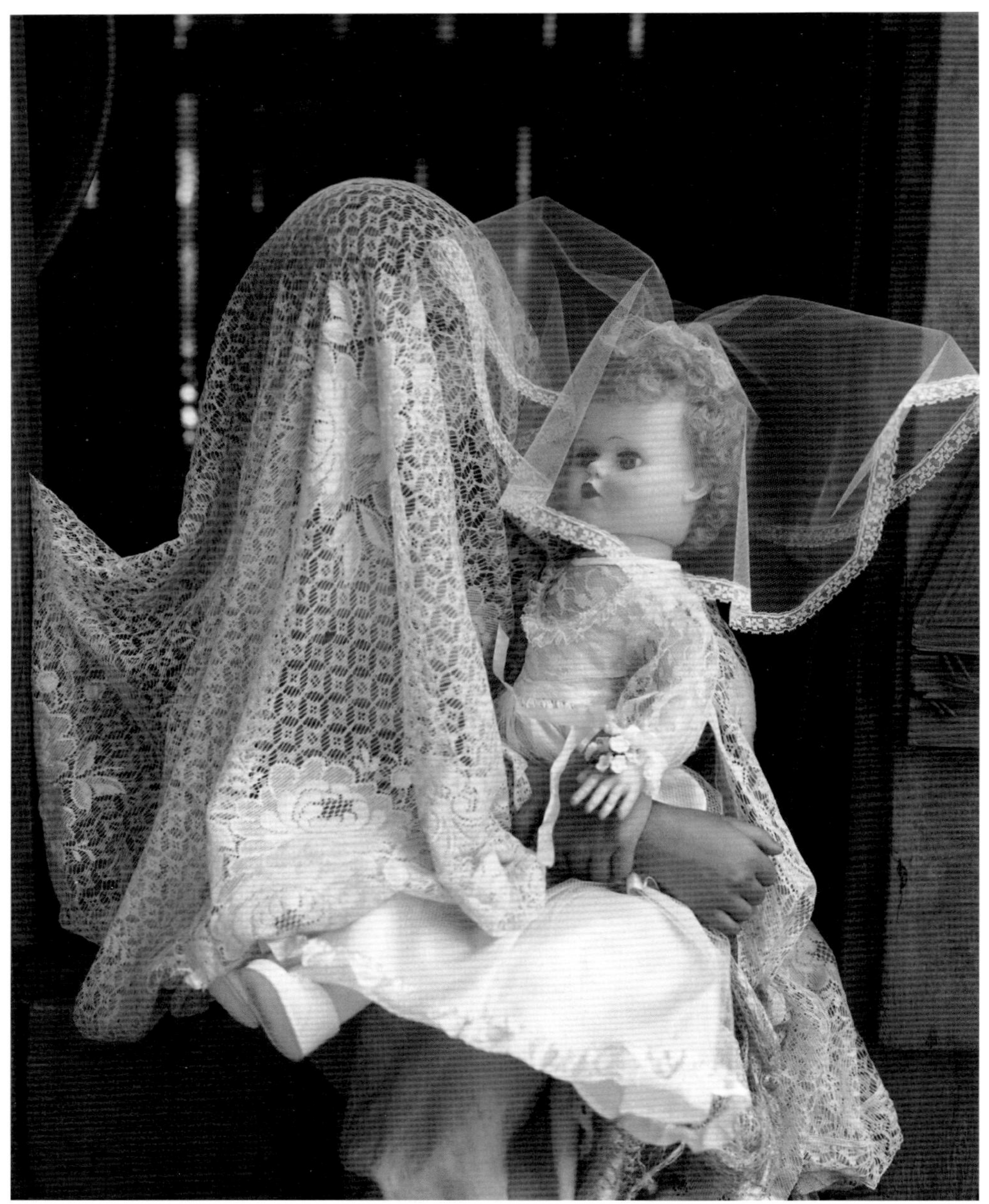

 | CHILD BRIDE, STINESVILLE, INDIANA, c. 1958

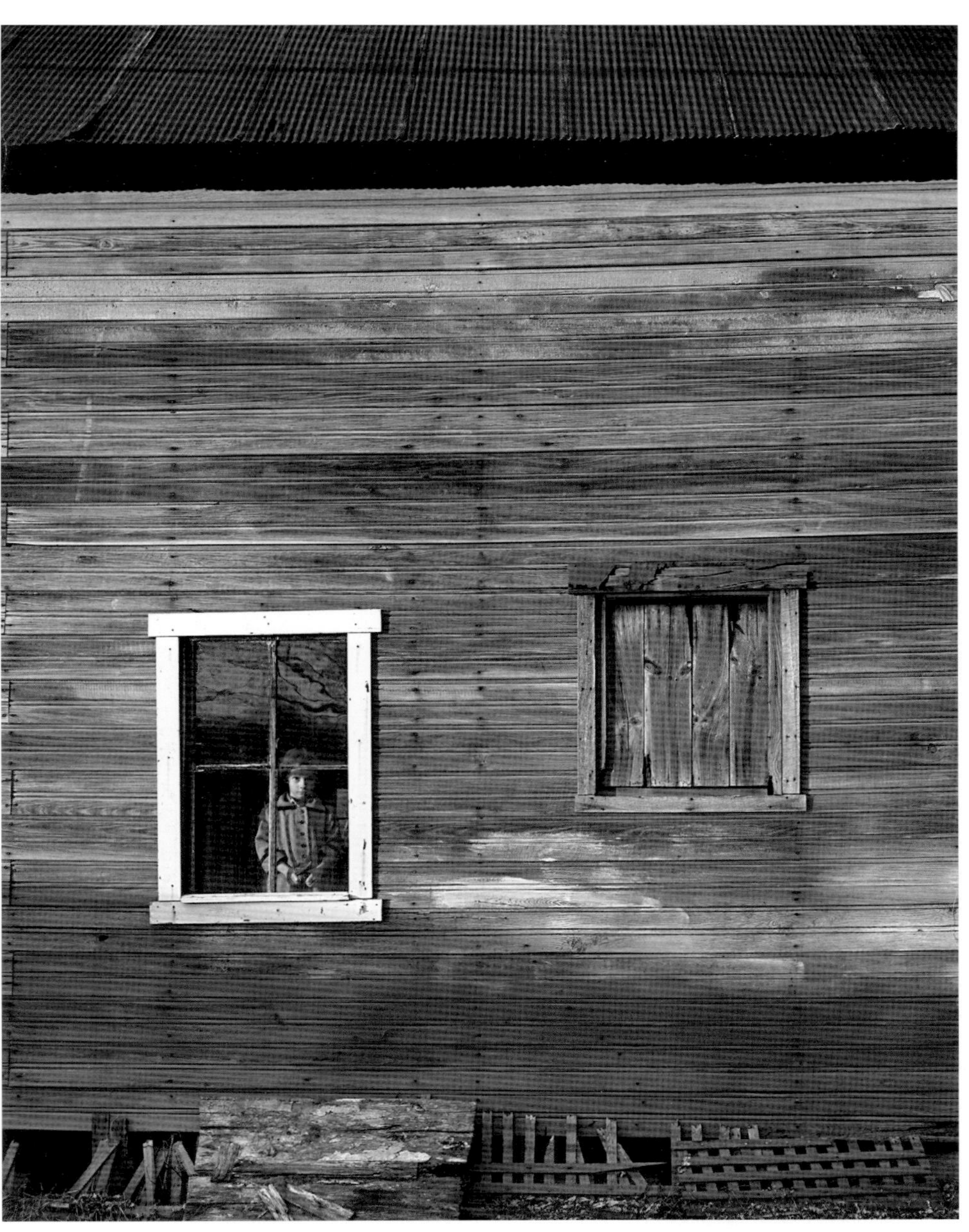

CHILD IN WINDOW, NASHVILLE, INDIANA, 1959

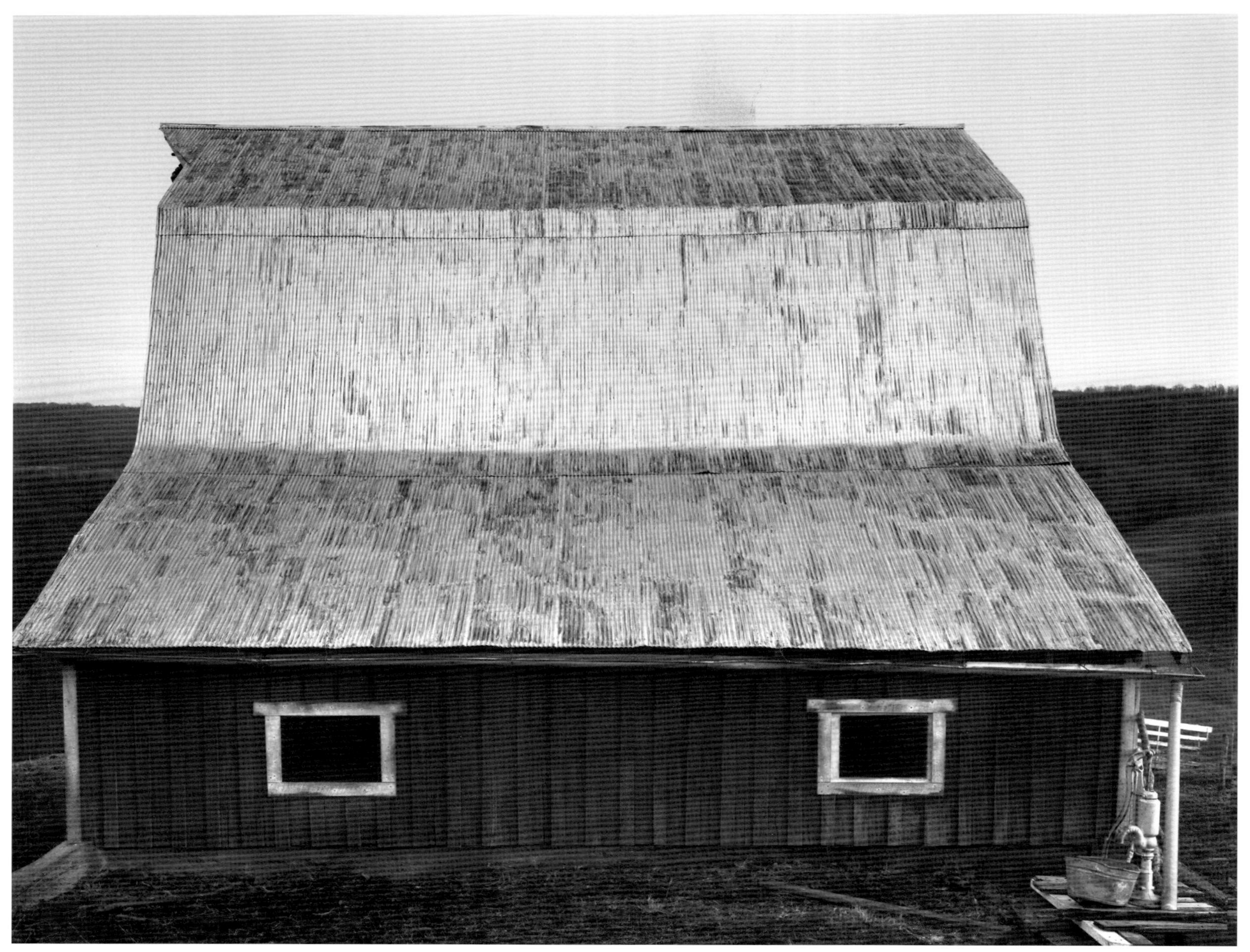

 | BARN NEAR NASHVILLE, INDIANA, 1958

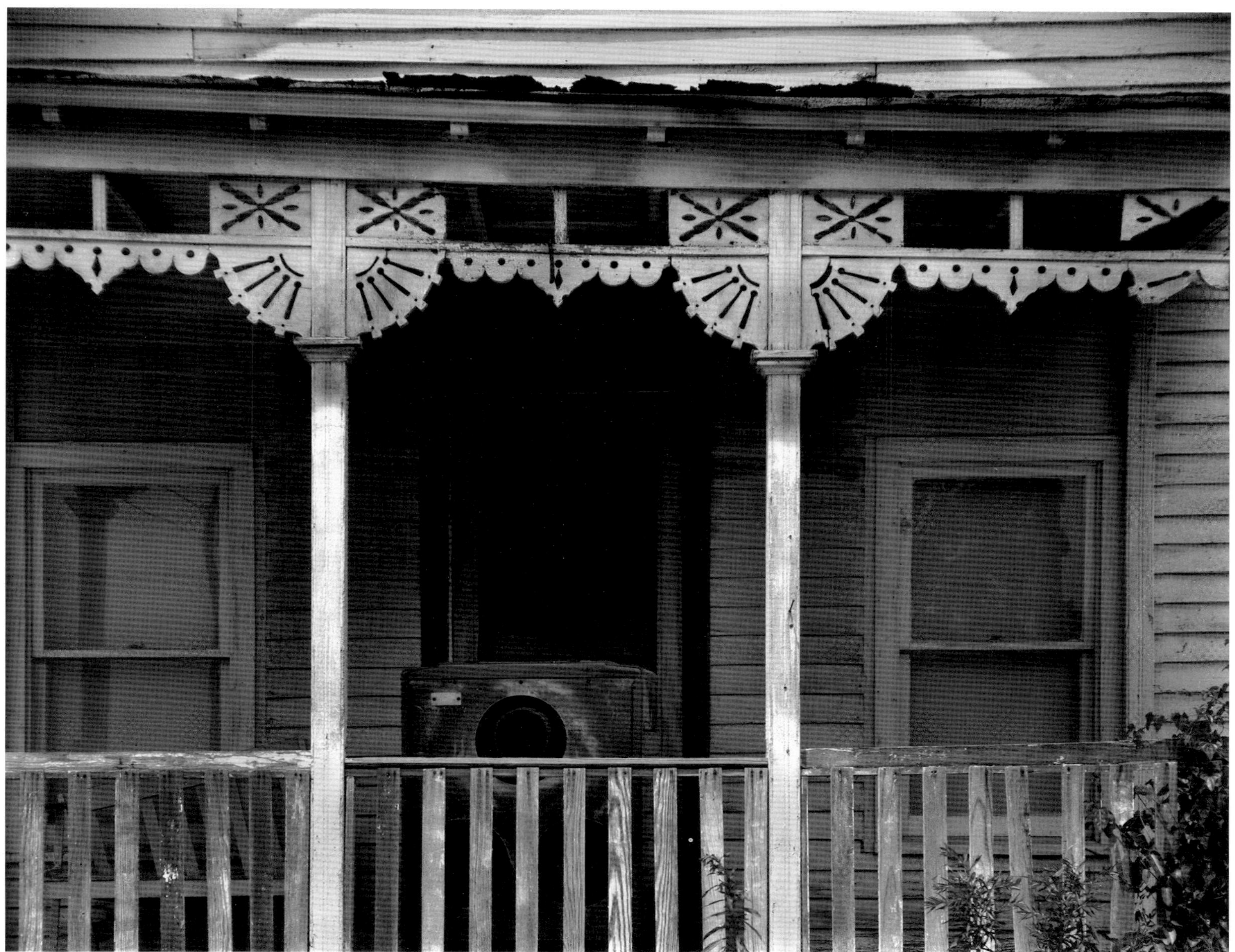

INDIANA PORCH, c. 1959

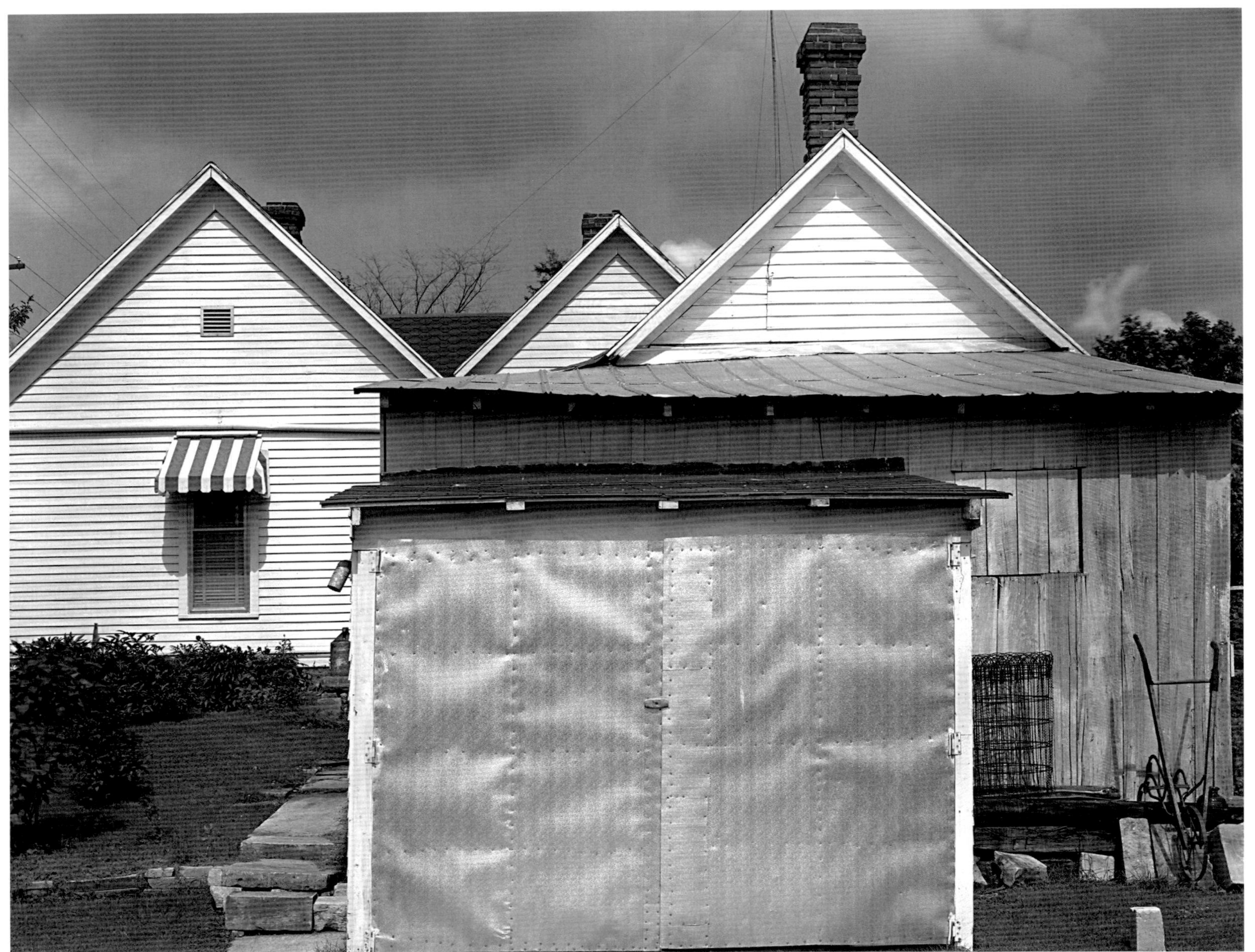

 | STINESVILLE, INDIANA, 1958

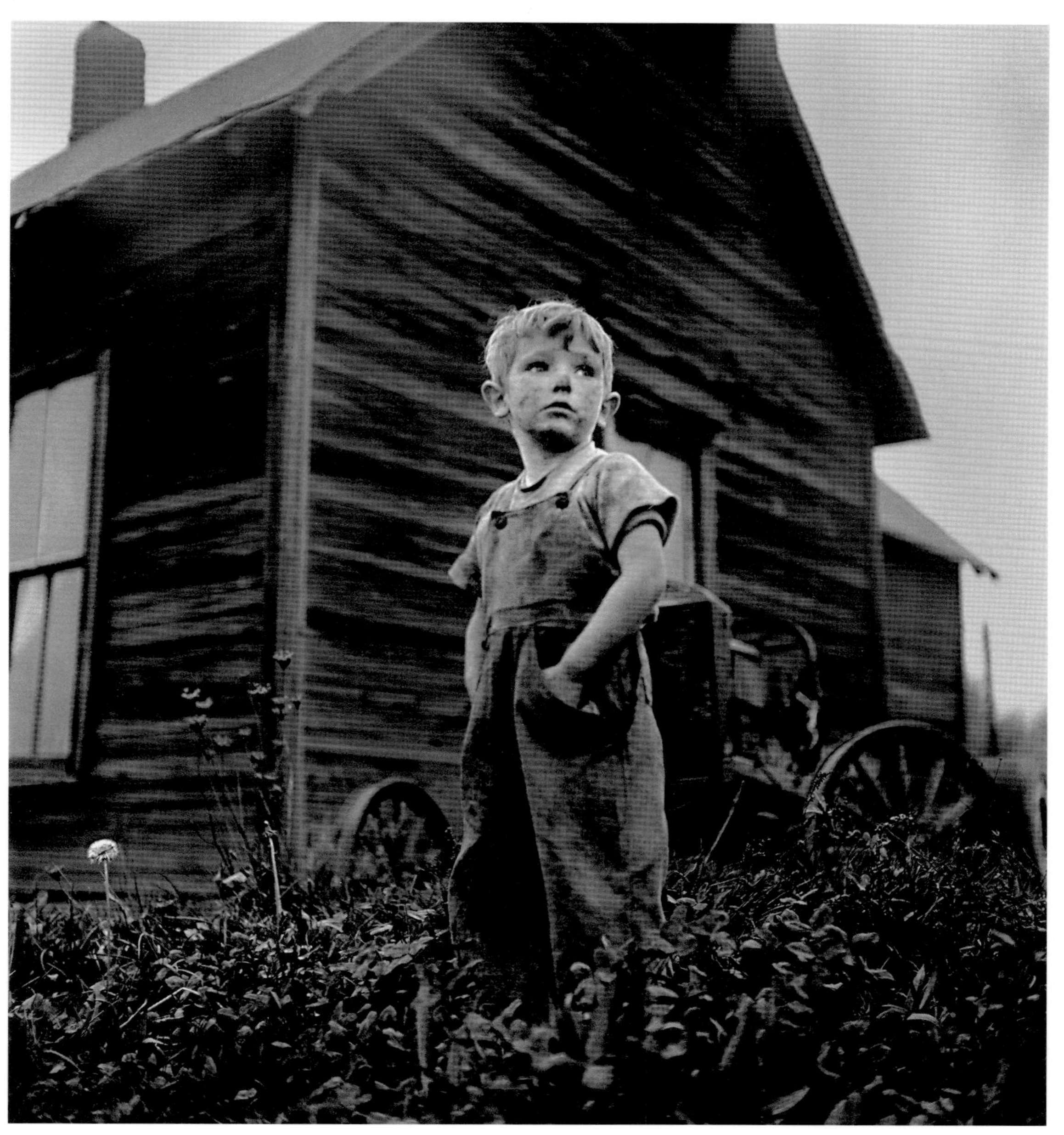

COUNTRY BOY, c. 1955

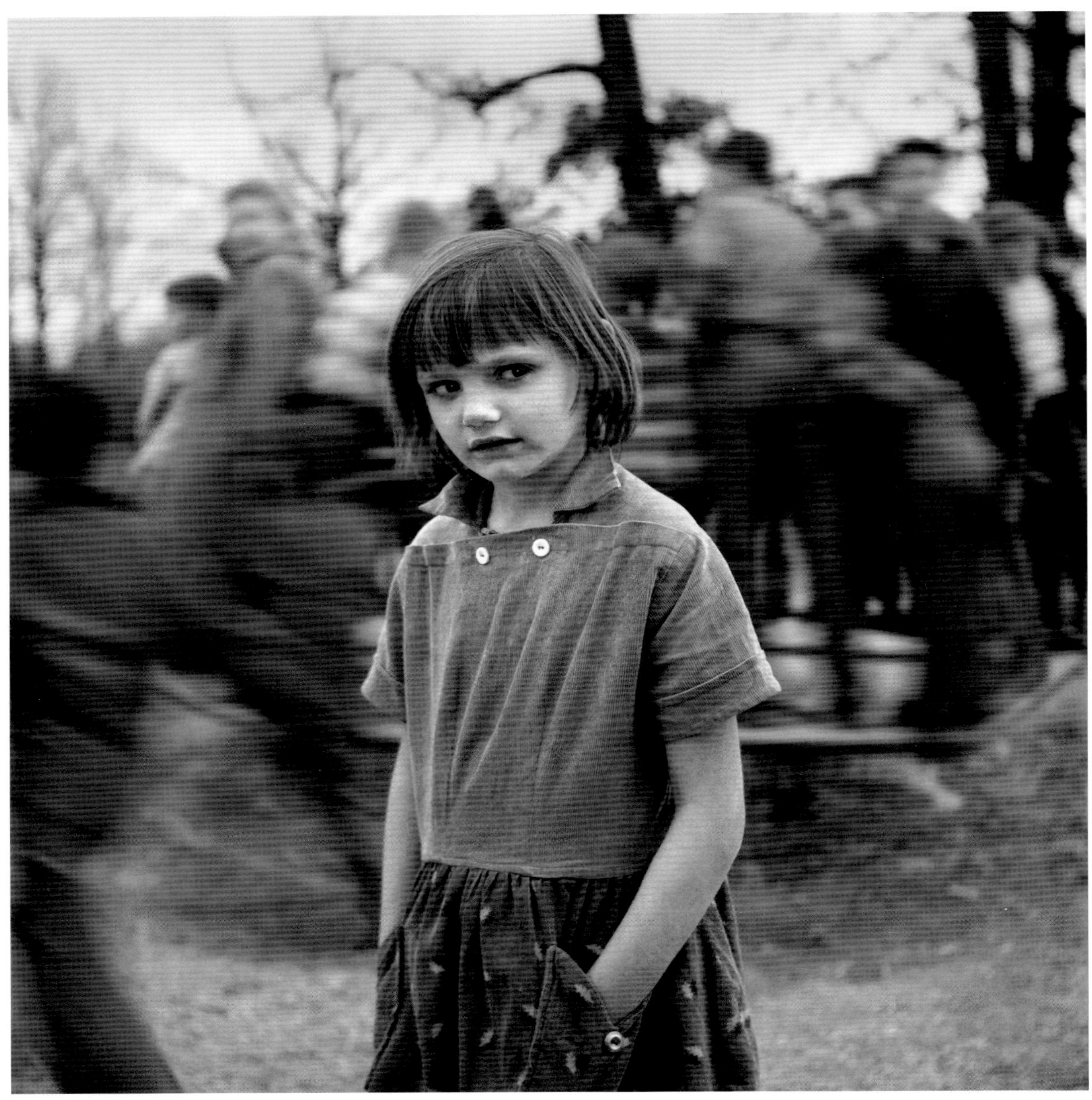

 COUNTRY GIRL, c. 1955

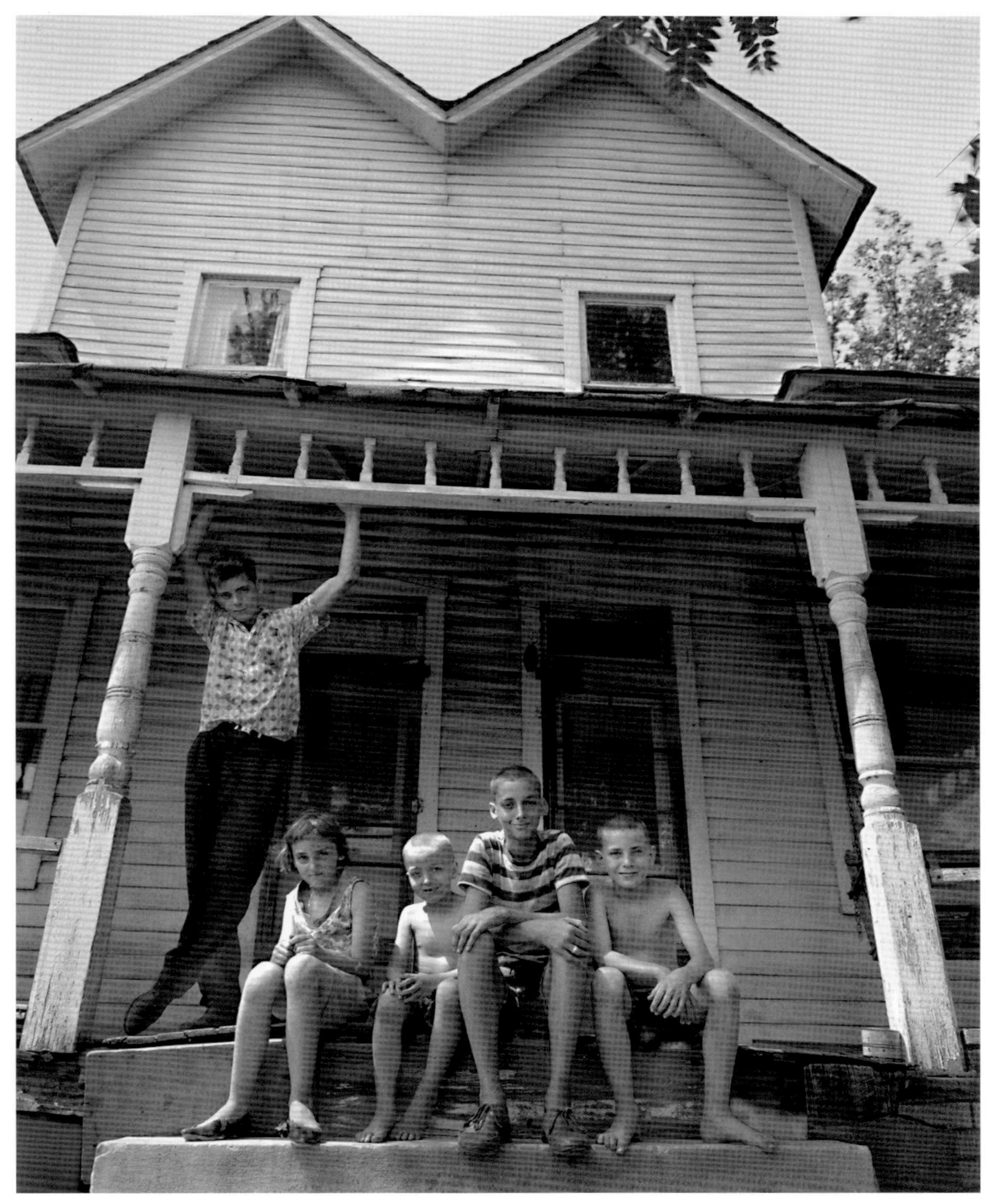

STINESVILLE, INDIANA, c. 1959

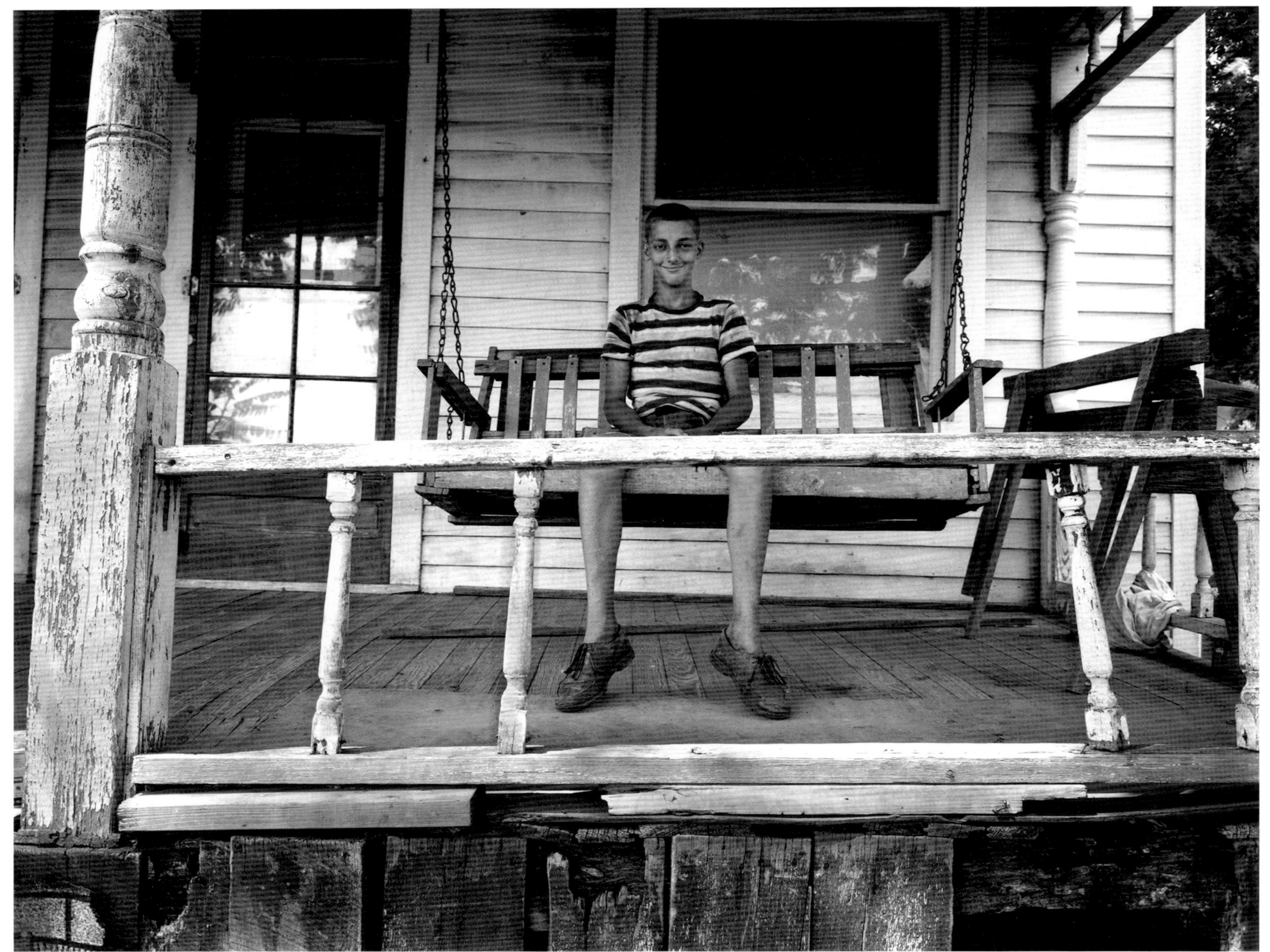

 | YOUNG BOY, STINESVILLE, INDIANA, c. 1959

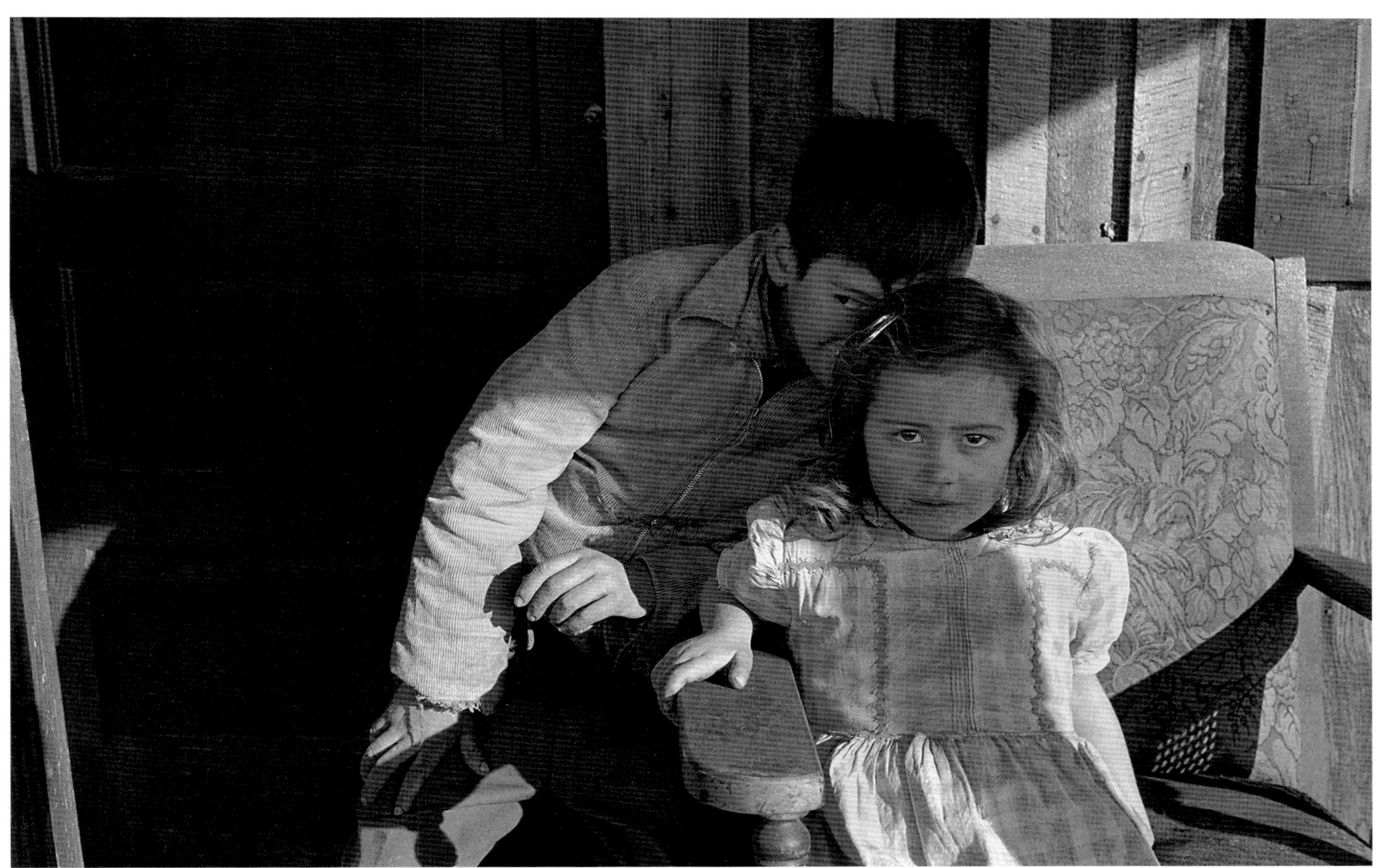

PIGEON HILL KIDS, BLOOMINGTON, INDIANA, c. 1955

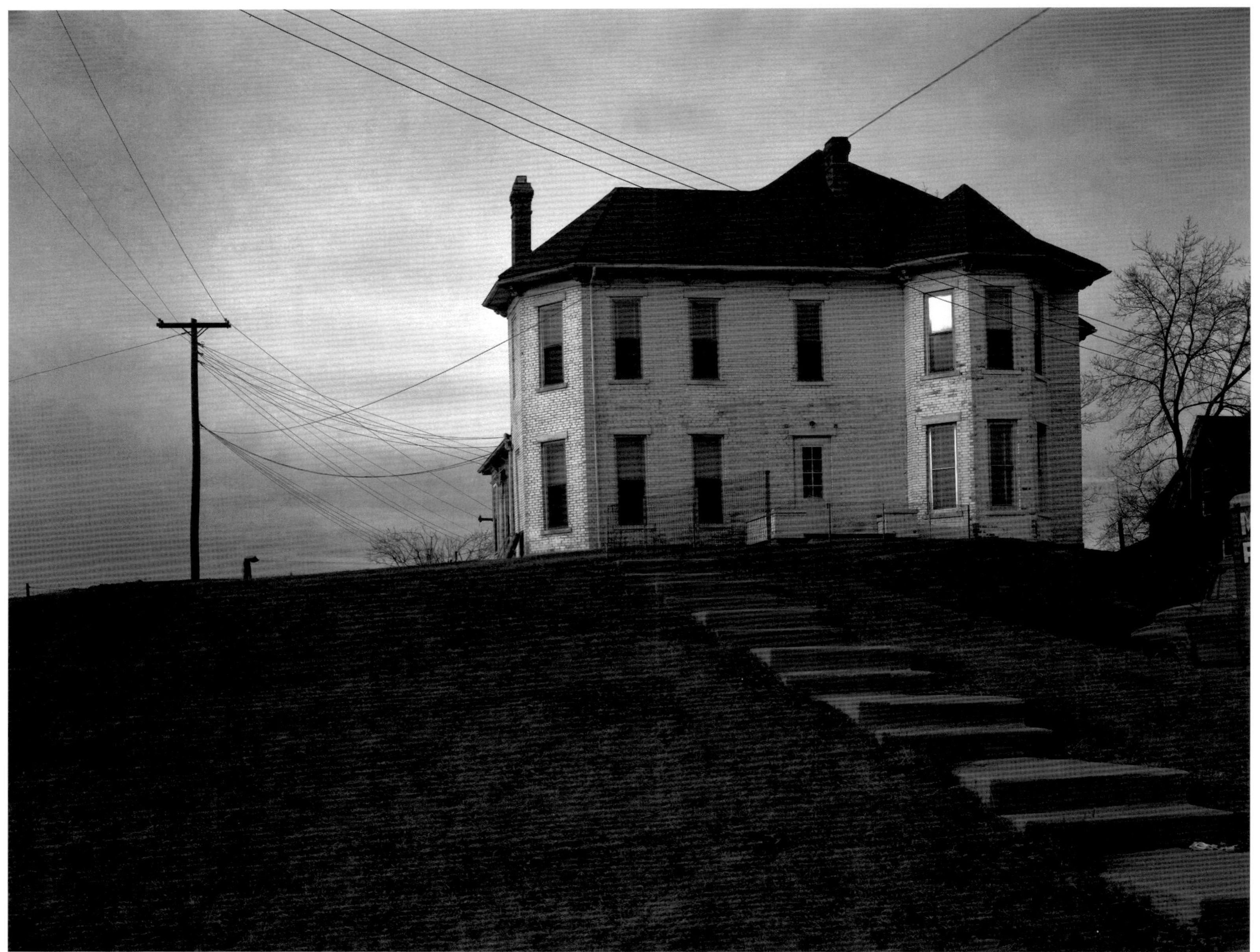

 | HOUSE ON THE HILL, BLOOMINGTON, INDIANA, 1957

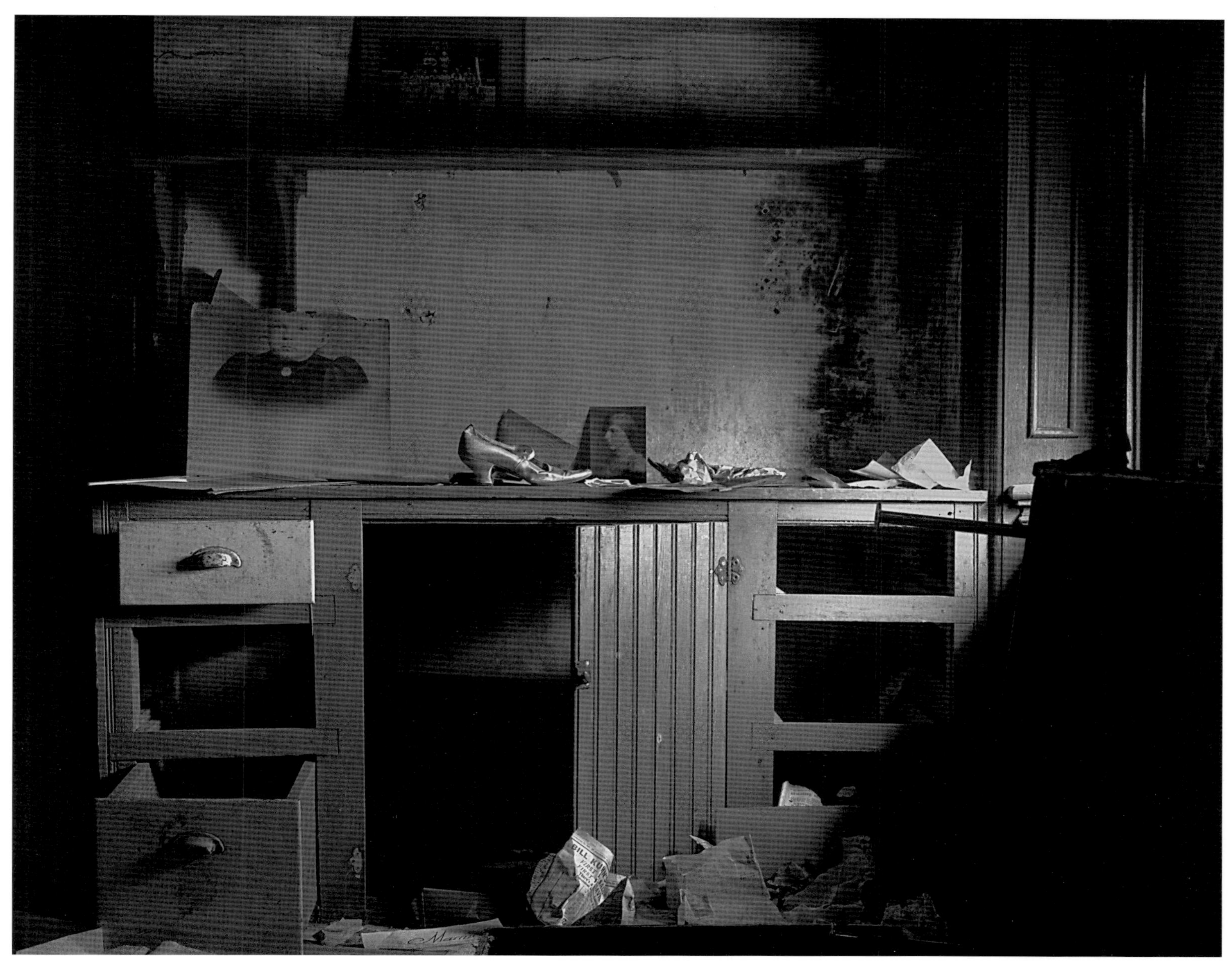

ABANDONED MATTHEWS MANSION, ELLETTSVILLE, INDIANA, 1948

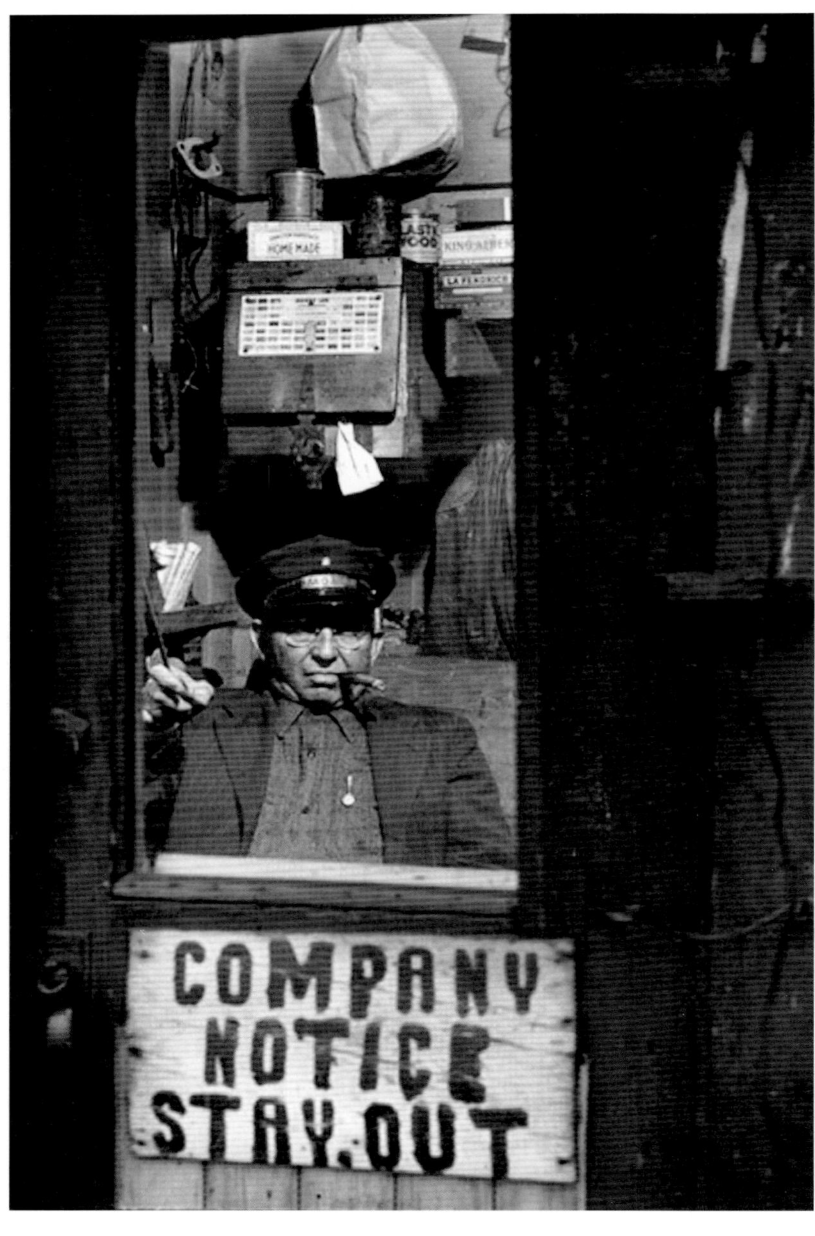

This gentleman was a crossing guard for the Monon Railroad.

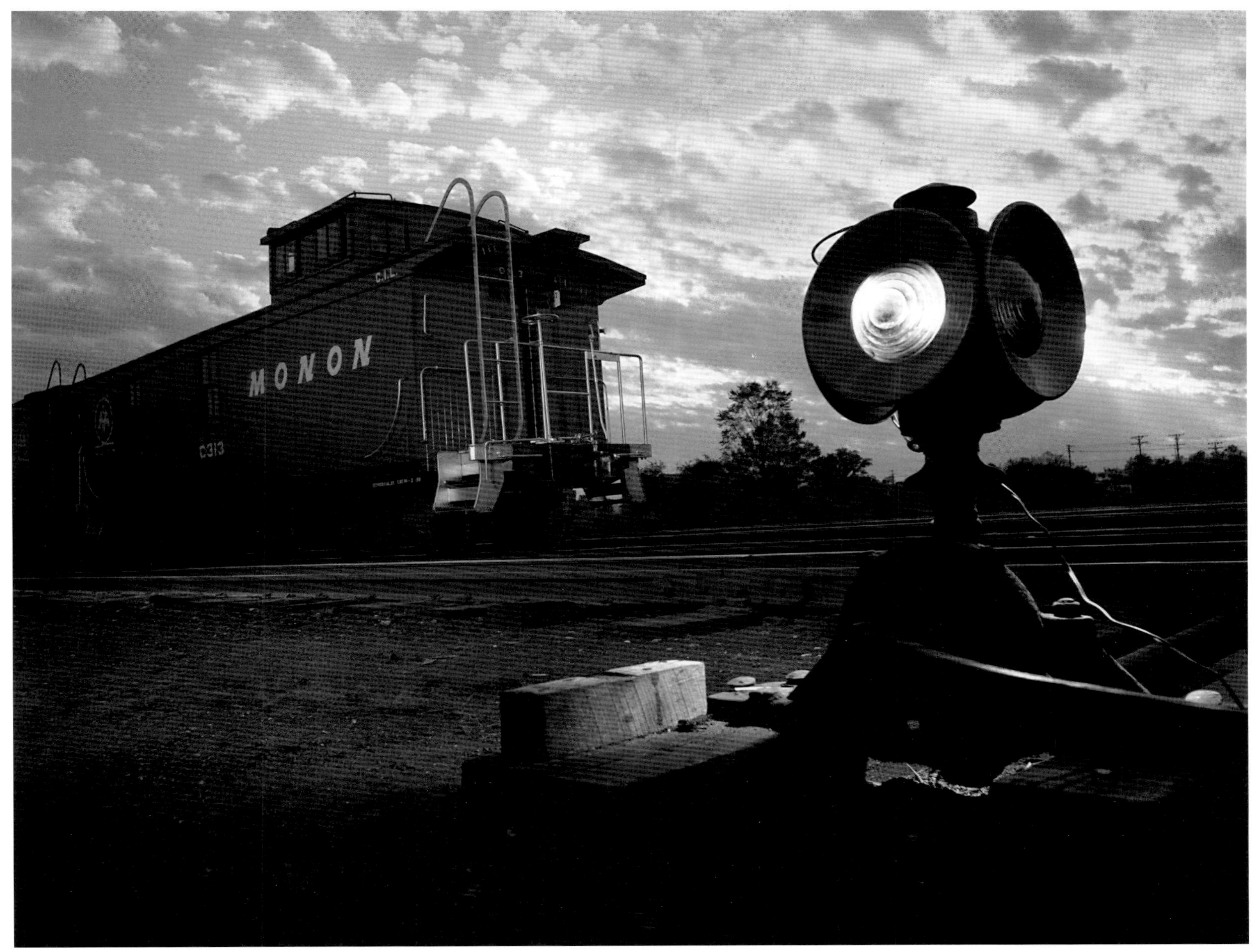

MONON RAILROAD, 1953

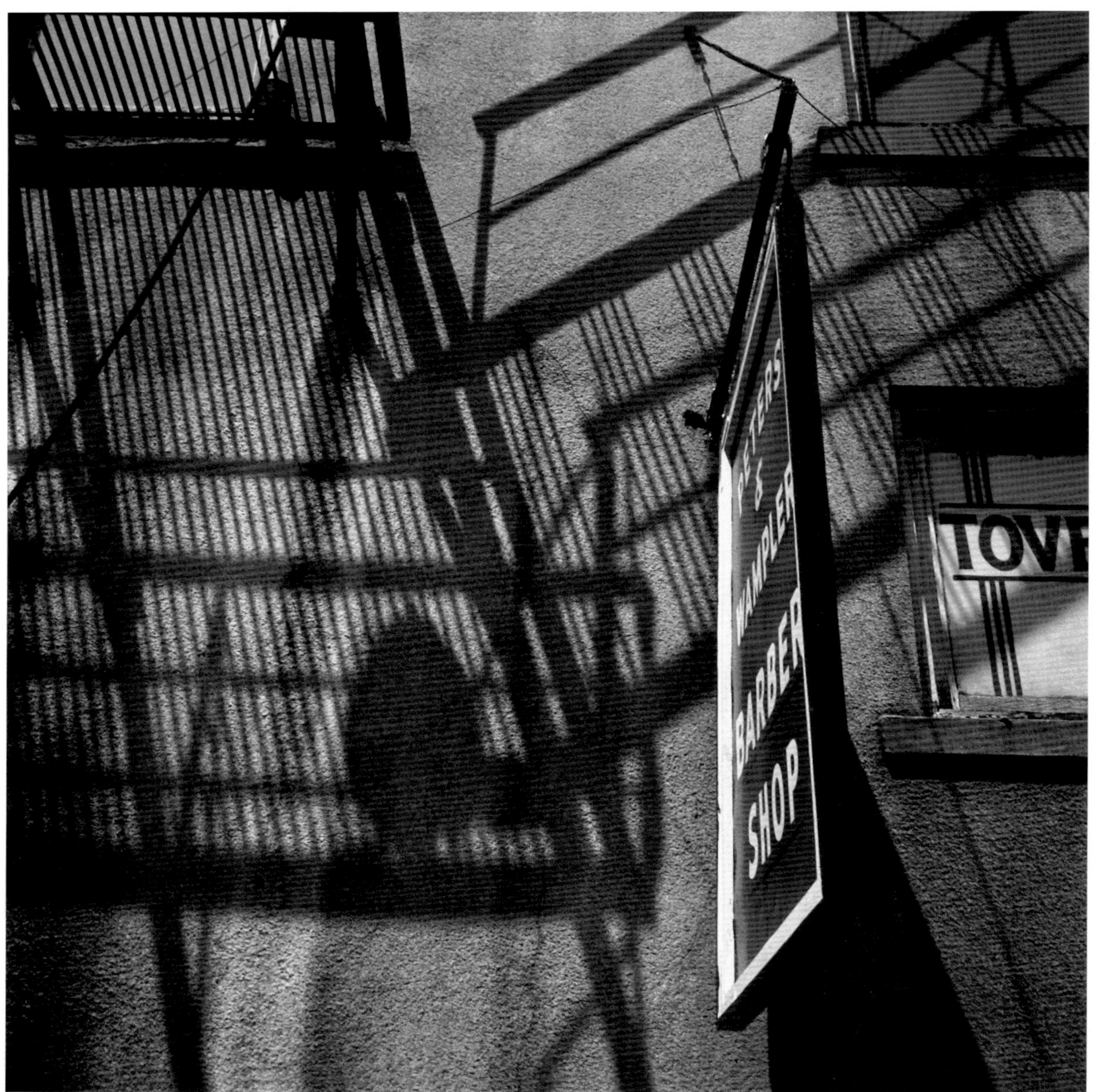

 | SIGN AND WALL, BLOOMINGTON, INDIANA, c. 1950

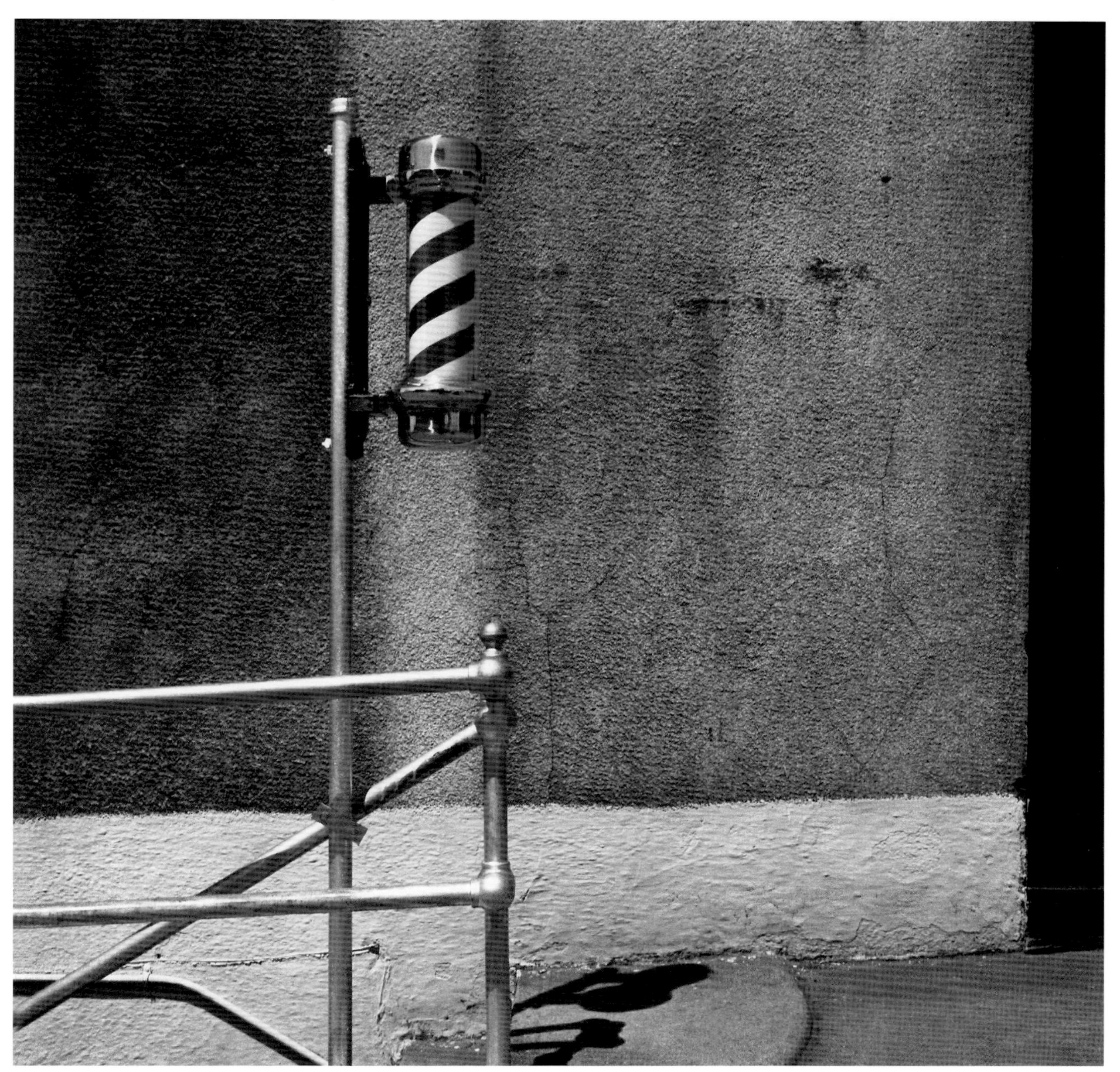

BARBER POLE, BLOOMINGTON, INDIANA, 1955

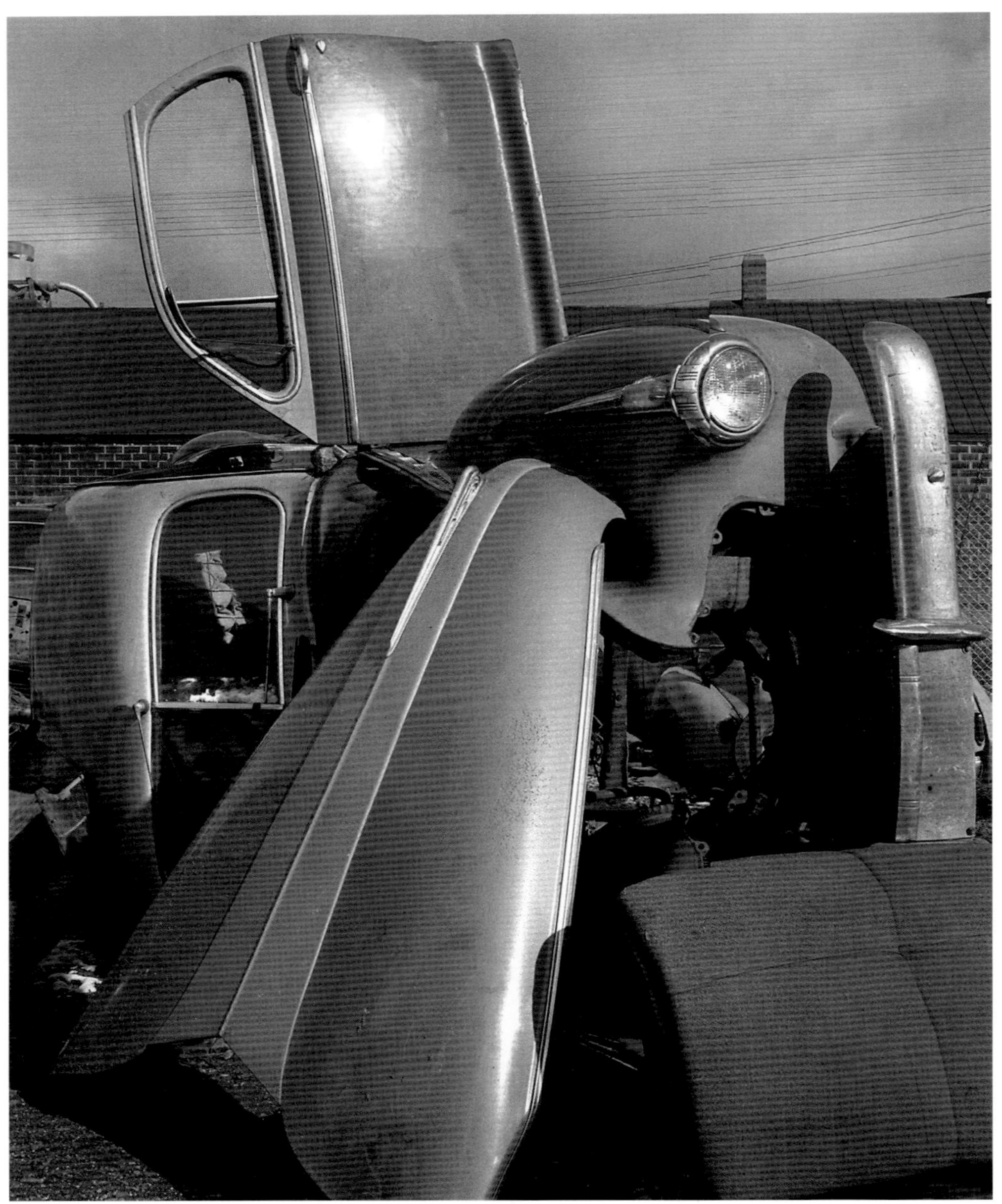

 | FAÇADE, FELL JUNK YARD, BLOOMINGTON, INDIANA, c. 1953

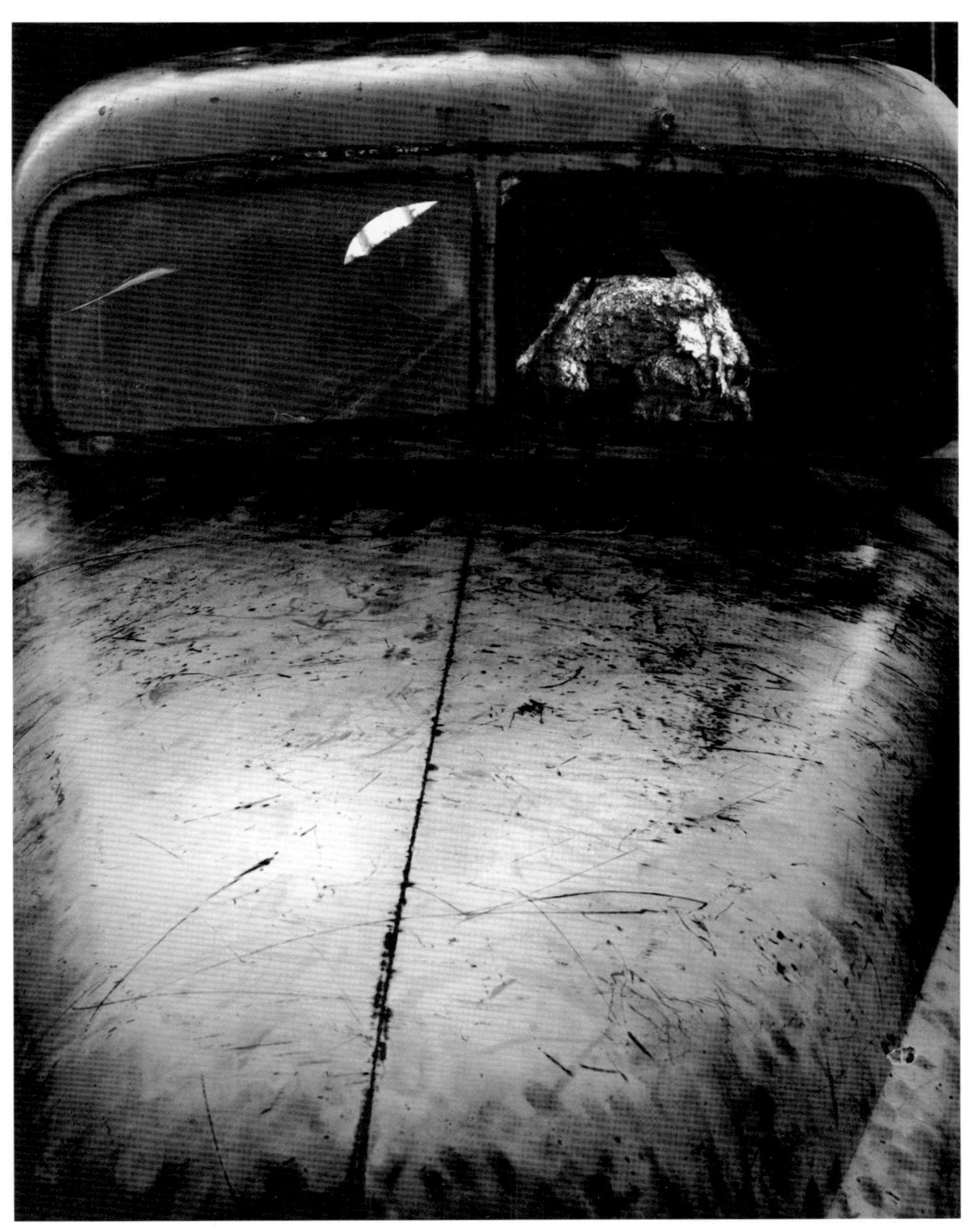

APPARITION, FELL JUNK YARD, BLOOMINGTON, INDIANA, c. 1955

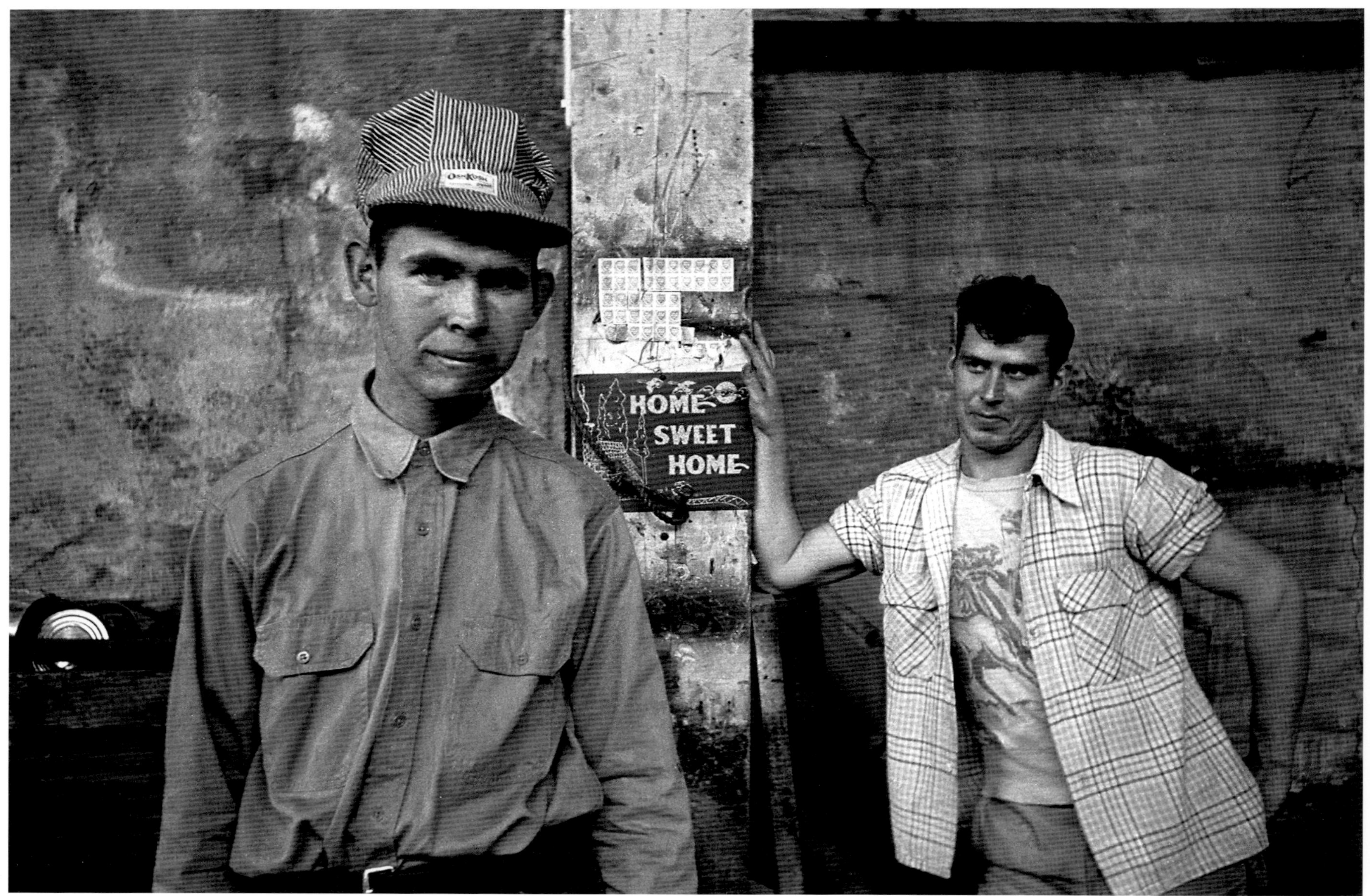

 | HOME SWEET HOME, FELL JUNK YARD, BLOOMINGTON, INDIANA, c. 1953

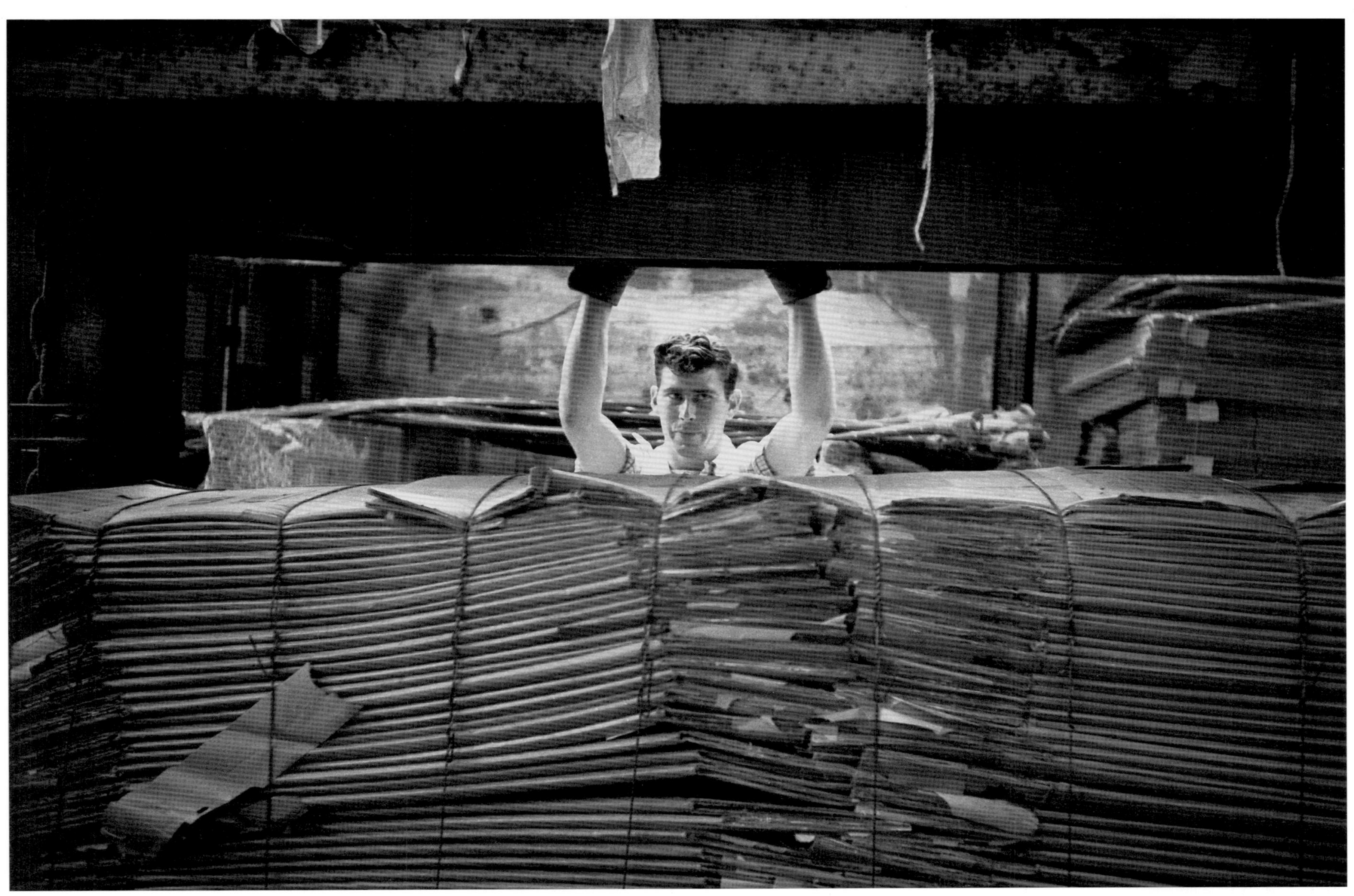

AT THE PRESS, FELL JUNK YARD, BLOOMINGTON, INDIANA, c. 1955

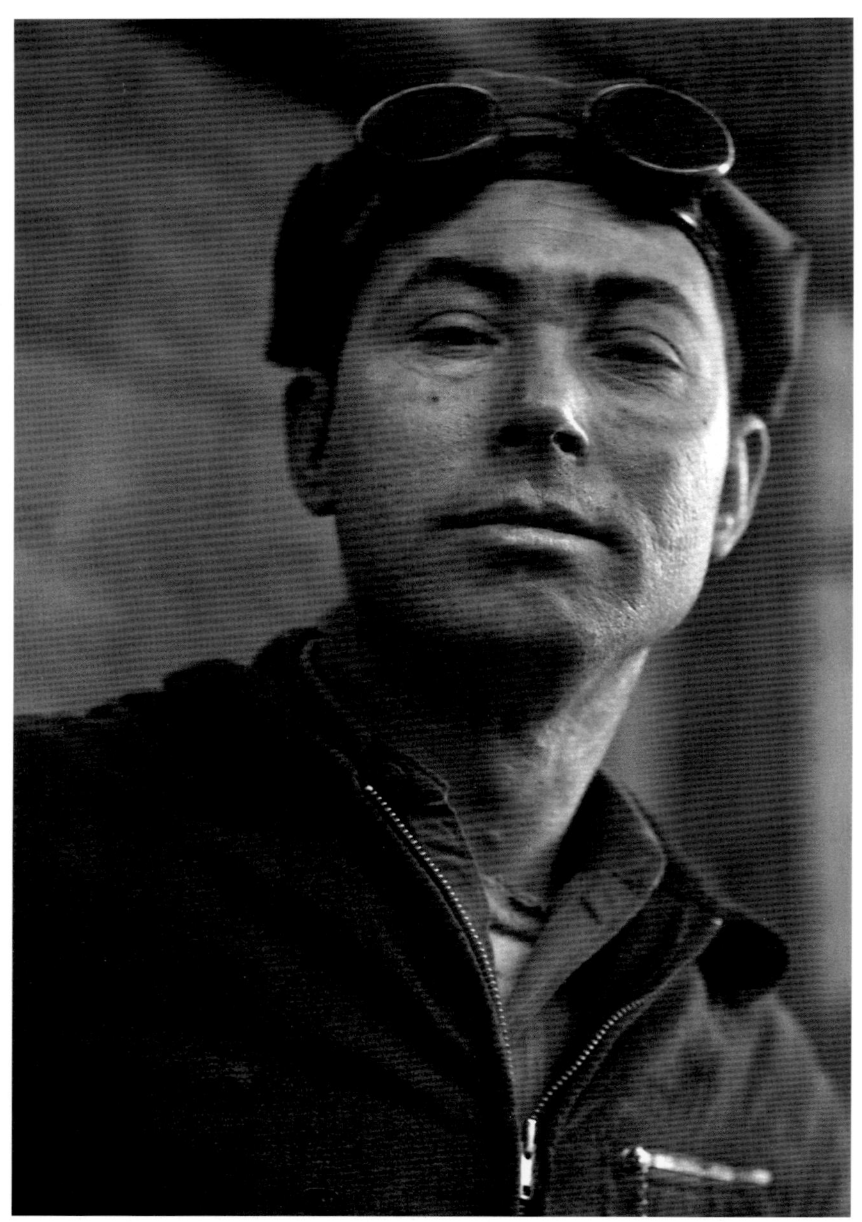

 | THE WELDER, FELL JUNK YARD, BLOOMINGTON, INDIANA, c. 1955

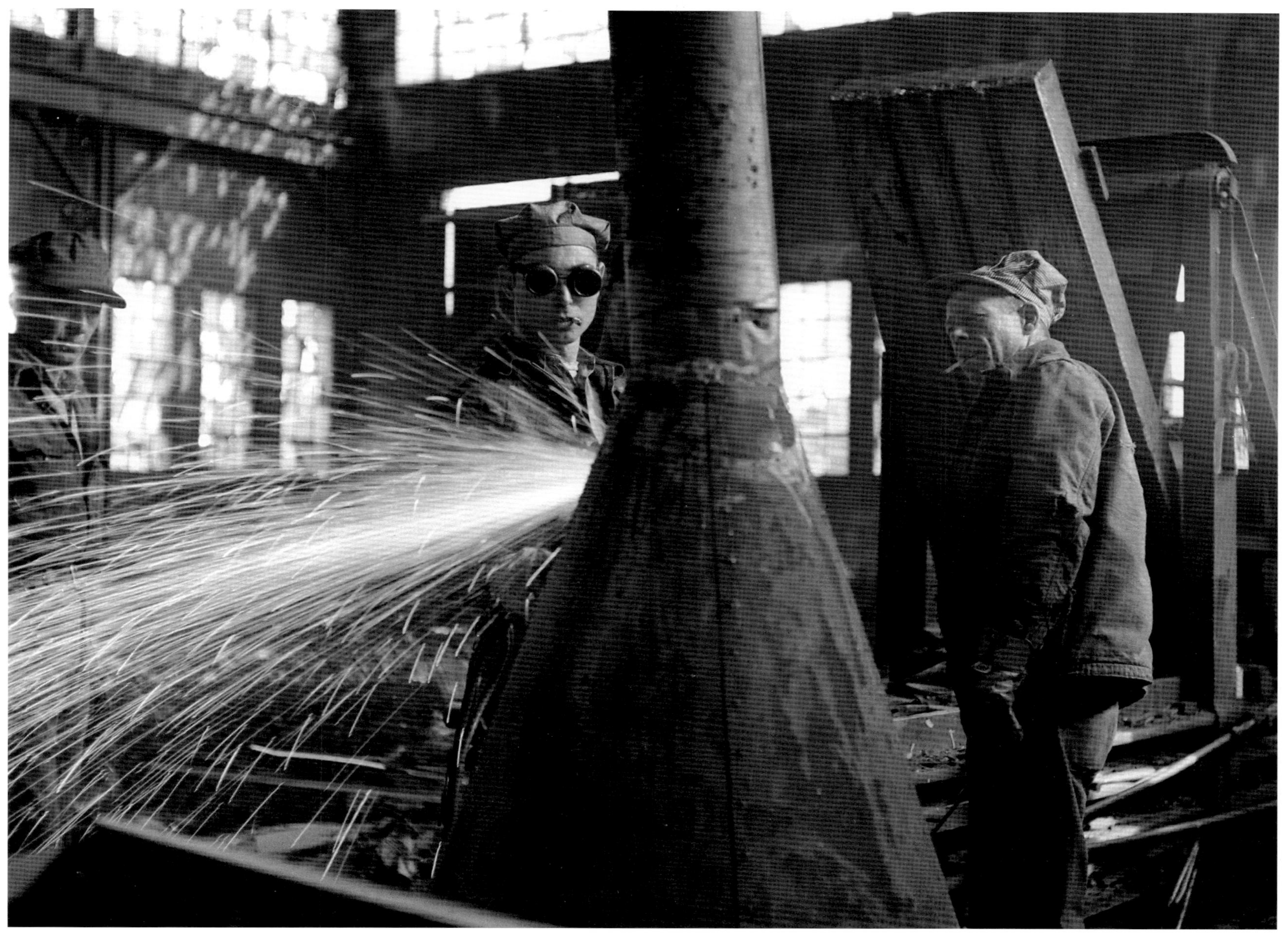

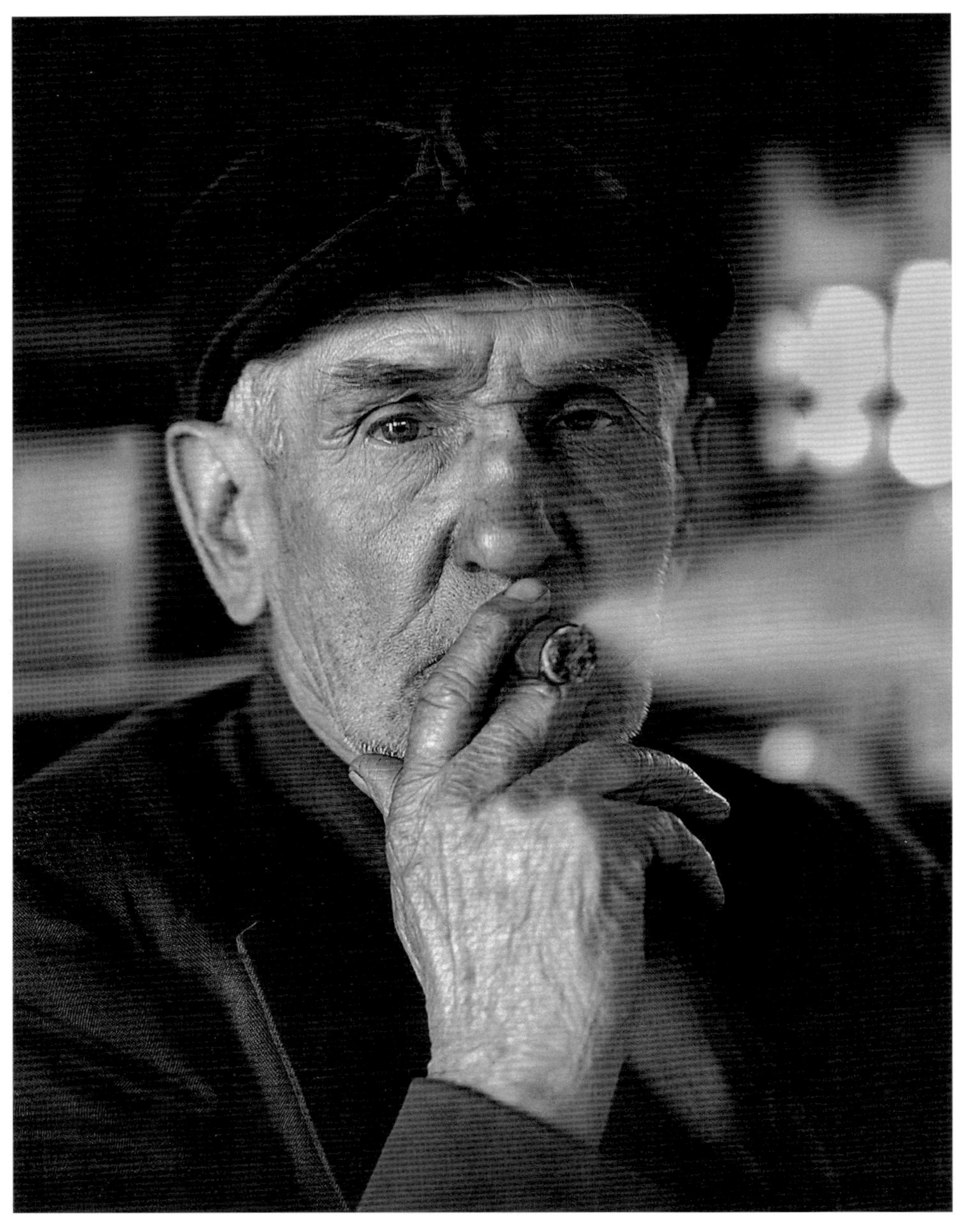

 | THE RAG PICKER, FELL JUNK YARD, BLOOMINGTON, INDIANA, c. 1955

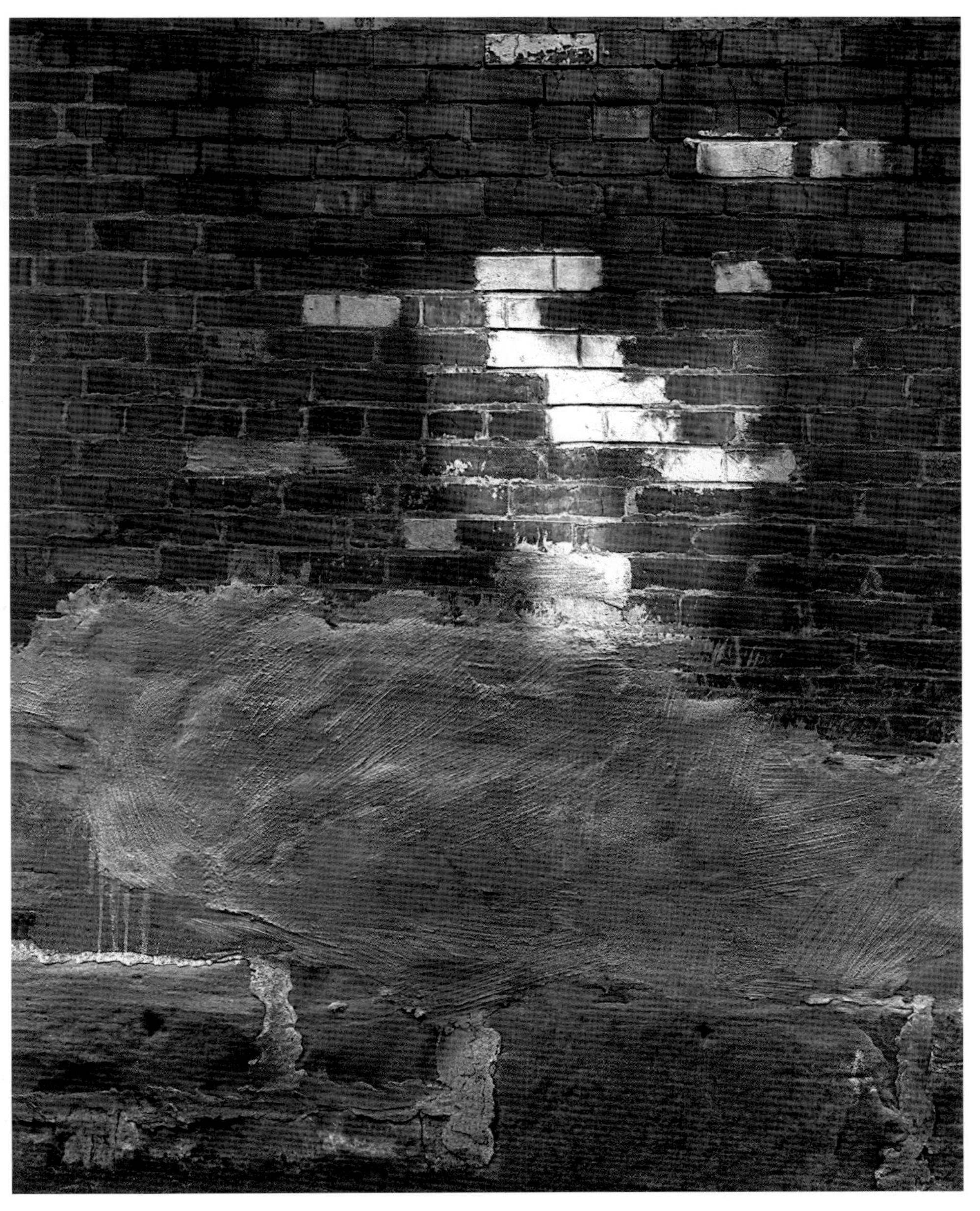

ALLEY WALL, BLOOMINGTON, INDIANA, 1959

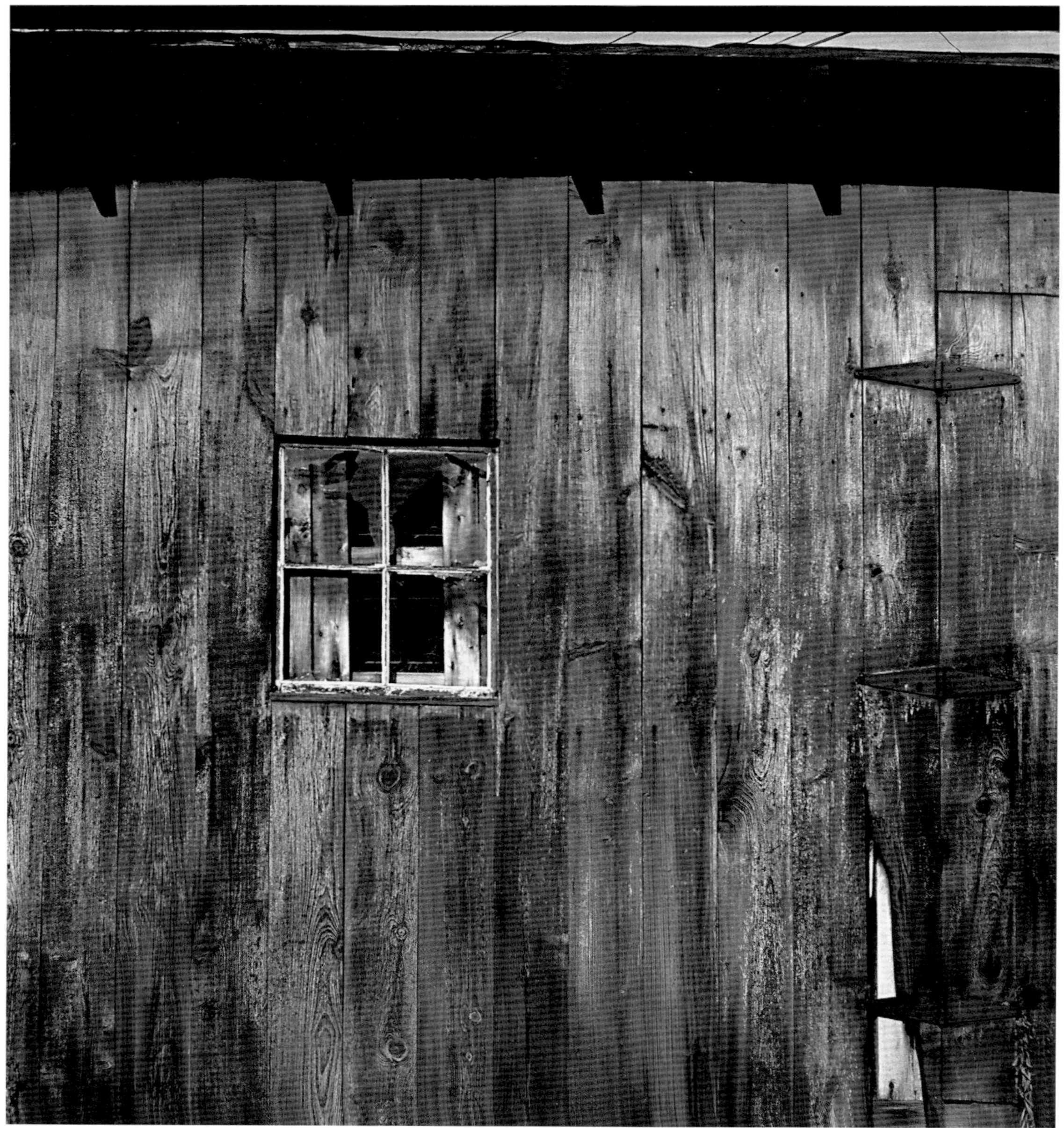

 | WINDOW, BLOOMINGTON, INDIANA, c. 1950

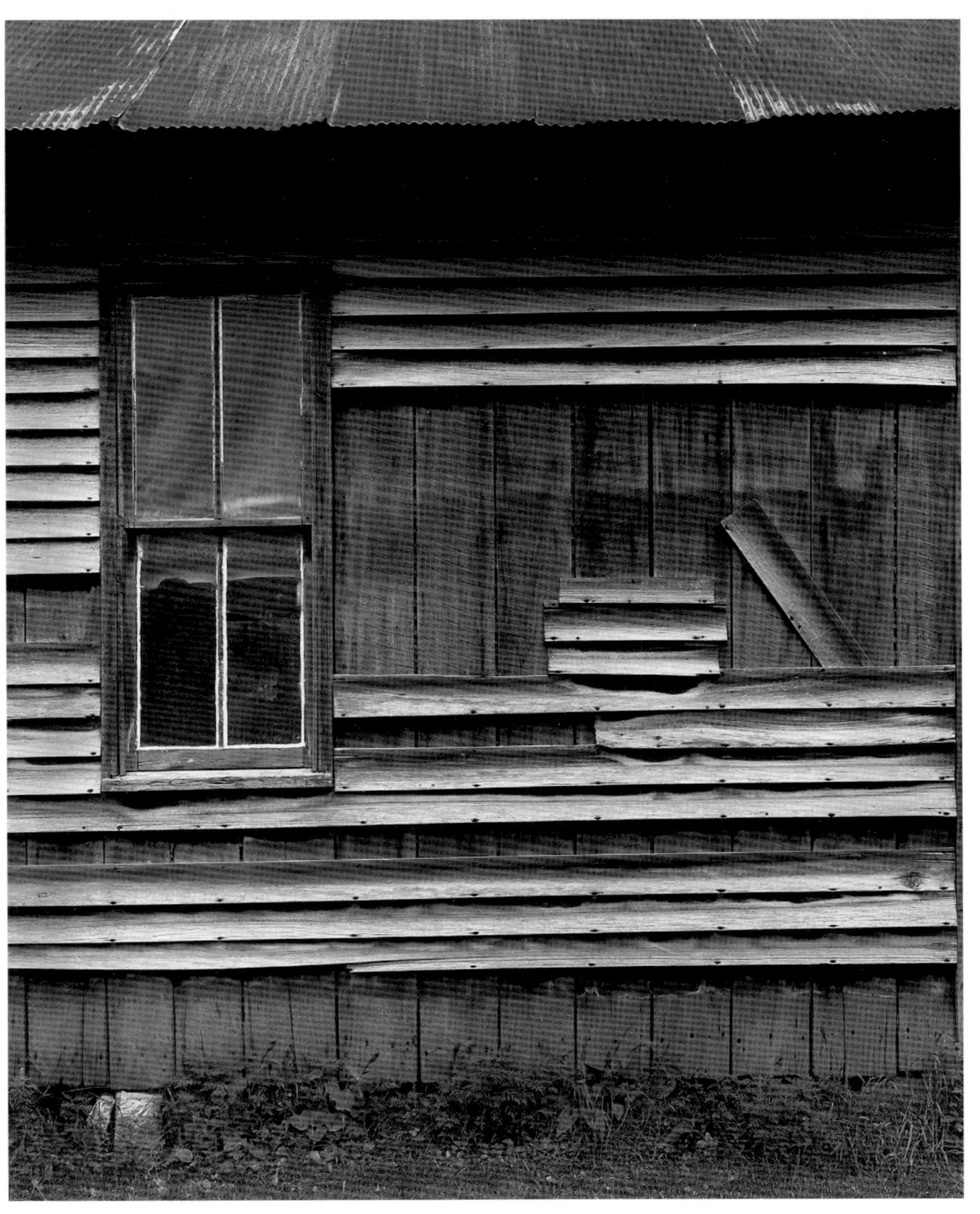

BLOOMINGTON, INDIANA, c. 1955

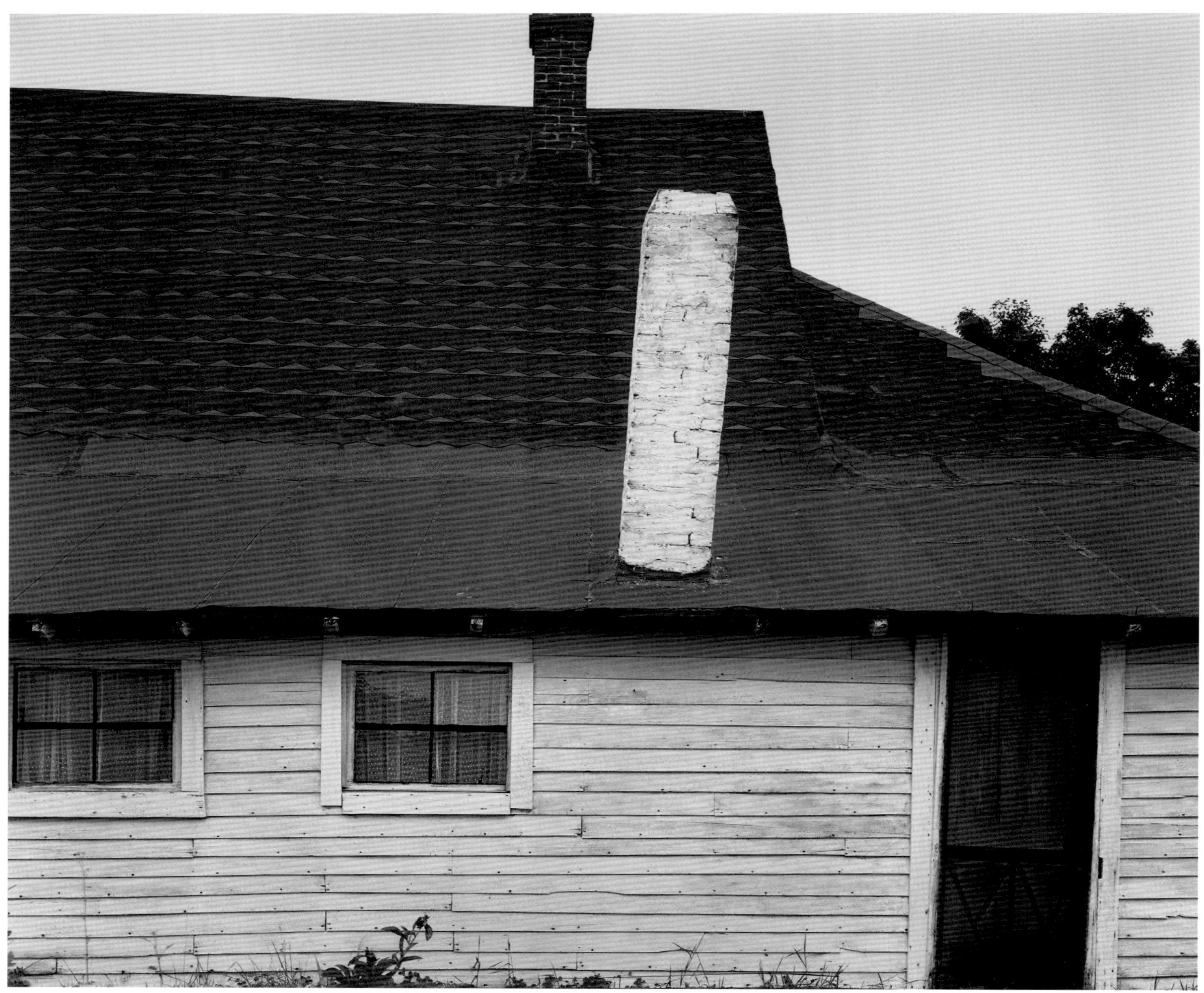

 | CHIMNEY ASKEW, BLOOMINGTON, INDIANA, c. 1955

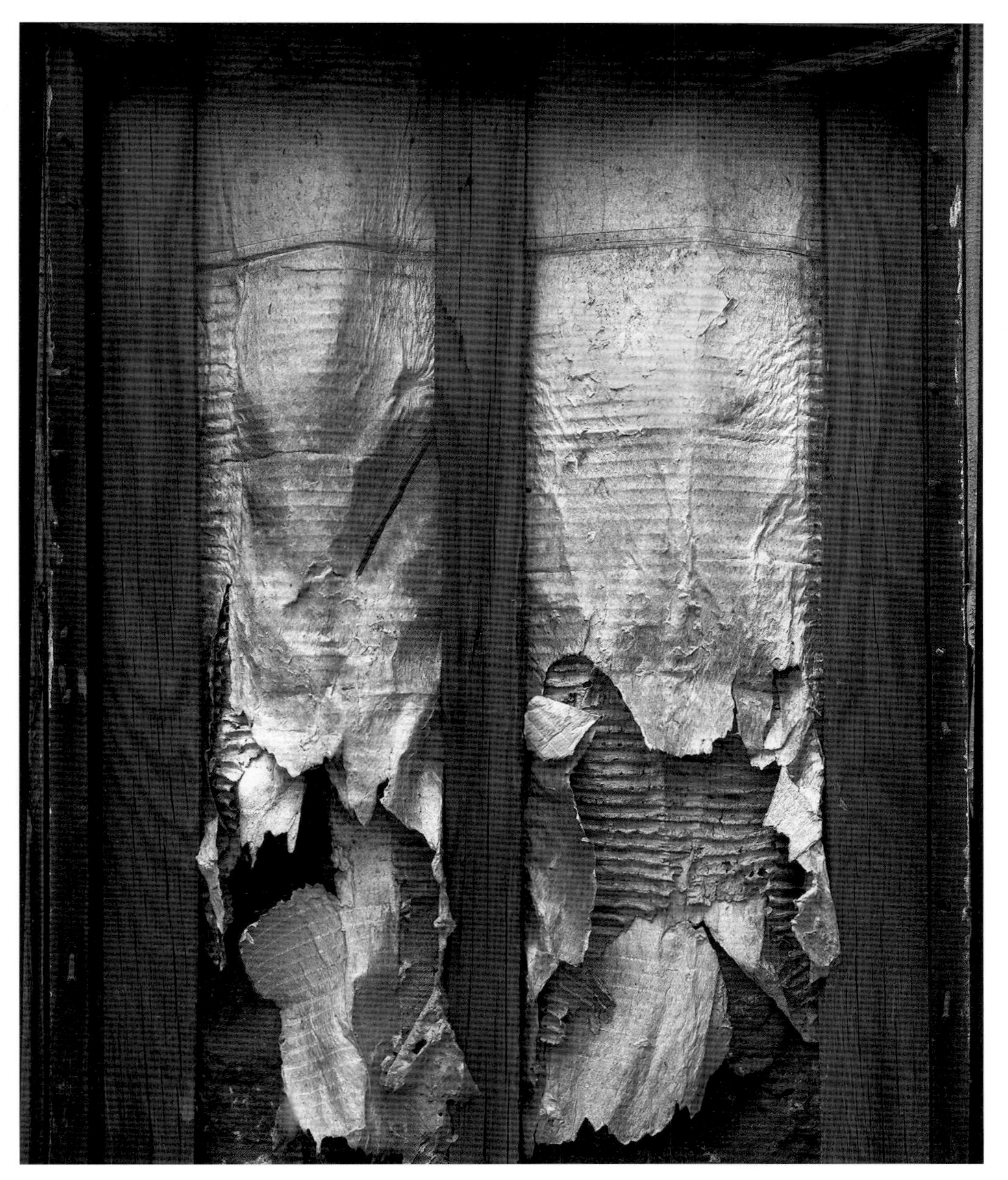

CARDBOARD WINDOW, BLOOMINGTON, INDIANA, 1958

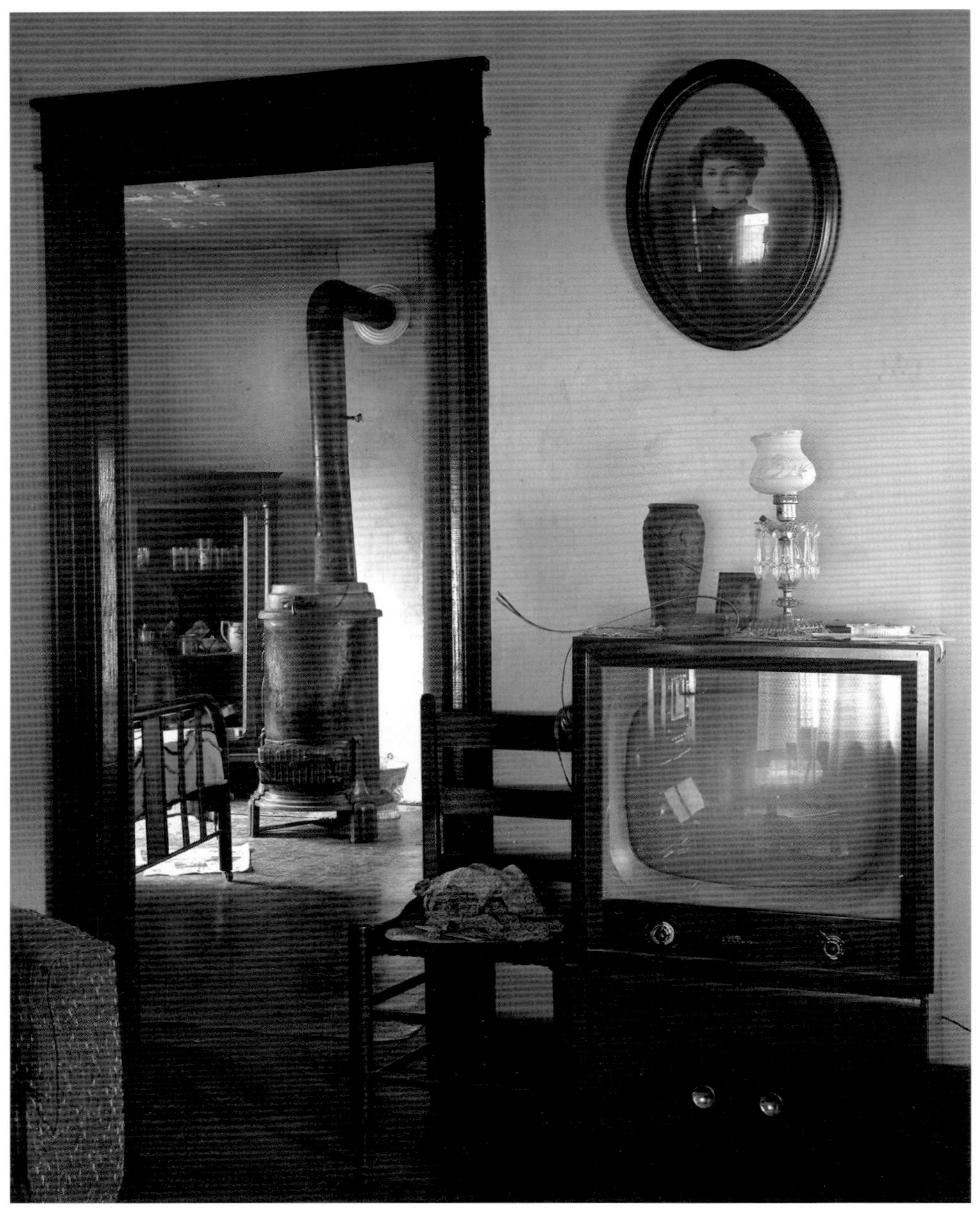

 | FARMER TWINS' INTERIOR, STINESVILLE, INDIANA, 1958

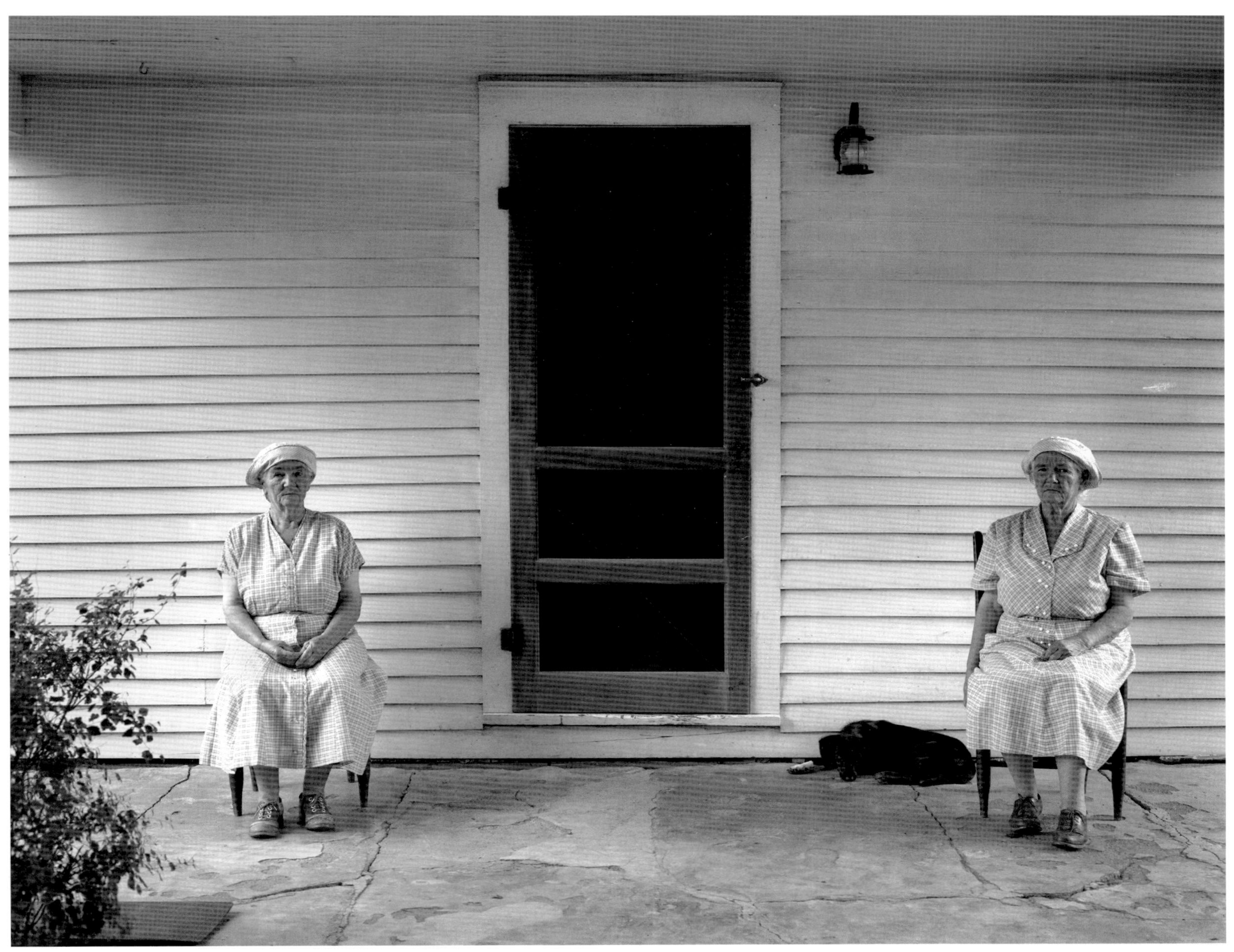

THE FARMER TWINS, STINESVILLE, INDIANA, 1958

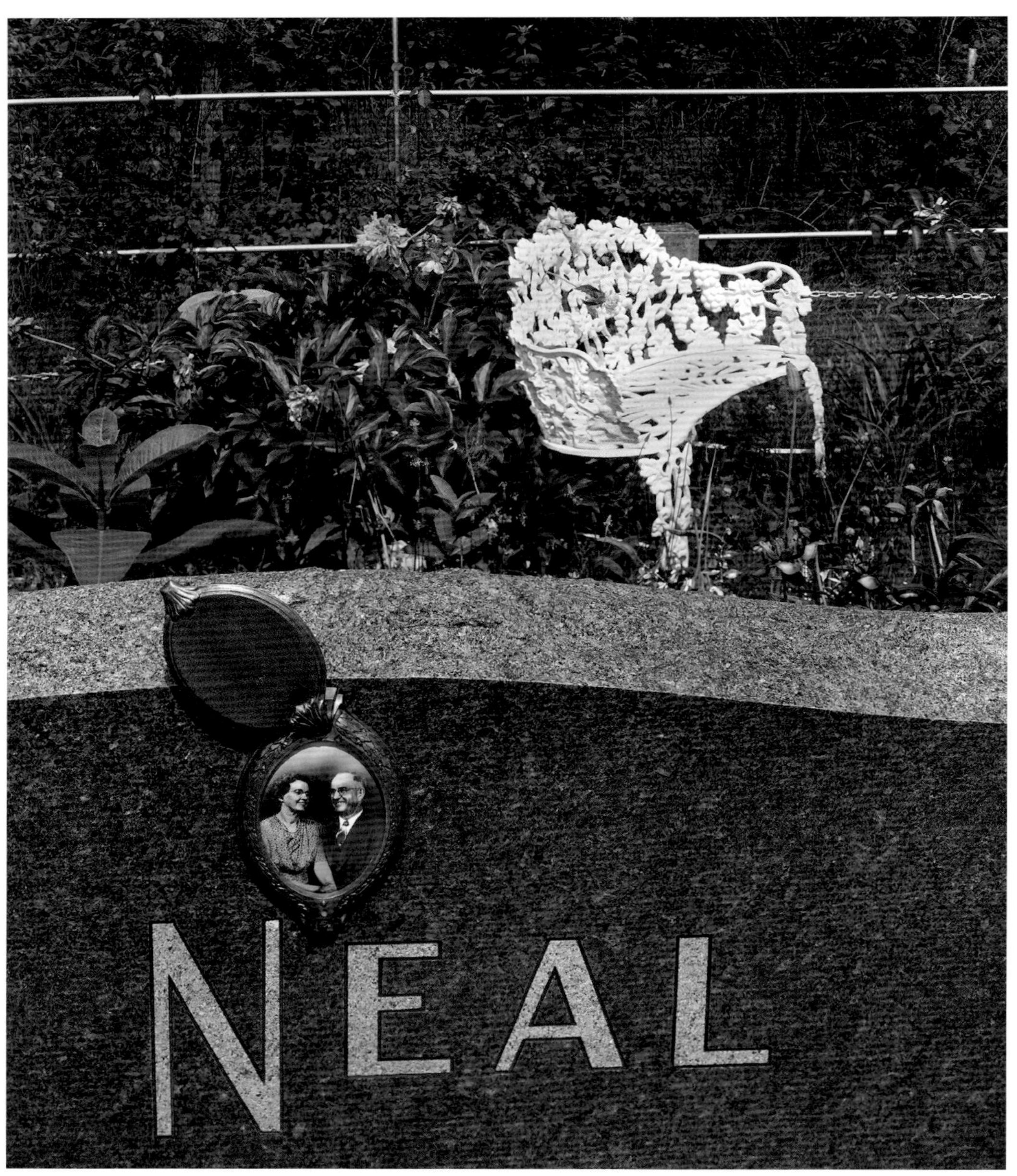

 | ROSE HILL CEMETERY, BLOOMINGTON, INDIANA, c. 1955

EIGHT | The Land

People have been the dominant interest throughout my photographic life. Even so, I began to develop an interest in landscape in the fifties. I was especially drawn to the land during winter months. Landscape photography is difficult—at best—in southern Indiana. As a rule, one cannot see the horizon for the trees, unlike in the west, where so much great landscape photography has been done.

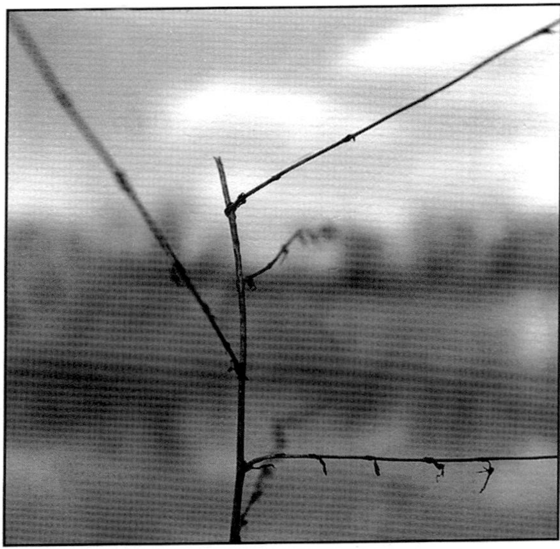

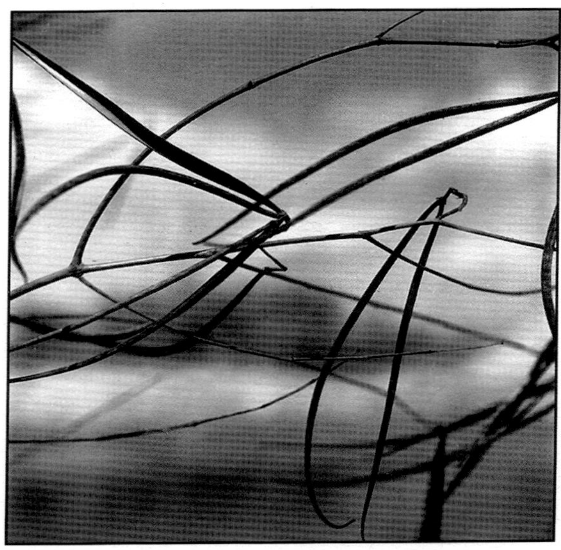

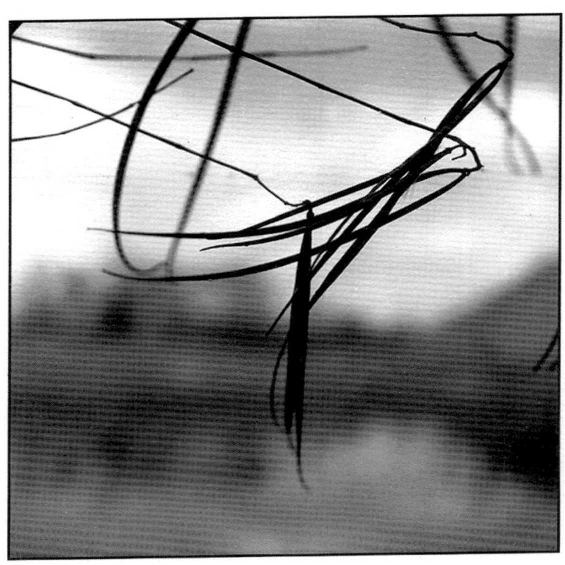

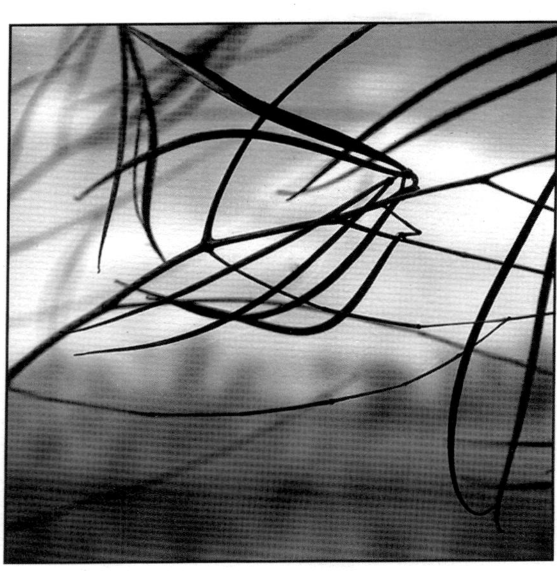

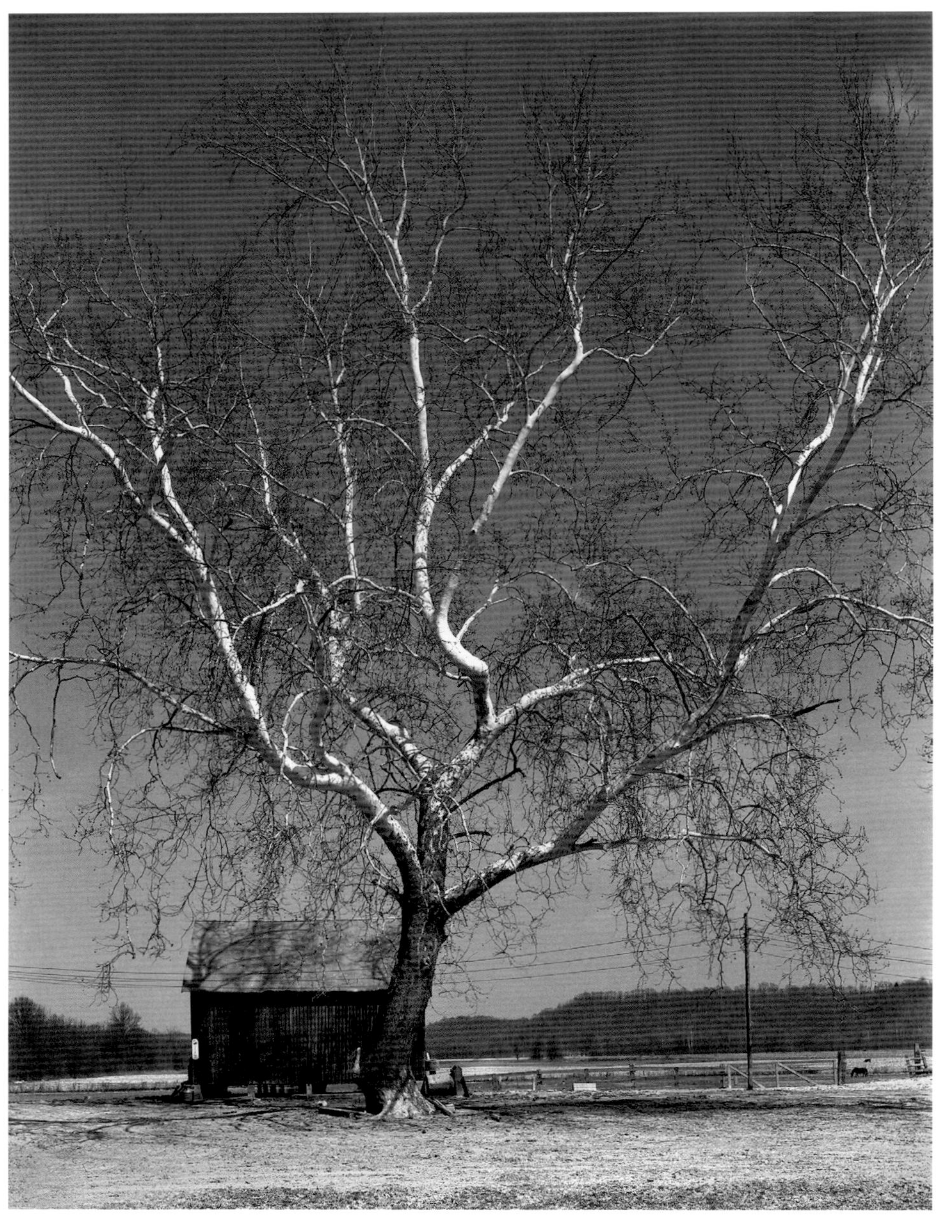

 | TREE AND BARN, c. 1958

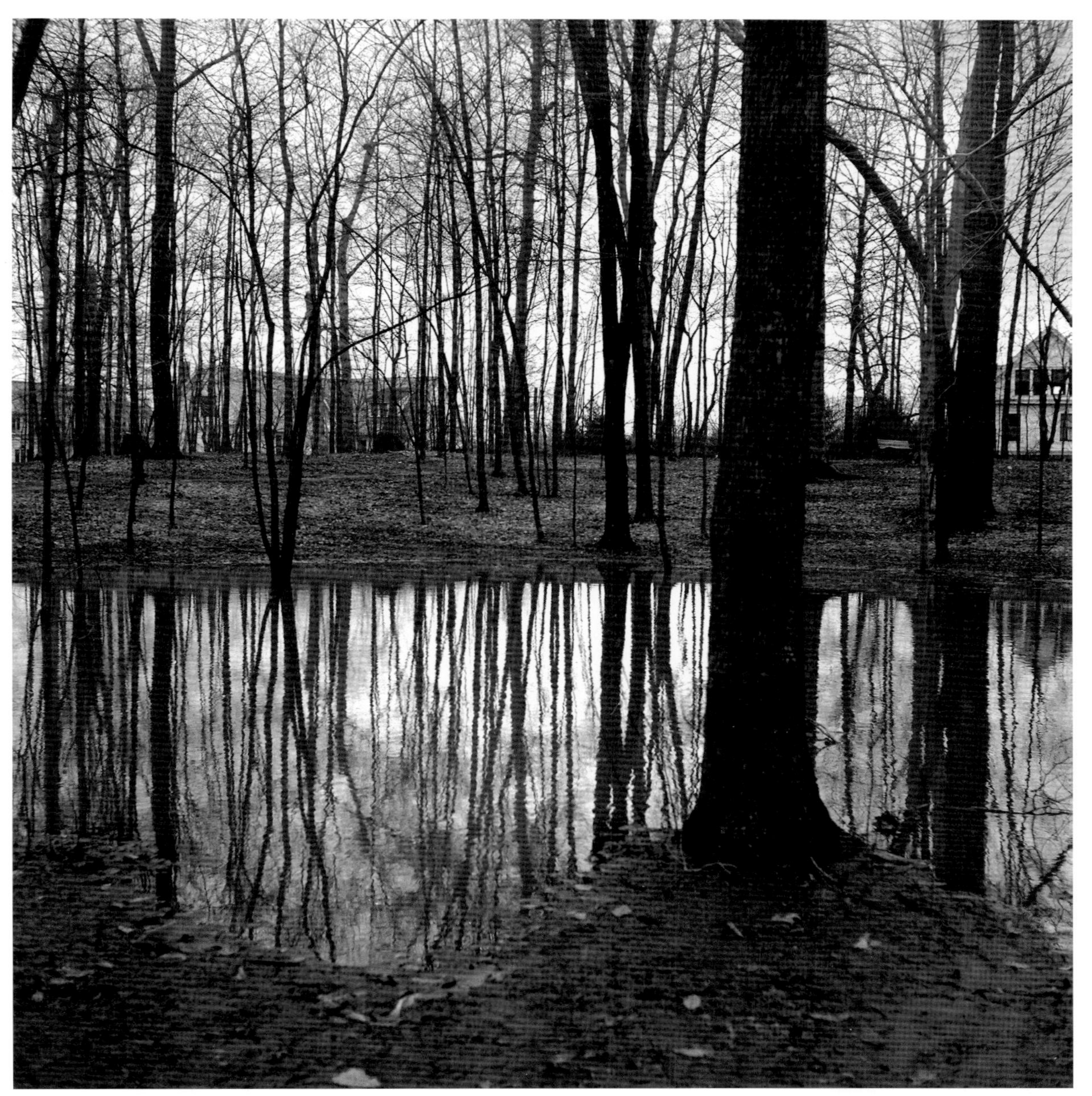

POND, c. 1950

 | GRIFFY LAKE, 1957

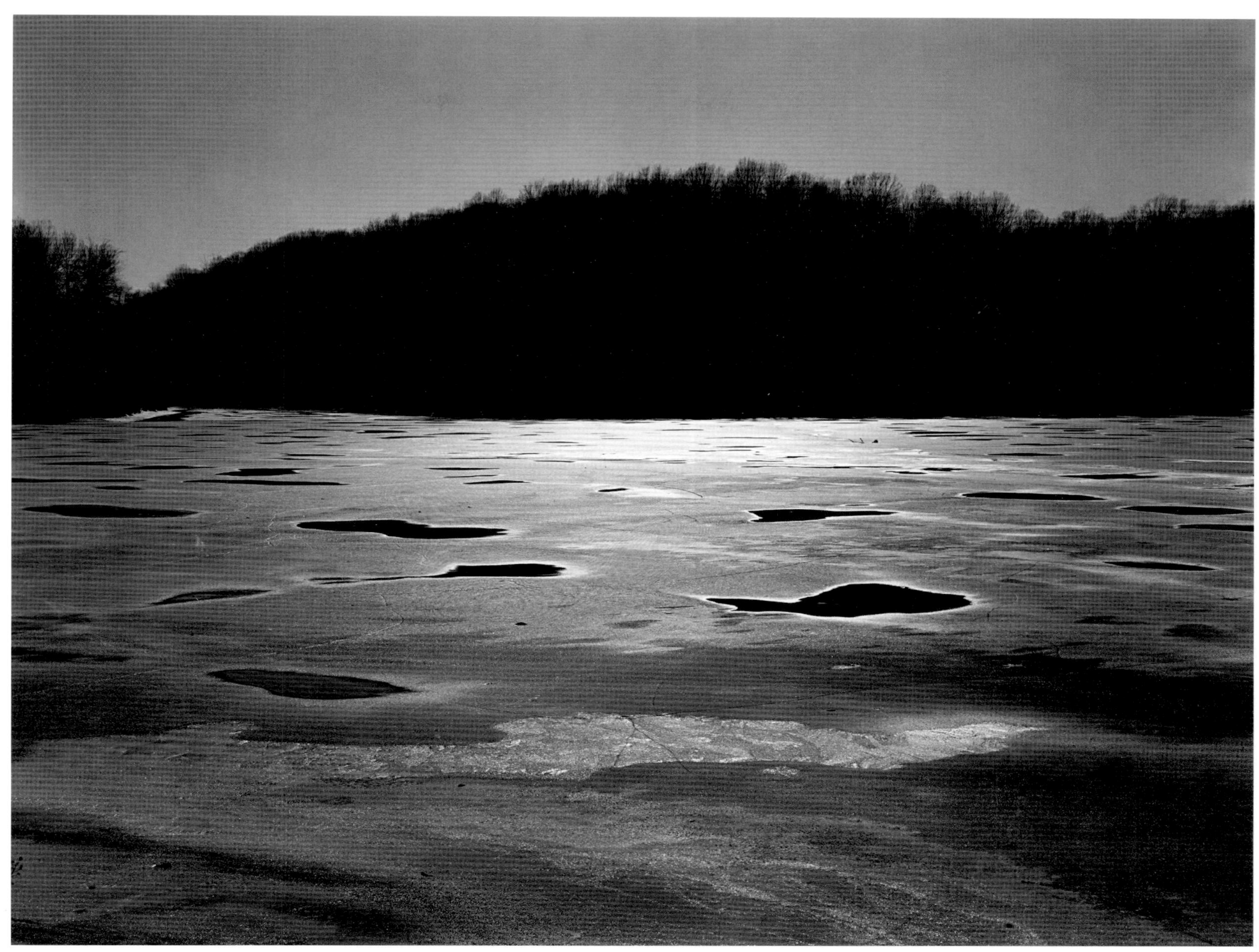

GRIFFY LAKE, 1958

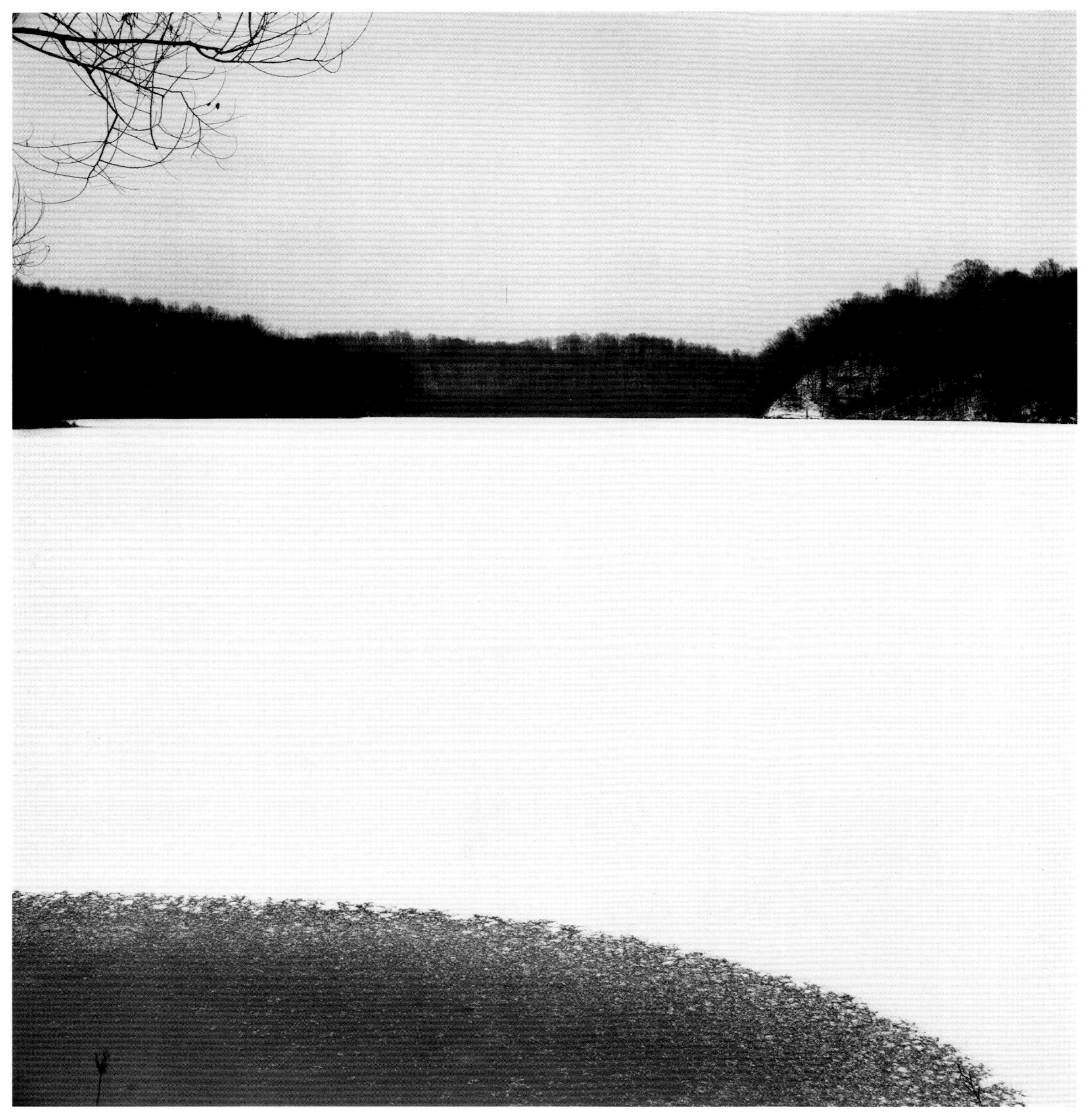

 | GRIFFY LAKE IN WINTER, c. 1957

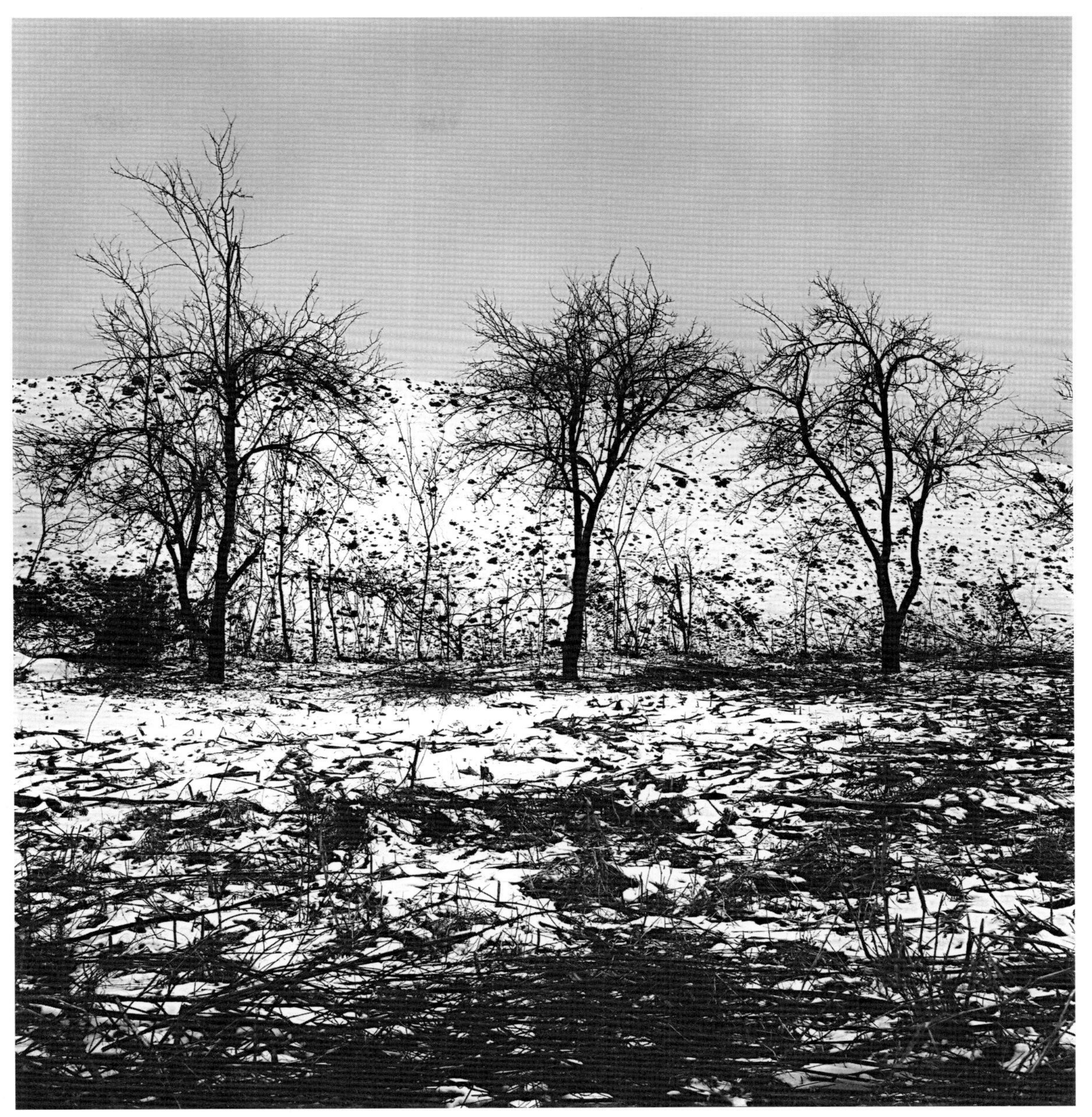

TREES IN WINTER, c. 1955

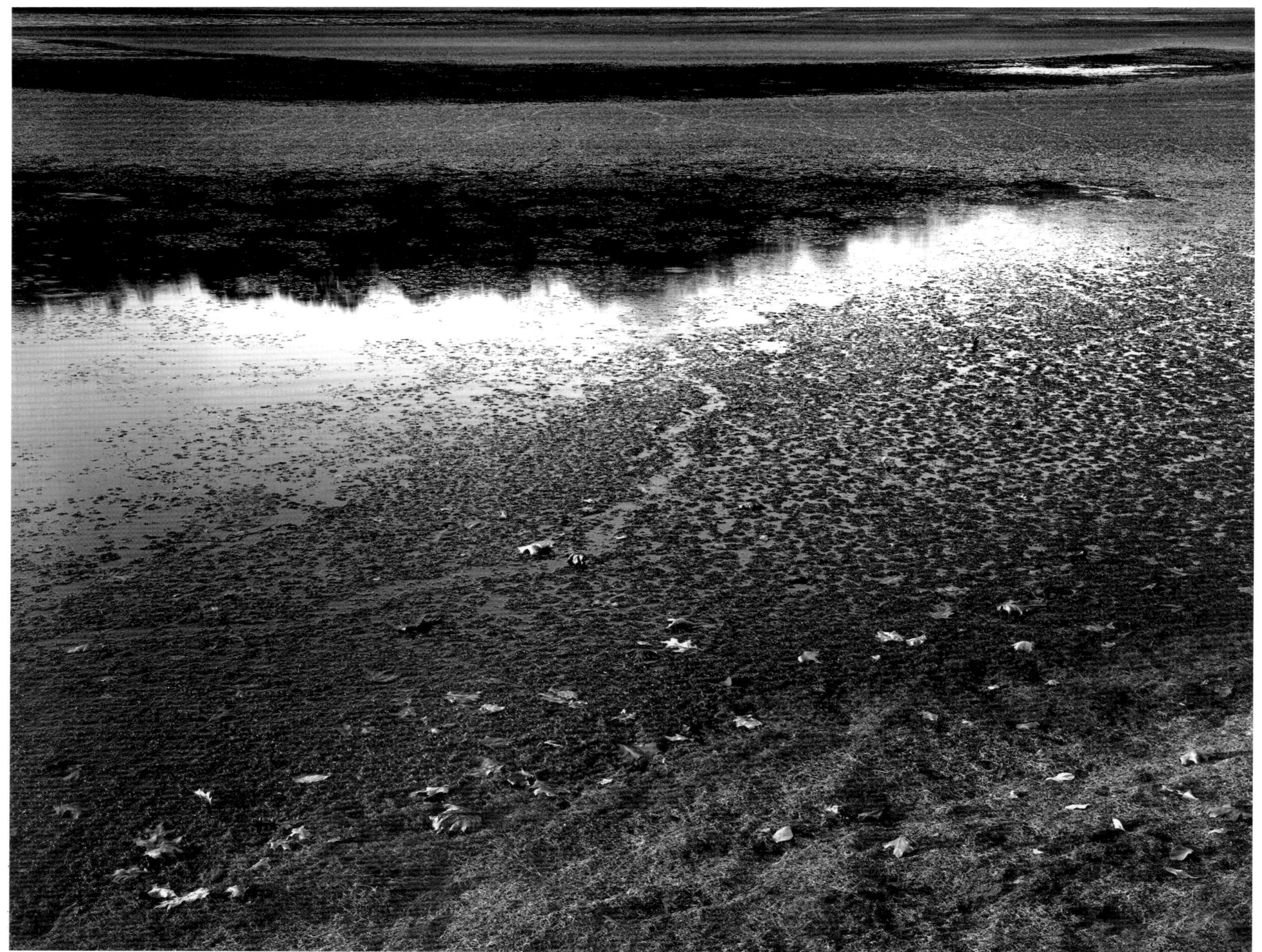

 | GRIFFY CREEK, c. 1958

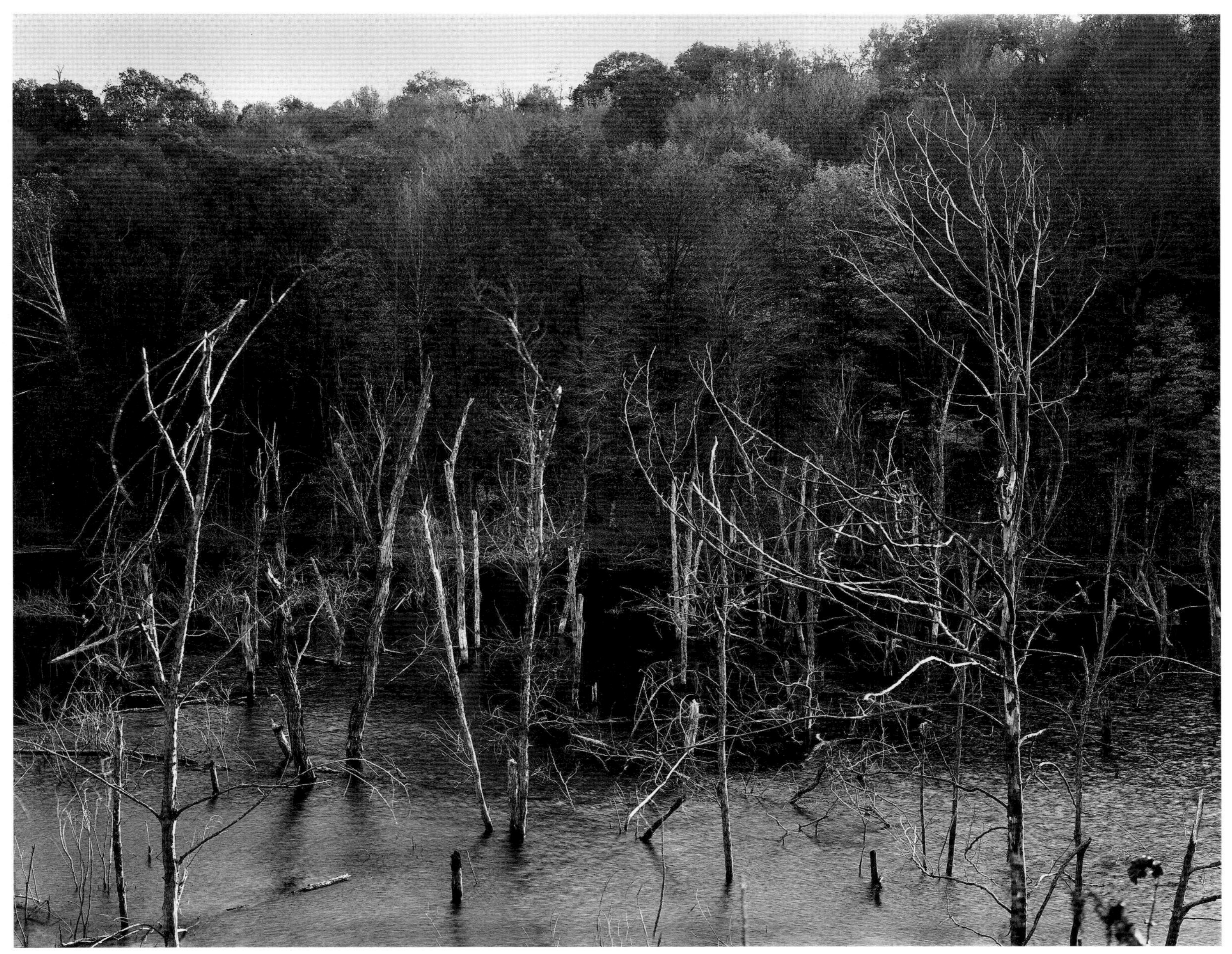

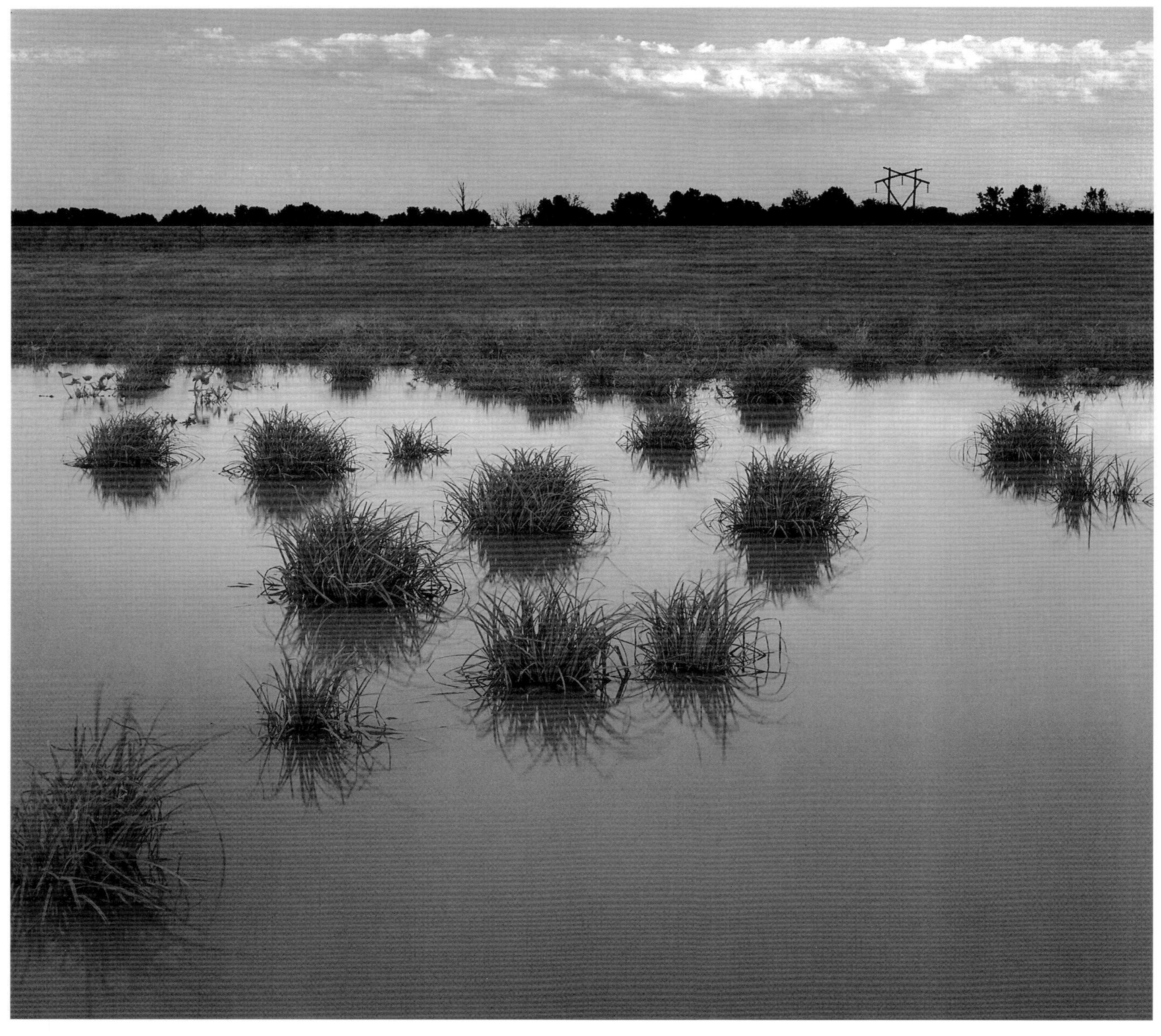

Sputnik had just gone up, and I began seeing weightless things in nature.

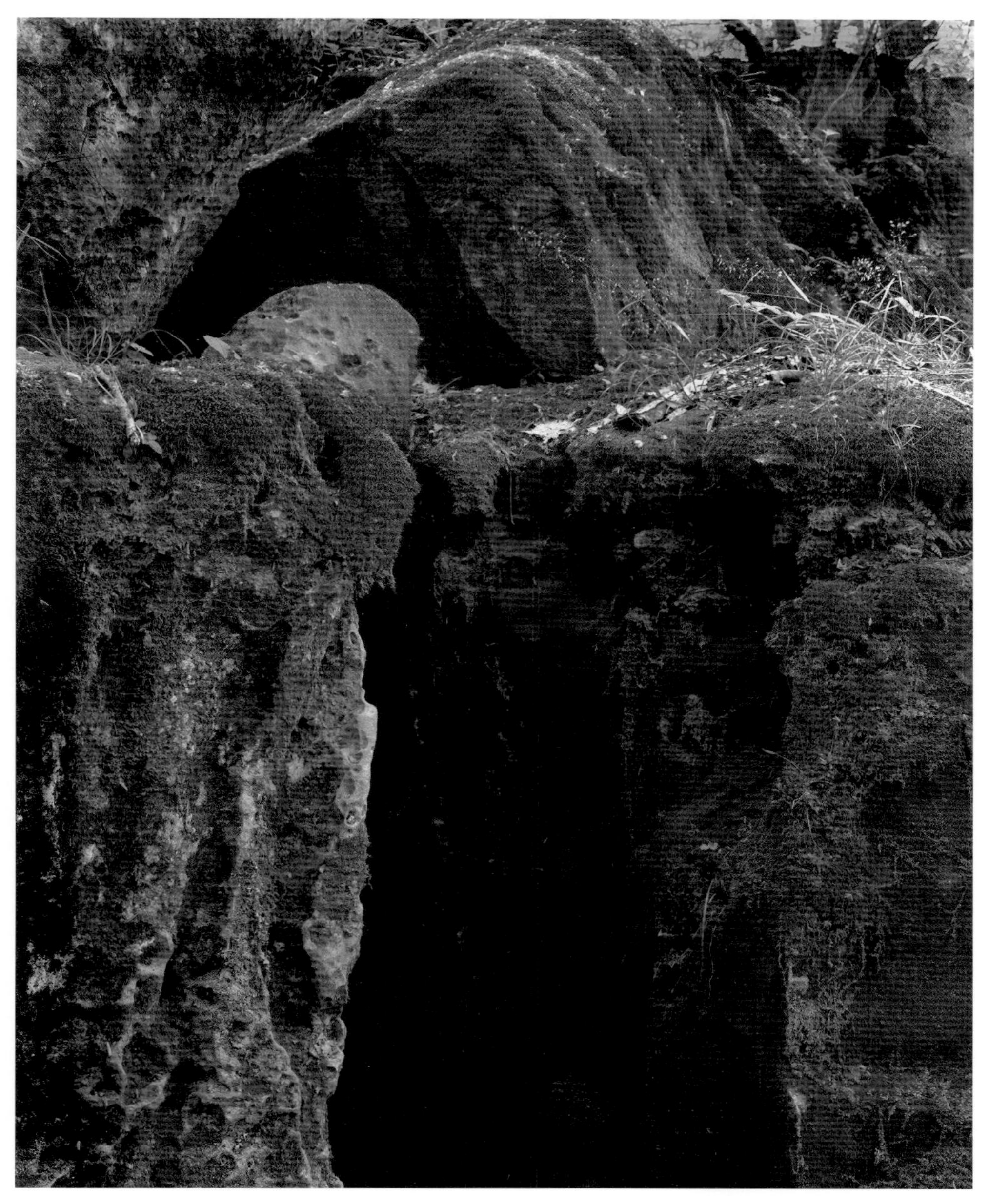

GROTTO, c. 1955

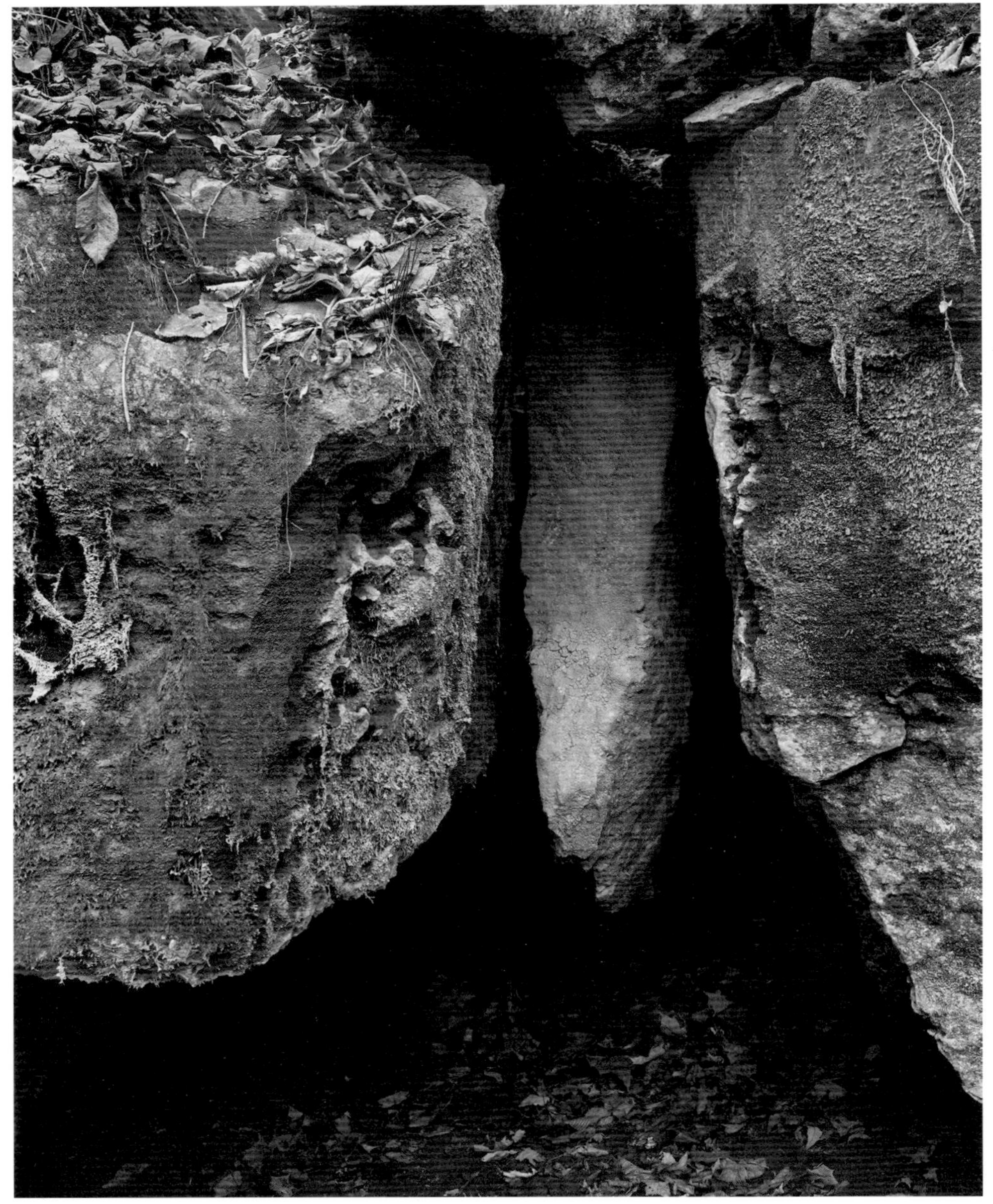

 | GROTTO, c. 1955

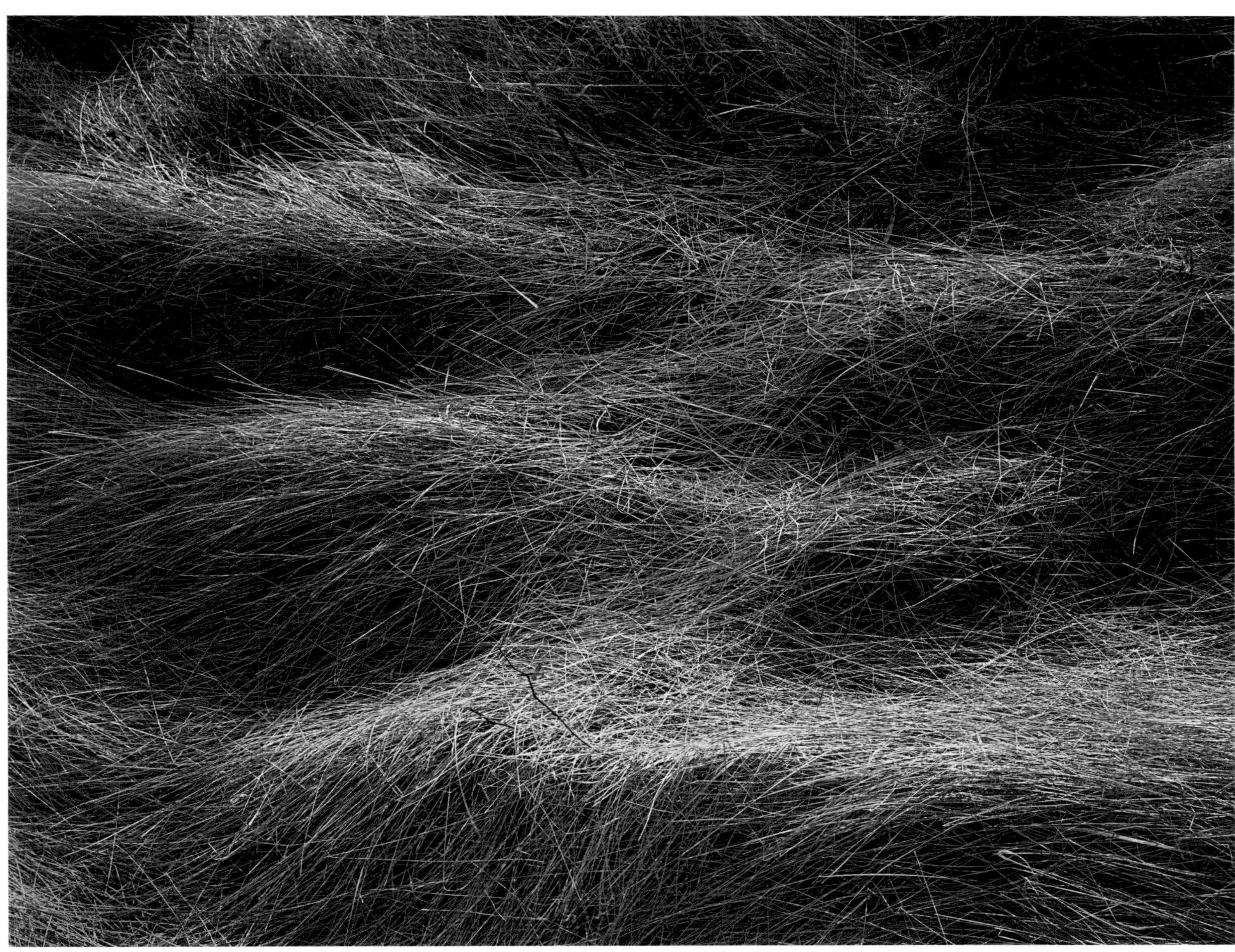

GRASS, 1959

List of Illustrations

JACK WELPOTT *is Professor Emeritus of Photography at San Francisco State University. Jack grew up in Bloomington, served in World War II, and studied under Henry Holmes Smith at Indiana University. His work is held in many major institutions both in the United States and abroad. He has exhibited in more than 200 museums worldwide, and aside from his long tenure at San Francisco State, he has taught workshops across the United States as well as in Mexico, Japan, England, France, and Switzerland. Jack Welpott lives in Inverness, California.*